# CHANGING LIVES:

## WORKERS' EDUCATION IN WALES,
## 1907-2007

EDITED BY

JOE ENGLAND

Llafur

Welsh People's History Society

Cymdeithas Hanes Pobl Cymru

2007

First Published 2007 by

Llafur:

Cymdeithas Hanes Llafur Cymru

Welsh People's History Society

The South Wales Miners' Library, Swansea

ISBN: 978-0-9514580-1-3

Cover Illustration: "At Home" by Robert Baker
(One of a series painted for Coleg Harlech in the 1930s)

Printed and bound by Cambrian Printers, Aberystwyth

# CONTENTS

## Reminiscences

James Griffiths, Thomas Jones, G. B. Owen, Derek Richards, Chris O'Connell, John Morris, Rufus Adams, J. Hefin Jones, Eddie Jenkins, Anne Thomas, Michael Shaw, Catherine Marvel, Julie Sarker, Terry Burns, Neil Kinnock

# FOREWORD

## GLENYS KINNOCK

The WEA and Coleg Harlech have many things to be proud of in their long history but the most significant is summed up in the title of this centenary volume, *Changing Lives.* I know from experience the startling and life-rewarding impact that these two closely joined institutions have had upon men and women in Wales, and the vitality they have brought to local communities. Change, they say, is the only constant; but despite the many changes that have affected the WEA and Coleg Harlech they have continued to be essential providers of adult education in a welcoming and democratic environment.

Wales is changing too. Its traditional industries have disappeared and new technologies are changing occupations and demanding new skills. Communities are changing rapidly. Patterns of family life are taking new forms. Yet parts of Wales remain amongst the poorest regions in Europe. The WEA in the twenty-first century is playing a major part in giving people the confidence and new skills that are the key to a prosperous future. These skills are necessary but not the end of education. In the age of digital television, jet planes and the internet, Wales is part of a global village where immigration, world poverty, religious fanaticism and environmental damage are brought to our doorstep. They bring new challenges to our intellect and imagination that we cannot and should not ignore. The WEA has always enabled men and women to face urgent contemporary issues and think their way through them. That capacity is needed today as much as ever, perhaps more so, and deserves the full support of funding agencies.

I am delighted to welcome this book of essays and reminiscences that tells us of the struggles of the pioneers as well as their successes, that speaks of vision and commitment, that through personal testimonies makes clear the life-changing work of Coleg Harlech and the WEA, and reminds us again of the contribution they have made to civil society in Wales. It deserves a wide circulation.

*Glenys Kinnock*

# ACKNOWLEDGEMENTS

I should like to thank all those who have contributed to this volume and made it possible by their efforts for it to appear in the centenary year of the founding of a WEA district in Wales and on Coleg Harlech's eightieth anniversary.

Hywel Williams played a major part in promoting the idea of such a volume and received essential support from Graham Price and Annie Williams.

The editorial skills of Ursula Masson, Paul O'Leary and Neil Evans and the administrative efficiency of Siân Williams, all of the Welsh People's History Society, were crucial in enabling this volume to appear.

Cathy Ives organized in 1996-7 the sending of questionnaires to former Coleg Harlech students, like herself, and gathered valuable insights, some of which have been used in this volume. It has not been possible to contact all those quoted and to record their current activities but their contributions are very much appreciated.

Thanks are due to Gwasg Gomer for allowing the use of Angharad Tomos's chapter which first appeared in her book, *Hiraeth Am Yfory: Hanes David Thomas A Mudiad Llafur Gogledd Cymru.*

A version of Neil Kinnock's contribution originally appeared in Stephen K. Roberts (ed), *A Ministry of Enthusiasm: Centenary Essays on the Workers' Educational Association* (Pluto Press, 2003).

Finally the WEA bodies in north and south Wales deserve sincere thanks for sponsoring this collection. None of the views expressed represent official South Wales WEA or Coleg Harlech / WEA (N) policy. All contributors have been free to interpret events as they appeared to them and any misjudgements or errors are entirely the responsibility of the contributors, but particularly of the editor.

*Joe England*

# ILLUSTRATIONS

COLOUR SECTION

*First page*
'Dip. Day' at Coleg Harlech 1993.
Coleg Harlech Entrance
Annie Williams: Principal Coleg  Harlech/WEA North Wales

*Spread*
WEA tutor organizers and classes
Graham Price: General Secretary South Wales, 1998-2007

*Last page*
Certificate presentation Maesglas, Newport, 1996
Risca delegates, International Women's Day, 1996
Risca ceramics class 1997

# NOTES ON CONTRIBUTORS

**Ron Brooks** is a former lecturer in History at the University of Wales, Bangor.

**Terry Burns** Terry Burns graduated from the University of Wales Institute of Science and Technology, Cardiff, and is WEA Learning Manager for the Valleys and Monmouthshire.

**John Davies** is the author of many books, including *Hanes Cymru* (1990) / *A History of Wales,* (1993) and is an Honorary Professor in the Department of History and Welsh History, University of Wales, Aberystwyth

**Joe England** was WEA tutor-organizer in south Wales, 1959-67 and warden of Coleg Harlech, 1981-1998. He is an Honorary Research Fellow in the Department of History, University of Wales Swansea.

**Neil Evans** was tutor in History and Director of the Centre for Welsh Studies at Coleg Harlech, 1971-2000 and is an Honorary Research Fellow in the School of History and Archaeaology, Cardiff University and at the Welsh Institute of Social and Cultural Affairs, University of Wales, Bangor.

**Jeremy Gass** co-ordinates a project within the Centre for Community and Life-Long Learning at the University of Wales, Newport, and is a former WEA tutor organizer.

**James Griffiths** (1890-1975) was President of the South Wales Miners' Federation (1934-1936), M.P. for Llanelli (1936-1970), Minister of National Insurance, (1945-1950), Colonial Secretary, (1950-1951), and the first Secretary of State for Wales, (1964-1966)

**Eddie Jenkins**, (1922-2006) was a WEA tutor-organizer and subsequently senior lecturer in the Department of Adult and Continuing Education, University of Wales, Swansea.

**Glenys Kinnock** represents Wales in the European parliament and is president of Coleg Harlech / WEA (N)

**Neil Kinnock** is a former WEA tutor-organizer in south Wales, M.P. for Bedwellty (1970-1995), leader of the Labour Party (1983-1992) and now sits in the House of Lords. He is Chair of the British Council.

**Richard Lewis** is Deputy Dean in the School of Arts and Media, University of Teesside, and author of *Leaders and Teachers: Adult Education and the Challenge of Labour in South Wales, 1906-1940,* (Cardiff, 1993)

**Catherine Marvel** graduated with first class honours from Brunel University and gained a masters's degree at University College London. She is a clinical psychologist.

**John Morris** studied at Coleg Harlech, 1970-1972, graduated with a degree in Economics from the University College of North Wales, Bangor, and was formerly WEA tutor-organizer for Dyfed.

**G. B.Owen** was Bursar at Coleg Harlech and subsequently Registrar of the University College of North Wales, Bangor.

**Graham Price** has recently retired as General Secretary of the WEA South Wales after nineteen years in post. An Oxford graduate he was formerly a tutor-organizer in West Mercia.

**Julie Sarker** graduated from the University of Sussex and after working in the Housing Department of Brighton Council became a primary school teacher. She is now an educational consultant for Brighton and Hove.

**Angharad Tomos** is a distinguished novelist and has published a biography of her grandfather, David Thomas, *Hiraeth Am Yfory: Hanes David Thomas A Mudiad Llafur Gogledd Cymru*

**Annie Williams** is Principal of Coleg Harlech / WEA North Wales. She has published a number of articles on Welsh women's history and was one of the authors of 'Project Grace' a set of teaching packs on Welsh women's history used extensively in adult education.

# INTRODUCTION

## JOE ENGLAND

'I feel that, scattered in all sorts of odd jobs, in all parts of the country, there are countless men and women with an intellectual passion or an undeveloped gift, and that in most cases these remain lost or half shaped, to their own misfortune and the general loss'. The words are those of the poet Edwin Muir; the thought, radical and disturbing, common to all who support and know the work of the Workers' Educational Association and Coleg Harlech, the Welsh long-term residential college for adults.

This collection of essays and reminiscences commemorates 100 years of the WEA in Wales and the eightieth anniversary of Coleg Harlech. They share eighty years of history and throughout that time their stories were intertwined. The same people served on their governing bodies. One man, the ubiquitous Thomas Jones, was instrumental in developing them both. They shared the same ethos. For three-quarters of the twentieth century Coleg Harlech was virtually the staff college for the WEA, receiving its students and returning them as missionaries, organizers, tutors and leaders in Wales and further afield. Both can claim to have changed the lives of thousands of men and women. And in August 2001 Coleg Harlech and the North Wales WEA District amalgamated to their mutual benefit.

It is in the nature of such collections as this that they should not only be commemorative but celebratory of difficuties overcome and achievements gained. These essays, however, also point to consistent themes, to present dilemmas and to potential difficulties. One theme that comes out clearly is the importance of the labour movement to these educational institutions, and their importance to it. Indeed, the two have grown up together for it was not until the early twentieth century that organized labour in Wales developed a consciousness of its independent strength and a radical social vision based upon an educated membership. The chapters by Brooks and Lewis show clearly the crucial part taken by trade unions in launching the WEA in both the north and the south. The miners'and railwaymens' unions withheld their support, preferring the important Central Labour College movement, but the quarrymen and the iron and steel workers were prominent WEA supporters from the beginning. The links continued and when, in the 1960s, the WEA in south Wales consciously targeted trade union members there were considerable benefits to all, as my chapter illustrates. Out of those courses emerged at least three trade union general secretaries and a high number of officials and executive members. And for the WEA there came a stream of tutors with trade union backgrounds that included Cled Phillips, Barry Moore, Terry Burns, Paddy Kitson, Gareth Morris and John Morris; all of them passing through Coleg Harlech. That work with trade unions and their members has continued in various ways and today, with education now a major trade union function, develops in co-operation with workplace learning representatives.

One not surprising consequence of the particularly strong link with the trade unions in the sixties and seventies was the number of WEA tutor-organizers who, in the south particularly, became Labour politicians. As that extraordinary generation of autodidacts who entered politics via the miners' union -- represented in this collection by James Griffiths – reached retiring age, they were replaced by a generation that owed its university education largely to those who had governed in the 1940s. Among them were the able ambitious young men whose work with trade unionists for the WEA had given them excellent contacts in the labour movement. A symbolic moment came when Neil Kinnock succeeded Harold Finch as MP for Bedwellty. He was followed into the Commons by Alan Rodgers, Ron Davies, Rhodri Morgan, Llew Smith and Wayne David, all former WEA tutor-organizers. Llew Smith had been a Coleg Harlech student but was not the first to become an MP; that was Tudor Watkins in the 1940s. Later Harlech students who entered Parliament include Sylvia Heal, Deputy Speaker of the Commons, Brian Jenkins, Albert Owen, with Jack Brooks in the Lords.

Another perennial theme is Funding: necessary but often double-edged for a voluntary organization like the WEA. In its early days, without the support of the powerful South Wales Miners' Federation, it turned to rich individuals for support and, as the essays by Lewis and Davies show, came under attack for so doing. From 1924 the WEA received state grant aid, although grants were subject to Treasury periods of 'restraint' in the inter-war depression or during the later fight against inflation. Coleg Harlech as a registered charity was initially funded by private subscriptions and donations. It was fortunate in having friends in high places – Thomas Jones and his daughter Eirene White who both possessed a talent for extracting money for the College from rich friends, Ben Bowen Thomas when a senior civil servant, and the unlikely pairing of Edward Boyle and Llewellyn Heycock. – they all were vital in securing funding.

A quite different regime was instituted in 1993 when, as the contributions by Gass, and Price and Williams explain, state funding became largely based upon the achievement by students of designated qualifications. Subsequently there has been an increasing emphasis upon the acquisition of skills as a factor of production. This focus on the wealth-generating aspect of education and training is essential to raising the standard of living in a Wales where former industrial skills are now obsolescent and where some areas are among the poorest in the European Union. Whilst retaining aspects of its traditional offering, particularly in the creative arts, the WEA has perforce successfully adapted to this new regime, helping to tackle the skills shortage and bring economically inactive persons back into the labour market. Although societal changes have always been reflected in the curriculum offered by the WEA and Coleg Harlech as the chapters by Davies, Brooks, and Evans demonstrate, this has been the first occasion when the state through a funding methodology has largely determined the nature of the curriculum offered.

But an emphasis upon skills has not been the only thrust of the funding methodology. Additional rewards have gone to institutions that recruit students from deprived areas. The WEA (with Coleg Harlech) has always seen this as part of its remit and initiatives in the south Wales valleys and Caia Park at Wrexham, aided by money from Europe, have enabled it to penetrate communities that other methods could not reach. As a result, the WEA in Wales now has more students than ever before; more students from disadvantaged communities; and more female students than ever before. In south Wales, where learning opportunities were male dominated for much of the twentieth century, the change to where a clear majority of students are female is startling.

Another recurring theme is the voluntary nature of the WEA. How many branches are there and how active are they? Branches have two functions: to organize classes in their area and, as part of a democratic structure of governance, to elect representatives to a governing body. Both functions have suffered from the growth of professionalization. Competition for funding through the expansion of student numbers makes it inevitable that the great majority of classes are organized by WEA employees. Price and Williams demonstrate that the need to comply with bureaucratic audit and funding regulations has put heavy demands upon voluntary workers. 'Marrying a democratic structure of governance to an effective management structure . . . has proved a difficult process'.

Does an absence of branches matter? For the organization of classes, probably not. In the 1930s branches flourished in north Wales whilst they were few and far between in the south. Nonetheless, classes grew in both areas and the essential democracy between students and tutor, where each has an input into what is to be studied and how, was maintained. For governance a democratic structure does matter. Not only because in its absence the result is likely to be a dictatorship, even if it is 'genial' as under John Davies between the wars, but because a democratic structure has been one of the defining characteristics of the WEA. Without it, what differentiates the WEA from other further education 'designated institutions'? In the current competitive environment a strategy for developing a strong voluntary input would seem desirable

One thing that used to differentiate the WEA was that it was part of an 'adult education movement' that encompassed university extra-mural departments, Coleg Harlech, and the WEA. Now, the term 'adult education' has virtually disappeared, subsumed into 'further education' for funding purposes and terminologically replaced by 'life-long learning', a phrase with connotations of constantly upgrading one's skills. Adult education meant something different and coupling it with the idea of a 'movement' was not accidental, for at birth and subsequently it was part of a general desire to create a better social order based upon learning and democratic values. This is not an ignoble ideal. And in its current practice, in reaching out to new disadvantaged students and undertaking difficult pioneering work the WEA in north and south Wales lives up to that ideal.

But there is an unease, expressed by Price and Williams, that the current policy framework in Wales does not encourage sufficiently the acquiring of knowledge in order to judge the world around us. Glenys Kinnock in her Foreword reminds us of the challenges to intellect and imagination that this globalized world brings to our doorstep. And here in Wales, where a process of nation building is taking place before our eyes, the need for an educated citizenry has never been greater. In this context it is ominous to learn that the future of Coleg Harlech is in some doubt as there are questions as to 'how its mission fits with current Welsh Assembly Government priorities'. In a philistine acquisitive society without social purpose it would not be surprising to find no understanding of the value to working men and women of a period of learning and reflection. But we are in Wales. The reminiscences of past students, printed in this volume, are eloquent on what that time gave to them. James Griffiths, a builder of modern Wales, understood it well. Those who follow in his footsteps surely understand it too.

Perhaps there is a belief that in the twenty-first century there are no more obscure Judes who have slipped through the comprehensive net and long to explore the world of the mind; or that the universities have captured all who are capable of applied study? The daily experience of the WEA and Coleg Harlech affirms that this is not so. And for all of us, even after a century of achievement, the WEA style of critically-questioning adult education is needed as much as ever in an age where commercialism is rampant and where the question 'where is society going?' is ever more pressing.

# 'THE GUIDANCE OF THE WISE'
## THE WEA IN WALES, 1906-1918

### RICHARD LEWIS

In December 1907, Henry Jones, the Welsh-born professor of moral philosophy at Glasgow University, visited south Wales to deliver a series of public lectures. Something of a celebrity in his homeland, his rise from very humble origins as the son a shoemaker in rural Wales to an academic with an international reputation attracted much attention. He personified the power of education, not just as an agency of individual mobility, but also as a means of wider social improvement and advance. For Professor Henry Jones was a leading advocate of neo-Hegelian idealism, a philosophical outlook that promoted action aimed at social improvement, reconciled religion and worldly advancement and gave a key but limited role to the state in securing progress in the conditions of humanity. It was an outlook that underpinned the world view of a number of influential academics and public servants who were to play a pivotal role in the early history of the Workers' Educational Association (WEA) in Wales.

For an academic, Professor Jones proved to be remarkably adept at attracting popular attention to his outlook and opinions. His previous visit to his homeland had coincided with the height of the Evan Roberts religious 'revival' of 1904/05. Although he had strong religious beliefs, Professor Jones made it clear in his public lectures at the time that he was disturbed by certain aspects of the 'revival' that he felt promoted irrationality and superstition amongst the mass of the people. His views gained good coverage in the south Wales press, and so in December 1907 it was with some anticipation that the local and regional papers waited on his assessment of the current state of Welsh society.

They were not to be disappointed. He very quickly announced that he was struck by the way that the great religious passions of 1904/05 had been replaced by a new 'great ideal' a new enthusiasm that was not religious but social and political. Rather like the Evan Roberts revival it was a development that he welcomed in many ways, but again feared that there were features of it that he found to be disturbing. He identified two key ones, the first was a tendency to stress the role of class conflict as the only effective mechanism for improving the conditions of the working class and secondly an over emphasis on the role of the state in securing such advances. It was a trend that caused Professor Jones to change the focus of his lecture tour from 'True and False Citizenship' to 'True and False Socialism.'

Many 'progressive' academics and public servants at the time were both encouraged and alarmed by the growth amongst the working class, especially amongst the active members of the labour and trade union movements, of a desire to raise the material well-being and the quality of life of the mass of the population. They became anxious to engage with these activists to ensure that such ambitions were shaped by 'sound' principles and methods. Whilst there were few signs in the mid-Edwardian years that the older Welsh radical political agenda, with its strong Nonconformist commitments to disestablishment of the Anglican Church and temperance reform, was in long-term decline, there were enough straws in the wind to concern the likes of Henry Jones. It was in the urban, industrial and anglicised areas of south Wales where the dangers were seen to exist most clearly, and it was precisely in this part of Wales that the first sustained efforts to establish the Workers' Educational Association were made. Subsequently the growth of the Association in Wales was ascribed to the way that its fundamental aims and objectives chimed in so closely with the essentially democratic principles that underlay Welsh (and especially rural Welsh-speaking) popular culture in the late nineteenth and early twentieth centuries, but as one acute observer of the WEA in south Wales observed in the 1930s, 'This historical fiction may gratify the urge to discover reputable national antecedents of the work, or it may serve as an approximate background to classes in rural areas, but it would tax the powers of our historians to trace the exact sequence between these essentially Welsh institutions and the modern tutorial class in industrialised south Wales.' The early WEA in south Wales had little or nothing to do with bardic circles, chapel-based literary groups or eisteddfodau.

### The Key Networks
The WEA as an institution arrived in Wales on 6 October 1906, at a conference attended by over 250 representatives from local councils, trade unions, the co-operative movement and the local University College, held at the Cory Hall in Cardiff. It is evident that the initiative for this conference came from the national leadership of the WEA and from its founder and first national secretary Albert

Mansbridge. Driven by an almost religious conviction that higher education would not just raise individuals out of poverty, but also help to eliminate want and ignorance and raise the quality of life for all working people, Mansbridge devoted his life to spreading this 'gospel' across all the great industrial and urban centres of the United Kingdom, and later the world. A dedicated trade unionist and co-operator, he used a network of influential contacts amongst these groups and amongst sympathetic academics, senior churchmen and politicians to build up the WEA from its foundation in 1903. At an early stage in this process he sought to establish a presence in the still expanding coalfield and coastal towns of south Wales.

*Albert Mansbridge*

In 1904 A.B. Badger, the Director of Higher Education for Newport, joined the national executive of the WEA as a representative of the Association of Directors of Education. It was Badger who, in July 1905 reported to the WEA executive that plans were already being made to establish a provisional committee for a District of the WEA to be created for south Wales. The south Wales provisional district committee held its first meeting in the Spring of 1906, and a full list of its members were included in press reports of the Cory Hall meeting in the following October. It is an interesting and revealing list that shows clearly the networks that Mansbridge was able to tap into to promote the WEA. There were leading co-operators such as T. W. Allen the Manager of the Blaina Cooperative society, who like Mansbridge was a director of the Co-operative Wholesale Society (CWS). Allen was also a Monmouthshire County Councillor. There were five other leading south Wales co-operators on the provisional committee, some like W.H. Brown, also a director of the CWS, from Newport and John Chappell from Cardiff were also local councillors and prominent local trade unionists. There were four other leading local trade unionists on the provisional committee, and significantly they all belonged to the long-standing Lib-Lab tradition that had sought to achieve the political aspirations of organised labour through a working alliance with popular Liberalism. Often tagged at the time with the name of 'Progressive' it was a loosely applied term that covered, in addition to such active members of the labour movement, a strand of social radical thought that had emerged in the ranks of Liberal politicians from the late 1890s.

However, in 1906, Lib-Labism and its 'Progressive' strategy was increasingly under attack in the industrial areas of south Wales from those who wished the Labour movement to pursue an independent strategy based on an explicit commitment to a socialist programme. Some of those on the provisional committee like the representative of the railwaymen's union, James Taylor, was a Liberal member of Cardiff City Council, who resisted the demands for an 'independent' and socialist strategy for Labour. Some such as Alfred Onions the representative of the largest and most influential trade union in the region, the South Wales Miners Federation (SWMF) 'the Fed,' went with the flow, and he eventually became Labour MP for Caerphilly in 1919. Others were only superficially reconciled with the change, the representative of Cardiff Trades Council, Samuel Fisher was as late as 1920 still describing his politics as 'Liberal now Labour.' The struggle between Lib-Labism and independent labour representation was the one issue that clouded an otherwise entirely successful founding conference for the WEA at the Cory Hall. The issue arose over representation of local trades councils (local committees of trade union branches) on the WEA district committee. In some areas where trades councils did not exist some of their functions were carried out by local Labour Representation Committees (LRCs), effectively embryonic local Labour parties. This was often the case in towns such as Barry, where advocates of 'independent' Labour political action were strong. An attempt to include representation from LRCs on the district committees was successfully opposed by the existing district provisional committee on the grounds that it ran counter to the non-partisan stance of the WEA.

It was a fine point. Trades Councils, the miners' federation and other trade unions often sponsored political candidatures and they were represented on the committee. It was a sensitive matter as on the very day that the WEA was being founded in Cardiff the miners' union was conducting a national ballot on whether or not to affiliate to the new Labour Party. It also reflected the rather ambivalent stance of the WEA on matters political, as their formal non-partisanship could be attacked by critics on the left as a reflection of its links with the established social and political order, but their desire for close association with organized labour was often cited as evidence by critics on the right that it was essentially an agency for promotion of a radical or socialist agenda. At a time when the tone of political debate was changing, and when as Henry Jones was to note just over a year later, the vocabulary of class conflict was becoming a feature of political debate in industrial south Wales, these issues took on a resonance they were not to lose for many decades.

Beyond the network of co-operators and trade unionists, Mansbridge was able to draw on sympathetic local politicians, educationists and academics. The man chosen to chair the provisional committee and the very embodiment of the 'Progressive' social radicalism that characterised the kind of people who supported the WEA in south Wales in its earliest days was P. Wilson Raffan, editor and proprietor of the *South Wales Gazette, a* weekly newspaper that circulated in the mining valleys of Monmouthshire, and a prominent Liberal member of Monmouthshire County Council, he was a staunch advocate of a working political alliance between the Liberal Party and organized labour. For men like Raffan, the WEA must have seemed an ideal agency for promoting an active dialogue between Liberal social radicals, who promoted a 'New' Liberalism that could accommodate the political ambitions and aspirations of organised labour, who could contemplate the use of the state to improve the working lives and economic security of the masses, and the active trade unionists and co-operators who were becoming prominent in the public life of south Wales.

In 1906 the 'Progressive alliance' in Wales was still essentially a highly plastic political continuum that stretched from men like Raffan to another prominent local political figure with radical and 'labour' associations, Peter Wright. Like Raffan, Wright was a Scotsman who had migrated to south Wales during the great expansion of the coalfield in the late nineteenth century and became a moderately successful businessman in the coal shipping trade of Newport. He developed good relations with the trade unionists in the town and was elected to the local council in the 'Labour' interest. Like Raffan, he was an advocate of state and local authority action to promote the welfare of working people. Unlike Raffan, he was willing to court support amongst the advocates of 'independent' Labour representation, he spoke regularly on the platforms of the overtly socialist Independent Labour Party (ILP). Probably the most colourful member of the WEA provisional committee, in addition to his business and political life, Wright was a well-known professional 'all-in' wrestler, a combination of activities that earned him from the *South Wales Argus* what must be the unique accolade of being 'a great wrestler and social reformer.' Wright was a significant figure on the provisional committee because his interest and enthusiasm for promoting higher education amongst working people had been developed by his admiration for fellow Scot and disciple of Hegelian idealism, J. S. Mackenzie, the professor of philosophy at University College, Cardiff.

Mackenzie, a keen advocate of extra-mural university education and of direct engagement of university staff with the social problems of the era, became chairman of the WEA in the later Edwardian period and Peter Wright served as his vice-chairman. Together with Ronald Burrows, the professor of Greek and the University College's representative on the WEA provisional committee, and economics lecturer Sydney Chapman (who later became prominent in the WEA in the north-west of England) Mackenzie was active in promoting university extension lectures and helped to establish a University 'settlement,' that promoted educational and social work, in the working-class Splott district of Cardiff. In its 1906-07 annual report the Splott settlement noted with satisfaction the way that the working men of the area 'capable of taking an active and intelligent interest in public affairs' were attracted to the lectures and debates arranged by the settlement. It was Mackenzie who defined the role of adult education in general and the WEA in particular as the promotion of the 'guidance of the wise subject to the criticism and control of all.'

University academics, such as Burrows and Mackenzie, did not operate in isolation. They were part of a wider coterie of socially conscious educationalists and public servants working or living in the coastal towns of south-east Wales who were driven by the same enthusiasms and concerns that exercised Henry Jones. One of the most notable was Miss Elizabeth Phillips Hughes. She represented Glamorgan County education committee — to which she had been co-opted, as women were not eligible for election to county councils at that time — on the WEA provisional committee, but her significance and influence went way beyond local government. Miss Hughes was one of the most remarkable Welsh women of her age; one of that small number of intrepid Victorian middle-class women who led lives of impeachable respectability but still managed to challenge the validity of the gender stereotypes of their times. She was the only female member of the committee that drafted the first charter for the University of Wales, and ensured that, unlike Oxford and Cambridge at that time, male and female students could be awarded degrees. She travelled extensively, was an acknowledged expert on American educational developments, had lived in Japan and taught at the University of Tokyo. At the age of forty-eight she climbed the Matterhorn. In 1899, following a very distinguished career in teacher education (she was the first Principal of Cambridge College for the Training of Women Teachers), Miss Hughes retired to her home town of Barry to devote her life to promoting the social and educational improvement of working people in general and women in particular. In 1920 she described her politics as 'Radical and Democrat'; a strong supporter of female political enfranchisement she was a critic of the civil disobedience tactics of the suffragettes. Always in demand to speak at educational conferences, she wrote and published extensively, mainly on educational matters and became a leading light of the influential coterie of social radicals that emerged in the Cardiff/Barry area in the Edwardian era, and remained a major figure in the work of the WEA in south Wales until her death in 1925.

### The First Branches

Although the leading lights of the early WEA in south Wales were drawn from this social radical coterie, they were acutely aware that if this new body was to make an impact on the working people of south Wales then it would have to draw on the leadership skills of the workers themselves. It would have to engage the enthusiasm of the 'secondary' leadership of the working class, the union branch chairman, the lodge secretary, the working men's club treasurer. This required them to find a strategy that would allow this engagement to evolve. Following the foundation of the south Wales WEA district an honorary secretary, A.C. Willis, was appointed to co-ordinate the development of the Association. He was an interesting choice. A lodge official of the South Wales Miners' Federation, he was also known to be an advocate of independent Labour representation, but as a local councillor in the valley mining town of Abertillery and as editor of the local Labour journal he maintained good working relations with leading Lib-Labs and progressives such as P. Wilson Raffan the Chairman of the WEA district and a fellow local councillor. Willis was, however, an archetypal Edwardian Labour man, he was like Keir Hardie a staunch temperance advocate and teetotaller. If Willis and Raffan may not have seen eye-to-eye on the issue of the merits of independent Labour political representation they shared a common belief that '...the democracy of this country will in the near future be called upon to play an important part in the affairs of this Empire' and that it was essential that this power was used 'wisely' and 'for the greatest good.' The WEA in south Wales therefore started a search for a pattern of activity which would exercise the interest and enthusiasm of their main target group -- the intelligent, active working class.

Initially, at the behest of the national WEA, the strategy was to establish local member WEA branches in the towns of south Wales where the Association could tap into the various existing voluntary and local authority initiatives to promote adult education. The very first of these branches, significantly, was established in Barry within a few weeks of the Cory Hall conference in October 1906, and its foundation meeting was addressed by E.P.Hughes. Barry was essentially a new town, a port created during the coal exporting boom of the late nineteenth century, with a population rather cosmopolitan and less distinctively Welsh than the mining valley towns. It had a vibrant associational life, with many clubs and societies including the Twentieth Century Club an organization set up in the town by the indefatigable Miss Hughes to promote amongst the young women of Barry an awareness of their rights and duties as full citizens of the nation. It was a town with a strong political culture, with many open-air 'soap box' meetings and a strong local branch of the Independent Labour Party (ILP), to which in 1906 Miss Hughes felt no compunction in giving a talk on the American prison and parole system. The local authority also provided a range of adult evening classes under the approving and pressurizing gaze of the redoubtable Miss Phillips, so it was into a local society which already displayed an appetite for public lectures and adult educational self enlightenment, that the first branch of the WEA offered its first series of public lectures.

Under the secretaryship of a local leading trade unionist, the class topics were aimed at working-class activists but by the autumn of 1907 the branch officers were already complaining that the workers were simply not attending in the numbers desired. The tone of statements from the Barry branch officials became increasingly plaintive: 'If the workers would only attend our meetings then we will know their requirements and progress to that perfect citizenship which is the ambition of all social reformers'. In the summer of 1909 Miss Hughes and the Barry branch of the WEA organized a series of lectures on the Royal Commission on the Poor Law which had just delivered its reports on how the state should address the whole question of poverty and destitution. Miss Hughes arranged for copies of the reports to be available at the public library. It is illustrative of the challenge that faced the WEA that, before the classes had started, the local branch of the ILP unanimously passed a resolution demanding the implementation of the minority report of the Commission with its demands for the wholesale break-up of the Poor Law system and its replacement by positive state action to tackle and eliminate poverty. Miss Hughes expressed her concern that such judgements should be based on 'solid knowledge' of the issues so that remedies were ones that 'would produce no fresh damage to society'. However, the local Labour activists knew what they wanted and did not feel the need to study the issues in such detail. The following year the WEA branch had ceased to function. The progressive dilemma remained -- how to secure reform without turning the world upside down. Poorly attended public lectures did not offer a resolution of that dilemma.

Between 1907 and 1914 twelve local branches of the WEA were established in south Wales, none west of the Afan valley. Only Cardiff had a continuous existence in that period, and none of the branches made the impact that the Association had hoped they would make. As a formula for promoting workers' education it simply was not working in south Wales. This is particularly well illustrated by the efforts to create and sustain a branch in Pontypridd. Situated at the confluence of the Taff, Rhondda and Cynon valleys it was in the heyday of the steam-coal mining boom a rapidly expanding town at the hub of the south Wales economy. The two most powerful unions in south Wales, the SWMF and the Amalgamated Society of Railway Servants (ASRS) were particularly strong in the vicinity and therefore this town was strategically important to the WEA if it was to embed its influence with the Welsh labour movement. It secured the services of a well known local trade unionist and town councillor, Moses L. Jones, as branch secretary. A radical progressive Moses Jones was the very embodiment of the ideal Labour activist for the regional leadership of the WEA. He had a good reputation amongst other trade unionists having been victimized for his union work by the notorious Taff Vale Railway Company. He was secretary of the local trades council, was an effective speaker, and knew how to gain access to the local press to propagate his views. He shared the WEA perception that '...to gain perfection the whole community must be educated. With the advance of democracy, the responsibility of the citizen increases, and this means increased happiness if intelligently carried out.' Moses Jones was keen to work with the local professional classes to promote local authority adult education provision, known as continuation classes. One prominent supporter was a local headmaster Dr R. D. Chalke who in 1909 addressed the Pontypridd branch of the Association and enthused about the work of Moses Jones and the need for such men and organizations to ensure that the 'ominous unrest' that he detected growing in the ranks of organized labour would not result in a 'rampant and unintelligent socialism' but that 'Labour rightly organized and rightly controlled, intelligent Labour would soon rule the destinies of this great empire.'

The ominous unrest noted by Dr Chalke was beginning to change the nature of debate within the ranks of organized labour in south Wales, just as Professor Jones had feared back in 1907. Men like Moses Jones, although trade union men to their finger tips, were now being challenged by younger more radical types who had a world view that sought not just social reform but a revolutionary change involving the rejection and replacement of the capitalist system itself. Pontypridd was one of the areas of industrial south Wales where these ideas were making their earliest impact. Part of the new radical agenda involved a specific rejection of the WEA perception of workers' education with its explicit desire to collaborate with the existing agencies of educational provision and their middle class leaderships. A new strategy of 'independent working class education' (IWCE) was emerging amongst these activists and they were to pose a direct challenge to the WEA in south Wales where the ideas of the IWCE movement were to find fertile ground for the growth of their ideas. It was, however, not the emerging IWCE or Labour College movement that really weakened the WEA branch strategy but the fact that the local authority classes they promoted failed to attract the workers targeted by the WEA. The class topics were often severely utilitarian, and often taught by tired and underpaid elementary school teachers seeking to supplement their meagre salaries. In addition, as in Barry, the WEA branches tended to be dominated by local professional people, teachers, doctors and lawyers, who would then criticize the workers for their failure to support the evening classes, and condemn their apathy or even their fecklessness. This was happening at a time when the willingness of the workers to listen to such strictures was rapidly diminishing. In 1908 Moses Jones replaced A.C. Willis as honorary district secretary, and at first the branch and continuation class strategy was maintained, but by 1909 it was obviously not succeeding. From 1909 onwards the initiative in the development of the WEA in south Wales moves away from the branches and collaboration with local authority provision to the district committee and collaboration with the University.

## Nil Desperandum

In October 1909 Professor J. S. Mackenzie replaced P. W. Raffan as Chairman of the South Wales District at its annual conference. The meeting was addressed by Albert Mansbridge who used the opportunity to discuss why the Association had failed to make a significant impact in the region. He also used the conference to promote the idea of the university tutorial class that had emerged out of a conference at the University of Oxford on the university and workers' education that also produced the influential report *Oxford and Working-class Education* published in November 1908. It was obvious that Mansbridge felt the future of workers' education rested with collaboration between the Association and the extra-mural work of the universities. There followed a series of three conferences sponsored by the South Wales District in 1910 that tried to find a formula that would attract workers to adult education and sustain a link with the universities. It was a triumph of organization by Moses Jones, who obviously used his networks amongst the local labour movement and local authorities to bring in some notable speakers. However, the problem had not been solved. Neither the education committees nor the University College in Cardiff showed any great enthusiasm for the work of the WEA, and this coincided with the spread of the influence of the Labour College movement and IWCE in industrial south Wales.

The Labour College movement was called into existence in 1909 following a 'strike' by students at Ruskin College, a working-man's college at Oxford. Amongst the leading lights of the strikers were Noah Ablett and Ted Gill, two members of the SWMF sent to Ruskin by their union and both very effective advocates of a new perception of workers' education which drew heavily on Marxist economic theory and a materialist conception of history. It reinforced rising anti-capitalist sentiment amongst Labour activists in the coalfield, and it also formed a key element in the 'syndicalist' outlook that animated so many of the young miners' leaders during the severe industrial unrest in the coalfield in the period after 1910. One of the factors that triggered the Ruskin College 'strike' of 1909 was a feeling among students there that the College's curriculum was being changed to meet the needs of the University of Oxford; that subjects and topics critical of the existing social order were being dropped, to be replaced by more orthodox subjects ideologically acceptable to the

University. As an institution, Oxford University was seen by the Ruskin rebels as quintessentially an agency of ruling class hegemony. Therefore, the WEA's attempts to build stronger links between the organized working-class and the Universities was anathema to this new breed of trade union activist. Ablett and Gill made every effort to block any working alliance between the SWMF and the WEA, and there were other IWCE advocates amongst the railwaymen who opposed the WEA. It was to be a conflict that would continue to haunt the WEA, especially in south Wales, until after the second World War.

By 1911 the two largest unions in south Wales, the miners and the railwaymen were unwilling to support the Association and in many cases were actively supporting the alternative Labour college classes with their explicit rejection of collaboration with 'bourgeois' agencies of adult education. It could not have come at a worse time for the WEA in south Wales for by then branch activity within the region had all but ceased. It was at this point that the district committee decided that if the WEA was to survive in the region then it required a full-time organizer to promote it. In July 1911 a recent economics graduate of Cardiff University College was appointed as organizing secretary for the Association. The man appointed was John Thomas, a Welsh-speaking son of the caretaker of a Congregational chapel in Aberdare. His impeccable credentials as a product of Welsh nonconformity were given a broader appeal by his active membership of the ILP and his staunch support for Keir Hardie. Hardie's ethical and spiritual commitment to socialism attracted Thomas as did his teetotalism. They all chimed in well with the WEA's vision of workers' education and Thomas brought considerable energy and enthusiasm to his new post. Any illusions he had that promoting the WEA view of workers' education would meet with universal approval were soon shattered. His appointment to the post was openly attacked in the local ILP journal the *Merthyr Pioneer* by a leading light of the Labour College movement, Wil John Edwards, who denounced the Association as an agency of ruling class propaganda. It is scarcely surprising that in his first annual report Thomas stated that 'In all aspects of WEA work "Nil Desperandum" is a good motto.'

John Thomas's remit ran for the whole of Wales, and he sought to follow up contacts already established between the WEA and the extra-mural work of the University College in Bangor among the quarrymen of the area. However, it was not until the Association established a distinctive district structure and appointed a full-time district secretary in 1925 that it made any real headway in north Wales. Things might have been different if an initiative by Dr R. D. Roberts, the Aberystwyth-born Registrar of the University of London Extension Board, and a tireless and internationally renowned advocate of University extra-mural work had come to fruition. An influential member of the University of Wales board of governors, Roberts used his position to promote the idea that the University should evolve as a peripatetic institution with class groups, open to all willing and able to use them, in every corner of Wales -- it presaged the creation of the Open University by over half a century. It was an ideal shared by another leading light of Welsh education -- Owen M. Edwards. It also enjoyed the support of the Principal of the University College in Bangor, Professor, Sir Harry Reichel who had been instrumental, as a close friend of Albert Mansbridge, in establishing the extension lectures for the north Wales quarrymen. Under pressure from these two very influential figures, the University of Wales in 1909 agreed in principle to establish a university-wide scheme of extra-mural classes that would cover the whole of Wales. There were many in the University who felt that this scheme would divert energies and resources away from the development of the University's intra-mural work, and little progress was made until 1911, when a sub-committee was established by the University, consisting of Roberts (now chairman of the governing body of the University of Wales), Reichel and John Thomas the WEA's organizing secretary in Wales, to finalize the proposals. In November 1911, R. D. Roberts died suddenly and the most effective advocate of the ideal of an 'open' University of Wales disappeared from the scene.

The Roberts scheme died with him and the WEA made only limited progress in promoting the university tutorial class idea in Wales before the 1920s, dependent as it was on the initiative and enthusiasm of each constituent college of the University. Bangor continued with their scheme with the north Wales quarrymen, Aberystwyth established a full scheme in 1911-12. Cardiff, ironically where the strongest advocates for such a scheme resided, proved the most reluctant and placed severe financial restraints on the provision of classes. This prevented a rapid expansion and meant that much of the time of John Thomas the organizing secretary of the WEA was taken up in seeking financial support for the classes and/or delivering them. Denied access to financial support from the big trade unions of the area by the supporters of the IWCE, the WEA became increasingly dependent on the financial goodwill of wealthy local benefactors, such as the mine owners David Davies and Lord Tredegar. This, of course, tended to provide further evidence for their critics on the left that the Association was an agency for ruling-class propaganda. In the period between 1910 and the outbreak of the first World War in 1914, industrial south Wales was seen as one of the great storm centres in a rising conflict between capital and labour. Denied the support of trade unions on any significant scale, to gain access to the industrial working class of the region John Thomas had to develop alternative tactics. One of the more successful was through the working-men's club movement which gave Thomas direct access to working men in the coalfield. The clubs also had financial resources that could be used to support educational initiatives largely outside of the influence of the advocates of IWCE. Often based on 'one-off' lectures and classes, they sometimes formed the basis of longer-term class groups and even the creation of local branches. By 1914 sixteen working men's clubs were affiliated to the WEA district compared with only three union branches, and they provided fifteen out of a total of twenty-four class venues. It was, however, a poor substitute for the full engagement with organized labour desired by the leading lights of the Association.

When the North Wales District of the WEA was established in 1925, the person appointed to the post of district secretary was the Reverend Robert Silyn Roberts. A noted poet as well as a non-conformist minister with strong socialist convictions, Silyn Roberts shared the radical ideals of the Cardiff/Barry coterie of social radicals. Indeed under the chairmanship of J. S. Mackenzie and his successor Daniel Lleufer Thomas, the WEA in Wales fell even more heavily under the influence and control of this group. With the effective collapse of the branch strategy, the fortunes of the WEA were now firmly in their hands. In addition to E. P. Hughes and J. S. Mackenzie, a key figure in the evolution of the Association at this time was Thomas Jones. Brought up in the south Wales coalfield from a working-class family Jones became something of a disciple of Henry Jones. As a student at the University of Glasgow, Thomas Jones became fully imbued with the neo-Hegelian ideals that pervaded the intellectual climate of the time. Driven by these ideals he became politically active in that Scottish city and he assisted his close friend Ronald Burrows in an 'anti-sweating' campaign and other social work in its teeming tenements. On his return to Wales initially to work for a charity and then for the Welsh National Insurance Commission, Thomas Jones became a leading figure amongst the Cardiff/Barry coterie. Whilst he was sometimes repelled by the beer sodden leisure pursuits of many working men, he was also inspired by their capacity for building up voluntary collective agencies of self-help such as co-operative societies, working men's clubs and trade unions. It was amongst those active in such bodies that he saw the hope for creating a socially cohesive and fairer society. As treasurer of the WEA in Wales, Thomas Jones built his contacts with wealthy benefactors that kept the Association afloat in the difficult years of industrial strife in the region and in the early years of the war. By 1914 the WEA in Wales was surviving mainly on subventions drawing on the coalowning wealth of the Davies family of Llandinam. It was through his friendship with the millionaire coal owner David Davies, that the Cardiff/Barry coterie of social radicals gained a voice in the form of the monthly magazine *Welsh Outlook*. Financially underpinned by Davies, Thomas Jones edited the journal from its inception until he left Wales to work in Lloyd George's cabinet office in 1916 and commence his career as a 'backroom boy' and chronicler of the high politics in inter-war Britain. This periodical became a platform for the neo-idealist reforming ideals of Jones and his allies in south Wales, and also a means of promoting the various agencies, such as the WEA, that were seeking to convert these ideas into practical action. Critical of the excesses of capitalism and the short-sighted greed of the employing classes, it also attacked and feared the 'nihilist spirit' of the revolutionary left, which Ronald Burrows stated in the very first edition of *Welsh Outlook* would be as cruel and relentless as the industrial order it sought to destroy. The anxieties originally flagged up by Henry Jones back in 1907 were now reinforced by the strikes and civil disturbances that convulsed south Wales society in the years immediately preceding the Great War.

Although John Thomas and his mentors amongst the group that dominated the district committee gave a sense of direction to the Association in Wales and did, to a large extent, give it a status within the academic life of the country, its existence remained precarious. The early years of the war were no easier for the WEA in Wales than in the preceding period, but to some extent the Association adapted to the new temper of the times. John Thomas became more openly radical in his criticism of the capitalist system in his economics classes, and he was able to fend off the Labour College critics as the products of his groups proved to be as militant as those produced by their class groups. Indeed in 1915 the *Plebs* magazine, the journal of the Labour College movement, had to acknowledge that John Thomas had made his hometown of Aberdare, in the centre of the coalfield, a stronghold for the WEA. Whilst Thomas's success in keeping the radical spirits of his part of the coalfield within the classes of the WEA was gratifying to many on the district committee it did begin to expose some tensions. One of Thomas's students responded to the *Welsh Outlook* article by Burrows in a letter published in the following issue stating that class warfare could not be wished away by the workers adopting the ideals of good citizenship, but only through the creation of a 'co-operative commonwealth.' Workers' education should be directed to that objective. The district committee could live with these views if it kept these active spirits within the classes of the WEA. Other conflicts were less easy to resolve. Following the lead of his great hero, Keir Hardie, John Thomas opposed the war on political and ethical grounds and became active in several anti-war movements in the region. By the autumn of 1915 Thomas Jones told John Thomas that his anti-war stance was causing problems for the association. One of his most vociferous critics on the district committee was Miss E. P. Hughes who Thomas described in an interview nearly sixty years later as 'A bloody minded warrior of the worst type.' In October 1915 Thomas resigned from the WEA, and, freed from the need to consider the position of the Association, increased his anti-war activities. He also became more radical in his political views. In April 1916 John Thomas was granted the status of a conscientious objector and directed to non-military war work and banned from taking classes. He eventually found ways around these restrictions and by the end of the war he had built up such a reputation in the coalfield that he was elected as a miners' agent for one the districts of the SWMF.

## A Very Useful 'Bogey'

The loss of John Thomas as organizing secretary coincided with the change in chairmanship of the district committee when Daniel Lleufer Thomas replaced J. S. Mackenzie. Lleufer Thomas was a major figure in Wales. The first Welshman to hold the post of chairman of the WEA district committee in Wales, he attended and graduated from Oxford in the 1880s and belonged to a generation of such Welshmen from that University anxious to promote a cultural and intellectual revival in Welsh life. A distinguished lawyer, and the stipendiary magistrate for the Rhondda valley, he was also a leading light in a range of voluntary bodies seeking to improve the conditions of ordinary working people in Wales. A believer in co-partnership and the co-operative movement, he promoted schemes to establish 'garden cities' in Wales and other types of housing reform and wrote sympathetically about the aspirations of the trade union movement. He was tied into every network associated with social reform in Wales and a severe critic of the forms of Welsh religious non-conformity that focused exclusively on the saving of individual souls rather than on raising the quality of people's lives in this world. The Edwardian era saw various attempts to re-invent nonconformity as a means of promoting social reform, but, much to Lleufer Thomas's annoyance, the Welsh protestant denominations proved to be remarkably resistant to such moves. In 1908 Lleufer Thomas organized a visit to south Wales by the Rev. R. J. Campbell the leading advocate of what was known as the 'New Theology' that laid as much stress on social reform as on individual salvation. Lleufer Thomas was disappointed in the response of the chapels to this message. In 1911 he founded the Welsh Council of Social Service as an inter-denominational body to co-ordinate and foster the work of the churches in Wales as agencies of social amelioration and progress.

It was Lleufer Thomas more than anyone else who sought to give the ideas of the coterie of the Cardiff/Barry radicals a strong Welsh tone. He argued that the efforts to create a fairer, less strife-ridden social order was part of a Welsh ideal of popular culture, essentially democratic in its aspiration, that underpinned the work of all the bodies he promoted whether for housing improvement or trade unionism. It was Lleufer Thomas who first promoted the idea that the WEA was the inheritor of an older Welsh tradition of adult education for ordinary working people. It was in an address at the National Eisteddfod in 1915 just after he became chairman of the WEA in Wales that he crystallized these ideas. All the current social ills he ascribed to the over rapid growth of industry and urbanization that had disrupted the older cultural cement that held Welsh society together. It was the task of the WEA in collaboration with the University to provide a comprehensive range of classes throughout Wales that would promote this Welsh ideal of popular culture and its democratic values. Failure to do so would, he feared, result in the spread amongst the workers of Wales of an 'illusory ideal of a cosmopolitan, and perhaps materialistic brotherhood.' This was, of course, an allusion to the ideas being promoted by the Labour College movement which was already beginning to see a major expansion in industrial south Wales. Instead he said that it was the mission of the WEA and the University to seek a true reconciliation of 'socialism and individualism - opposite, yet complementary, standpoints, both deeply rooted in the character and life of the people.' The WEA would drive this movement, give it an intellectual coherence and become the main propagator of this ideal. The WEA would be transformed from being an import from England into being a key cultural institution of Welsh life and thought.

As the war progressed the industrial conflict which had subsided in the immediate aftermath of its outbreak returned to the valleys of south Wales. In 1910, as stipendiary magistrate for the Rhondda, Lleufer Thomas had presided over the trial of many of those arrested during the riots in Tonypandy associated with the great coal strike of that year. Many in government, and especially in the Home Office, felt that Lleufer Thomas had been unduly lenient with those convicted. However, among the trade union radicals, and especially those associated with the Labour College movement, he was seen as a lackey of the capitalist state. It was yet more evidence in their eyes that the WEA was just a 'handmaid of capitalism.' Lleufer Thomas was concerned about the growing influence of the Labour College classes in the region, and when the District submitted evidence to the Royal Commission on University of Wales under the chairmanship of Lord Haldane, he made use of the growing influence of the classes to advocate the need for a firmer commitment by the University to adult education to counter the spread of their 'illusory materialistic ideals.' In oral evidence to the commission Lleufer Thomas stated that in 1916 over 500 students were attending IWCE-type classes in industrial south Wales and that he confidently expected that number to rise quite significantly. Cuts in provision occasioned by the war, for example due to the enlistment of tutors, meant that 'orthodox' adult education had all but ceased to be provided in the region. Whilst there can be little doubt that Lleufer Thomas was anxious about the spread of IWCE workers' education, it is difficult to avoid the conclusion that it was also a very useful 'bogey' with which to frighten government into devoting more resources to adult education in Wales.

It was a theme to which Lleufer Thomas was to return in 1917 as chairman of the Commission into Industrial Unrest in Wales that was set up by the Lloyd George government to find out why the region had once again become a centre for strife between capital and labour. As much concerned with the ideological as with the social and economic causes of the unrest, as chairman of the Commission he seized on evidence from witnesses about the influence of the Labour College classes. By 1917 it was reliably estimated that over 1,200 students were attending over forty Labour College classes in south Wales, almost all such students being active within their unions. The Unrest Commission probably marked the high point of the political influence of the south Wales social radicals. The secretary to the committee, Edgar Chappel, another member of the Cardiff/Barry coterie, who had been both a WEA tutor and someone who had worked with Lleufer Thomas on his various housing schemes, used the commission to expose the iniquitous nature of coal owner control over the industry. So that when it reported, it not only advocated more resources for adult education provision, it also favoured a semi-corporatist restructuring of the major industries and the institutional recognition of the rights and responsibilities of both employers and employed. This would see an end to free market capitalism, but it was well short of full nationalisation and nowhere near the workers' control advocated by the most advanced 'syndicalist' elements in the coalfield. It was all too much for the coal owners and other employers in south Wales and the proposals encountered far more virulent hostility from this quarter than they ever received from the socialist left.

The last year of the war was one in which many hopes were raised that the end of the conflict would create an opportunity to address many of the social ills of the time, not least in the area of education. The appointment of H.A.L. Fisher a progressive academic as President of the Board of Education raised great hopes and the WEA district committee prepared a memorandum for him demanding greater expenditure on adult education. The great hopes of 1917 started to turn into disappointment when the Education Act that came from Fisher failed to make the radical changes demanded and seemed to make too many concessions to the desire of the Treasury to curb public expenditure in the aftermath of war. By the end of the war the WEA was still in existence in Wales, class and branch activity had resumed and it had re-invented itself as the custodian of a distinctively Welsh perception of workers' education. It was not, however, to be the start of a new era of harmonious industrial relations and social cohesion in Wales. Class divisions in Welsh society were deeper than ever and were to be made more bitter by industrial disputes that were to dwarf anything that had occurred hitherto. These conflicts, combined with the new phenomenon of chronic structural unemployment, were to pose challenges for the WEA beyond anything envisaged by those that had founded the Association in south Wales in 1906.

## Bibliography:

This chapter is based on research I originally undertook in preparation of a postgraduate dissertation that was subsequently published as *Leaders and Teachers: Adult Education and the Challenge of Labour in south Wales, 1906-1940*, (University of Wales Press, 1993). That publication contains a very detailed list of primary and published sources for the study of the early history of the WEA in south Wales. More detailed information on the challenge to the WEA in industrial south Wales from the Labour College movement can also be found in *Leaders and Teachers*. Further biographical information on Elizabeth Phillips Hughes, Thomas Jones, Ronald Burrows and J.S. Mackenzie can be found in the latest edition of the *Dictionary of National Biography* (Oxford University Press). There is an entry for Daniel Lleufer Thomas in the *Dictionary of Welsh Biography* (University of Wales Press). Both of the above biographical sources can be accessed 'online'. For the wider influence of the Cardiff/Barry coterie see Richard Lewis 'The Welsh radical tradition and the ideal of a democratic popular culture' in E. Biagini (ed) *Citizenship and community: Liberals, radicals and collective identities in the British Isles, 1865-1931* (Cambridge University Press, 1996). A useful introduction to the early history of the WEA and especially of the role and personality of its founder Albert Mansbridge can be found in Stephen K. Roberts (ed.), *A Ministry of Enthusiasm: Centenary Essays on the Workers' Educational Association* (Pluto Press, 2003).

# JOHN DAVIES AND THE WEA IN THE INTER-WAR YEARS

## JOHN DAVIES

'The war,' wrote the district secretary of the south Wales W.E.A. in 1930, 'created such a break in the continuity of this organisation that it might be said that it had to be established afresh in 1920.' John Thomas, the District's tutor/organizer appointed in 1911 was an opponent of the war and had been forced to resign in October 1915. In the following year there was virtually no class activity; in 1917, an attempt was made to revive the movement with the appointment of John Davidson as full-time tutor/organizer and with the convening of a conference on educational reconstruction which attracted three hundred delegates. Davidson, who succeeded in organizing fifteen classes in 1918–19, departed to work for the London University Tutorial Committee in July 1919. When his successor was appointed in November, his office was a cubby hole at Gresham Chambers in Cardiff's Kingsway. The district had an overdraft of £98, the letterbox had not been cleared for weeks and, until a typewriter was borrowed from the Welsh Housing and Development Association, the office had no facilities at all.

The newly appointed secretary was John Davies, and he remained in the post until his death in December 1937. He was born on 5 May 1882 at Blaenpennal, Cardiganshire; his birthplace, his maternal grandfather's smallholding of Bryn-bedd, had been built on land which, forty years earlier, had been described as 'unenclosed waste'. Within a year, the agricultural distress of the 1880s had forced his parents, Jane and William Davies, to move to Maerdy, where William became a collier. A second son, Daniel, was born in October 1885; two months later William, along with eighty others, was killed in the Maerdy explosion of 24 December.

Jane and her two sons returned to Cardiganshire where they lived in a one-roomed mud cottage in Llangeitho. 'My mother's income,' wrote John to Thomas Jones of Rhymni in 1937, 'came from the Miners' Permanent Fund....five shillings a week on her account less four pence poundage on the postal order....and 2/6 for the two boys until we were thirteen years of age. Periodically a representative of the Fund would come to Llangeitho to assure himself that we were still alive; that my mother was single and, cheek of cheek, to make certain that she was of good repute. Further, she had now and again to get a minister or a magistrate to report in like manner. My mother supplemented this income by work, hard work too, in the fields, at the wash-tub and was the recognized midwife of the district....She was a woman of iron nerve, but that was only when there was call for nerve. Ordinarily she was *tyner* [tender], ever so *tyner,* and everybody in trouble came to her for comfort and everyone regarded her with great affection.'

At the age of thirteen, John was apprenticed to a draper in Porth, Rhondda, and later served in shops and department stores in Barry, Cardiff, London and in and around Swansea. The life of a store apprentice – the boys sleeping among the rolls of carpet and being dismissed if they pocketed sixpences secreted among merchandise in order to test their honesty – disgusted and sickened him. He developed a hatred of drapers comparable with that of Caradoc Evans. The living-in caused him to have a chest complaint which necessitated lengthy periods of recuperation at Llangeitho. While in Porth, he was witness to the 1898 lock-out, an experience which led him to interest himself in social and political questions. In later years he was to claim that he was the first to borrow and read the Porth Public Library's copy of *Das Kapital.* In 1900, he moved to Swansea, working initially for Lewis Lewis and then for Ben Evans. Already a member of the ILP, he first attended its annual conference in 1904. He also attended the conferences of the Shop Assistants, Warehousemen and Clerks' Union; at that of 1903 he was photographed alongside Margaret Bondfield. He moved to London in 1904. While there, he was a member of the Willesden Green Welsh Calvinistic Methodist Chapel where he came under the influence of the religious revival of 1904–05. That experience, together with his upbringing in Llangeitho, caused him to be a life-long adherent of Calvinistic Methodism, despite his frequent exasperation at the behaviour of what he called the 'Corphites'. Also while in London, he attended a demonstration at the Queen's Hall to greet the twenty-nine Labour MPs returned in the general election of 1906. Thereafter, his allegiance to the Labour Party was absolute. His first loyalty, however, was always the ILP tradition and to the concept of Labour as being a movement rather than merely a political party; that, he informed Thomas Jones, 'is the greatest formative influence in [my] life'.

Driven from London by ill health in 1906, he took up, after further convalescence in Llangeitho, various jobs in Swansea and the upper Tawe valley. The Labour movement came to absorb all his leisure hours. Among his priorities were his efforts 'to relate the working-class movement to the cultural past of Wales', an issue he discussed with Keir Hardie. Along with the distinguished educationalist, David Thomas, he arranged a meeting in 1911 at the Carmarthen National Eisteddfod to seek to give the I.L.P. a more distinct Welsh identity, a meeting condemned by the veteran Liberal, Llewelyn Williams, as 'an attempt to bring politics into the eisteddfod'. He became a close associate of James Griffiths, who remembered in 1937 'the great rally [John] organized at Brynaman when young Victor Grayson, fresh from his triumph at Colne Valley, came down'. The secretary of the Brynaman I.L.P, he would, recalled his obituarist in *The South Wales Voice*, 'mount the platform which was usually an old dray in the open air with only about half a dozen to encourage him….He used to taunt the local Liberals that once disestablishment of the Church of England in Wales was on the statute book they would have nothing left to shout about.'

It was *The South Wales Voice*, then entitled *Llais Llafur*, which first gave John a wider sphere of activity. 'Discovered' in 1909 by W. H. Stephenson, the paper's chief reporter, John, then aged 27, became a staff writer for *Llais Llafur* while still serving as a shop assistant. His link with the paper lasted until September 1914 when he volunteered for military service. Rejected on health grounds, he spent the years 1914 to 1917 as a hut leader with the Y.M.C.A. on Salisbury Plain, an open-air life which did much to restore his health. He then became the organizer of the Agricultural Labourers' Union in Pembrokeshire, Cardiganshire and Carmarthenshire at a crucial period in the history of rural radicalism. By the end of 1918, the union had almost three thousand members in the three counties and approaches had been made to John to stand as Labour candidate in Cardiganshire. During his campaigning he gave vent to memorable attacks on the much vaunted radicalism of the small farmers of Wales. His work won literary recognition for he provided the model for the rural trade union organizer, Gomer Davies, in J.O. Francis's *Cross Currents*, and also, so he believed, for Gwilym in Francis's *Change*. While working for the union, he represented farm labourers on the Agricultural Wages Committee, chaired by the Llangeitho scholar, Methodist and landowner, J. H. Davies, assisted E. J. Chappell in his inquiry into agricultural wages and worked for Seebohn Rowntree's survey of rural housing needs.

## A Daunting Prospect

Such was the background of the man who, out of 131 candidates, was appointed to the Cardiff office of the WEA in the autumn of 1919. At the time, he was responsible for the whole of Wales, for the northern district was not established until July 1925. John faced a daunting prospect. The district was more or less bankrupt. The chief task of the new secretary was to coordinate courses for the working classes provided and financed by the colleges of the University of Wales; this presented difficulties, for many of the leading figures in the largest of those colleges, and the one which was on John's doorstep, the University College Cardiff, were notoriously unenthusiastic about such ventures. In Cardiff, while *The South Wales Daily News* was supportive of the WEA, its better financed competitor, *The Western Mail*, was hostile to any form of workers' education. Even more challenging was the fact that a rival grouping, the advocates of Independent Working-Class Education (IWCE), was rapidly winning support in the south Wales coalfield. To them, the WEA was a middle class conspiracy which sought to use education to ensure that the working class did not revolt against capitalism.

Yet the situation did not lack its positive aspects. Among them was the support provided by what Richard Lewis has called the Cardiff/Barry coterie. Idealists with views varying from New Liberalism to Fabian socialism, they included D. Lleufer Thomas, one of the truly great figures in the history of modern Wales. Chairman of the Welsh WEA from 1915 to 1919, Lleufer Thomas was the author of the WEA's submission to Lord Haldane's Royal Commission on University Education in Wales and chairman of the panel which produced the report on Wales for the Commission on Industrial Unrest. In both these roles he used the challenge of the IWCE movement as an argument for providing resources for non-partisan working-class education. An earlier member of the coterie was Thomas Jones, by 1919 the deputy secretary of the cabinet and the conduit for innumerable useful contacts for the WEA; perhaps the most important was his association with the wealthy coalowner, David Davies of Llandinam, and Davies's sisters, Gwendoline and Margaret Davies of Gregynog. The ventures established through the Jones/Davies connection included the monthly journal *The Welsh Outlook* which, until its demise in 1933, gave unstinting support to the WEA.

Equally important to the growth of the WEA was the fact that, although the IWCE movement had strong support among the south Wales miners, there were other groups of workers which were virtually immune from its influence. Chief among them were the iron and steel workers with their traditionally moderate leadership. Coincident with John's appointment was the establishment, through the initiative of Arthur Pugh, the leader of the Iron and Steel Trades Confederation, of the Workers' Education Trade Union Committee (WETUC), a body eager to have the closest association with the WEA. Immediately upon his appointment as district secretary, John also became secretary of the two south Wales committees of the WETUC, one based in Swansea and the other in Cardiff. In September 1920, a full-time organizing tutor was appointed for the Swansea district. He was Illtyd David, who did much to raise the profile of the WEA in west Glamorgan and east Carmarthenshire.

But perhaps the greatest asset of the south Wales WEA in the difficult days of the early 1920s was the personality and experience of its district secretary. John was not a great administrator. As his old friend, W. S. Collins, wrote in 1937: 'I would not call him a first class ledger clerk.' Indeed, as Ernest Green, the general secretary of the WEA, put it in his obituary: '[John] believed that the only barriers to the new Jerusalem were constitutions, fixed rules and committee meetings.' Thomas Jones agreed: 'No one quite knew what was happening or how. Once a year there was a business meeting, an array of nominations and voting papers, an election and a tea party. We all guessed that the proposers and seconders were puppets gladly obeying the promptings of the Secretary. There was an Executive of quite worthy and responsible public figures, professors and the like, but they too were equally obedient to the nods of the genial dictator.'

'Genial dictatorship' may have been the only way to run the south Wales WEA in the 1920s. The most pressing problem was the lack of money. In 1919–20, when the expenditure of the WEA as a whole was £5,212, its income was £3,720, so Wales could not expect extra help from headquarters. In his early days, 'wrote W. S. Collins in 1937, '[John] saw more pay days than pay packets'. 'The WEA in Wales is bankrupt', wrote John to Thomas Jones in December 1920. 'We have just negotiated an overdraft of £150 so that [I] can be paid for the last four months or so.' He was paid, but two years later his salary was six months in arrears. Matters improved in the rather more prosperous years 1923–5 and in its report for 1924–5 the district stated that for the first time it was not in debt. The following year was calamitous. 'The District owes me five months salary', John informed the Association's vice-president, Professor A. D. Lindsay, in December 1926. 'I have had to arrange a personal overdraft to carry on. The WEA overdraft of £250 is fully drawn upon. This means that the liability of the District is at the moment in the neighbourhood of £500' – that is, some £40,000 by today's values.

The ability of the south Wales WEA to limp along financially in the early and mid twenties depended on the generosity of middle class patrons, for, with the onset of depression, little could be expected from trade unions, working-men's clubs and working-class members. Professional men gave what they could; in 1920–21, for example, R. T. Jenkins gave £5, despite his distrust of 'the mission theory of education'. Comfortably off Cardiff families were persuaded to give, with Mabel and Lilian Howell of Llandaf being particularly generous. John's ability to raise money owed much to his membership of the KKK, the Kardomah Koffee Klub, a group of businessmen and others who met daily in the Kardomah Cafe in Cardiff's Queen Street. His habit of carrying on much of his work in the cafe was to Illtyd David a mark of his eccentricity, although the contacts he made there were central to the ability of the WEA to survive. The crucial contributors to the WEA, however, were the Davieses of Llandinam and Gregynog. In 1920–21, David Davies gave £500 and his sisters made an unsecured loan of £300. In subsequent years John, through Thomas Jones, succeeded in persuading the sisters to pay their substantial annual contributions four years in advance.

That a working-class movement should be so reliant upon the largesse of capitalists –particularly the Davieses, the chief shareholders in the Ocean Coal Company – made the WEA vulnerable to the attacks of the IWCE movement. In response, John was always ready to stress his socialist links, partly no doubt in order to deflect left-wing opposition, but fundamentally as an expression of his own convictions. He kept up his links with the Agricultural Labourers' Union, publicly urging its members to support Labour candidates in general elections. He made it known that he was a friend of A. J. Cook, although the friendship consisted largely of urging Cook, unsuccessfully, to curb the language of his overhasty letters to the press. He was a close associate of Alfred Zimmern, the professor of International Politics at Aberystwyth and Lloyd George's Labour opponent in the general election of 1924. In his *My Impressions of Wales* (published by Mills and Boon in 1921), Zimmern paid him a warn tribute; indeed, it was John who suggested to Zimmern the concept of the coalfield as American Wales, a concept which would become something of a mantra for later generations of Welsh socialist historians. On occasion, John could sound very much like an ardent supporter of the IWCE movement. 'I have always deprecated', he wrote in 1934, 'the tendency to apologize for the place Economics and Industrial History occupy as subjects taken in Adult Classes….The further you get from these subjects, the further you get from the real and fundamental interests of working people….Leadership ….never comes to the type of worker who spreads his interests over many fields….The ever widening range of subjects in Adult Classes is having the effect of attracting…."tame students"….What the students need is a soaking in Economics and History.'

John's commitment to the Labour movement was at its most apparent during the General Strike of 1926. Following its collapse, J. M. Mactavish, the general secretary of the WETUC, anxious to refute any accusations of capitalist collaboration by his organization and by the WEA, sought information from all the district secretaries. John informed him that 'our students, of course, were involved up to the neck'; the chairman of the Cardiff Strike Committee was a WEA tutor, he himself had acted as the committee's minutes secretary and the committee's bulletin had been produced on John's own gestetner duplicator. 'I do not think', he added, 'that we have anything to fear from NCLC criticism….in this connection.'

Yet, emphasising its political radicalism in order to stave off criticism from the ICWE movement made the WEA vulnerable to attack from the other end of the political spectrum. Among the critics were leading figures at University College Cardiff and, above all, *The Western Mail*. Urged by John, Thomas Jones in 1925 wrote privately to Sandbrock, the paper's deputy editor, arguing that the WEA, far from being an ally of Bolshevism, was a bulwark against it. 'The original purpose of the WEA', answered Sandbrock, 'was admirable [as]….a strong protection against vicious propaganda [but]….many friends of the University do not regard [it] as so conservative a force today as you appear to believe it is.' The issue had become more acute from 1924 onwards, for changes introduced by the first Labour government meant that the WEA henceforth received direct grants from the Board of Education. In his correspondence with Sandbrock, Thomas Jones acknowledged that 'there had been sharp criticism of bias on the part of one or two of the WEA tutors….These are evils which require handling firmly.' Criticism reached a crescendo in 1926 when sympathetic Board of Education inspectors and even *The Welsh Outlook* expressed disquiet. When it became known that Thomas Jones intended to establish an adult education college in Harlech, primarily as an extension of the work of the WEA, *The Western Mail*'s hostility became even more palpable. John, one his closest associates in the venture, lamented that 'all this business in the Mail will have the devil's own influence on our projects'. 'You can render us a signal service', he informed Thomas Jones, 'if you could write me an article for publication in the Western Mail on the relation of the WEA to the universities and to Labour.' Thomas Jones defended Coleg Harlech with vigour in *The Western Mail* and also wrote to leading figures in south Wales asking whether one should infer that 'the policy of the Mail and its proprietors is to fan the flames of class war and to do all they can to make more difficult the task of the conciliator'.

In stating that the WEA was a socialist organisation, *The Western Mail* was not indulging in a groundless attack – although it may be pertinent to ask what else a movement offering education to socially aware members of the working class could have been in the south Wales of the inter-war years. Some of its classes were covertly if not overtly Marxist in their teaching, for there were tutors who had one set of notes for teaching purposes and another for showing to the Board of Education's inspectors. The district secretary was undoubtedly aware of such stratagems and was content to connive in them. Yet, he was skilful in piloting his ship between the Scylla of the IWCE movement's criticism and the Charybdis of *The Western Mail*'s hostility. In this he was assisted by the public perception of his character and convictions. Although having some sympathy for Marxism, he saw little virtue in the Soviet Union. Unlike Silyn Roberts, the WEA's north Wales district secretary, who in 1930 longed to 'live for another forty years in order to see the fruit of this stupendous experiment in Russia', John was convinced that he and his kind would have been among the first to be assassinated by Stalin. His socialism had none of the dogmatic certainties of many of his contemporaries, for, as E. L. Chappell put it; '[John's] urge to socialism was religious and humanitarian rather than political'. His rural background and experience, his deep immersion in Welsh literary culture, his loyalty to Cardiff's Pembroke Terrace Calvinistic Methodist Chapel and his ability to associate with all manner of men and women made him an unconvincing harbinger of Bolshevism.

### Responsible Body Status
On his appointment, John's first task was to energize the Joint Tutorial Classes Committee of which he and the registrar of University College Cardiff were co-secretaries. Progress was encouraging. The number of tutorial classes in Wales trebled between 1919 and 1924, although, initially, the growth in the Cardiff region was less than it was in the regions served by Bangor and Aberystwyth. A major factor in the expansion was the enthusiasm shown by the newly established University College at Swansea, where 388 students registered for tutorial classes in 1920–21. Cardiff's role increased in the mid 1920s, partly because the University

Extension Board established as a result of Lleufer Thomas's submission to the Haldane Commission, was by then fully functional. (The college became much more supportive from 1929 onwards, when J. F. Rees, the tutor of the first WEA class in Gwynedd and a one-time treasurer of the Association, became its principal.) In 1926–7, the University financed 136 tutorial and preparatory classes in association with the WEA, with Swansea responsible for 25, Aberystwyth for 29, Bangor for 31 and Cardiff for 51.

By the mid 1920s, the WEA was not merely organizing courses financed by the university colleges, for in 1924 it had been accepted as a responsible body for state grant aid. The aid was not great – in 1925–6 the Board of Education granted £220.0s.11d. to the south Wales WEA – but it did allow the Association to establish courses wholly under its control. By the late 1920s, John had responsibility for five different types of courses: preparatory courses which ran for twenty-four weeks; tutorial classes divided into a first, a second and a third year; lecture courses of between three and ten weeks; terminal courses of up to eighteen weeks; one-year courses of at least twenty weeks. The first two were financed by the university colleges and the last three were the direct responsibility of the W.E.A. The university courses, which paid a tutor's fee of £3.6s.8d. for a two-hour session, were generally given by tutors with higher degrees; David Thomas, the founder and editor of the WEA's magazine *Lleufer*, obtained an M.A. specifically in order to conduct a tutorial course. The WEA's courses, which were less well remunerated (usually a guinea per class), drew on a wider range of tutors, some with formal qualifications and others with none.

Organizing these courses, together with innumerable day schools and special conferences, was a formidable task, especially in view of the fact that, although the WEA office had a telephone, hardly any of the tutors and class secretaries had one. In 1922, the WEA moved into more commodious offices at 38 Charles Street, sharing the building with E. L. Chappell's Welsh Housing and Development Association. John only spent a small proportion of his time there, for he believed that his main task was to visit classes, not only to undertake that quintessential WEA task, the checking of the registers, but also to give the inspirational addresses which were remembered with such gratitude by those who paid tribute to him after his death. Visits to evening classes, particularly in west Wales, could involve an absence of up to three days. His wife recalled in 1951 that he hardly ever spent a night at home. The problems of the pre-car era were common to all those involved in adult education; R. T. Jenkins wrote a delightful essay in which he described how he travelled to classes by a combination of train, bus and cart or was passed like a parcel from crossroads to crossroads by car-owning well-wishers. The Association equipped John with a car in 1936. Although the car greatly increased his mobility, it caused him much heartache; in places like Dowlais in the mid 1930s, drivers of cars, even very modest ones like his, were considered to be capitalists, and his vehicle was stoned on more than one occasion.

Already vastly well acquainted with west Wales, Swansea and the anthracite coalfield, John's work with the WEA gave him an intimate knowledge of Cardiff and the valleys of east Glamorgan and Monmouthshire. His association with Coleg Harlech and his friendship with David Thomas and other northern socialists made him familiar with much of the north. As a result he seemed to know everyone in Wales and everyone knew him. As W. J. Gruffydd put it: 'After the demise of Sir John Morris-Jones and John Williams Brynsiencyn, there was only one John in Wales.' He came to be acknowledged as the prime authority on all matters relating to Wales, knowledge which he put to good use in the mid 1930s in his weekly gossip column in the Welsh edition of *The Daily Herald*. 'No one was better informed on Wales', wrote W. S. Collins. 'His encyclopaedic knowledge of Wales and its people' wrote *The South Wales Voice*, 'was unsurpassed.' 'I got to know and appreciate', wrote the distinguished writer Glyn Jones, 'his vast and detailed knowledge of every branch of Welsh life; there seemed to be no aspect of Welsh life and culture and institutions with which he did not have an intimate acquaintance.'

But the more he knew about Wales, the more his knowledge distressed him. As his correspondence with Mactavish shows, he was shattered by the events of 1926. By the late 1920s, his reaction to the depression was causing friends such as E. L. Chappell to consider him 'morose and despondent....As he approached his late forties, we feared that he might develop into a soured surly cynic.' Then, in 1929, at the age of 47, he took a wife. Ruby Part, a native of Portsmouth, was the woman organizer of the Workers' Union and the Labour candidate for Wells in the 1929 general election. 'We were staggered by the marriage', wrote W. S. Collins, while E. L. Chappell declared that it 'revolutionized his entire outlook and led to a great improvement in his health and appearance'. Ruby shared his convictions, although some of his Cardiganshire acquaintances found her baffling. Until recently, there were still in Llangeitho those who remember their surprise when a son of Jane Maerdy (as his mother was known) brought to the village a cigarette-smoking, Eton-cropped, eyebrow- plucked wife who sought to convince the inhabitants of that heartland of abattoir agriculture of the virtues of vegetarianism.

The year 1929 was also a year of considerable expansion in the work of the WEA. 'I took the chair', wrote Thomas Jones in March 1929, 'in the rooms of Captain Ellis of the Council for Social Service. He has secured £5000 from the Carnegie Trust and we shall spend £3000 in south Wales and £2000 in Durham on works of cheerfulness.' 'What', he asked John, 'is the best way of spending this money?' John became the secretary of yet another committee, the joint committee for the promotion of educational facilities in the south Wales coalfield. Two tutor/organizers were appointed: D. E. Evans, the editor of the WEA's Welsh journal, *Cambria* (1930–32), and the future distinguished economist, Brinley Thomas. Afternoon lectures with a rather lighter content were organized as were singing sessions and free drama and musical performances. Concerned at the decline in the ability of workers' libraries to buy books, John arranged for Brinley Thomas to make a survey and, through Thomas Jones, obtained a grant of £1000 from Carnegie to restock them. The Carnegie-funded activity proved hugely successful, with the number of sessions organised by the WEA rising by ninety per cent between 1928 and 1930. In 1929, 161 concerts attracting 72,673 people and 89 singing sessions attended by 5,801 singers were held. Afternoon lectures drew large audiences with three hundred listening to a Welsh-language talk at Cefncoedycymer. Dora Herbert Jones's Saturday school on Welsh folk singing at Maerdy, an occasion when John broke down remembering his father's death, was later recalled by her in a memorable broadcast.

The Carnegie grant continued until August 1933. Among the developments it financed was the appointment in 1931 of a full-time WEA organizer based at Swansea. The post went to Mansel Grenfell (brother of D. R. Grenfell, the Labour M.P. for Gower from 1922 to 1959), a man whose devotion to the WEA enabled him to build upon the achievements of Illtyd David and the WETUC. The Carnegie activities involved close cooperation between the WEA and the YMCA and the National Council for Music and with figures such as E. H. F. Mills, the education officer for the BBC's West Region. (John acquired a wireless in 1932 and quickly 'learnt some of the possibilities of Radio'.)

The south Wales district secretary's involvement in activity outside the immediate control of the WEA caused the Association central office to write to John to express disquietude. 'Until Carnegie', answered John, 'we were really at the end of our resources as a grant-earning body....If you decide upon non-cooperation, you will isolate the WEA....The glory of the WEA has been in its capacity to cooperate with all kinds of organization and yet retain its own integrity....If we pulled out, our classes would be reduced by two thirds and I would have to consider seriously my position as district secretary.'

With the cessation of the Carnegie grants, the joint committee became the education committee of the south Wales Council for Social Service of which John was secretary until 1936. The leading figure in the council was Percy Watkins, another member of the Cardiff/Barry coterie. John had doubts about Watkins. 'We who have been born to the purple', he informed Thomas Jones, '[the reference was to the fact that he was a Rhondda collier's son] have many misgivings that Percy, born and bred in a border town [Llanfyllin], does not understand.' In turn, Watkins, who was virtually apolitical, chided John: 'You are a little disposed to consider it almost improper for any of us who do not happen to be within the working-class movement to interest ourselves in the working class.' John, however, had more basic suspicions of the social service movement. 'What I fear above everything else in the....movement', he wrote in 1937, 'is the creation of a class with a vested interest in it and who will represent its activities, always having at the back of their mind that a case has to be made because their livelihood depends upon it.' He was frequently outraged by references to the working class 'as if they were a race apart'. 'I am in dread', he informed Thomas Jones in 1933, 'of this feeling conscious of well doing. I met it during the war in the YMCA I meet it in the WEA.' What annoyed him most was what he considered to be the voyeur element in the social service movement. Writing to Percy Watkins shortly before his death, he referred to those who stressed 'the value of sending down young men from Balliol to Maes-yr-haf [the settlement in the Rhondda]. I am sick and tired of this kind of attitude. The depression did not come to south Wales for their good.'

Grants from the Social Services Council and the Board of Education and further contributions from wealthy patrons – above all, from Gwendoline Davies – together with subscriptions from members and fees from students, caused the south Wales WEA by the mid 1930s to have a more secure financial basis. Nevertheless, the two most powerful institutions in south Wales, the Glamorgan County Council and the South Wales Miners' Federation, refused any assistance, the former because it maintained its own network of adult classes and the latter because a substantial number of its members remained committed to the IWCE movement.

The WEA's ability to receive state grants was a major factor in allowing it to outdo its more radical rival. The antagonism of the IWCE enthusiasts lasted throughout the interwar years. When the WEA celebrated its coming-of-age in 1924, Raymond Postgate, the chairman of the Plebs League Executive Committee, declared: 'It is no fault of ours that you have reached your twenty-first birthday. We would be much happier to attend your funeral.' Hostility became so great that in 1926 A. D. Lindsay suggested that in the Rhondda Valley 'some educational body not involved in this wrangle should be employed'. Reciprocal hostility from the WEA was less common, for there were those within it, John among them, who welcomed the competition, partly because they shared at least some of the views of the IWCE movement, and partly because the movement's successes were a telling argument for state aid for more moderate organizations. In 1953, John Thomas, Wales's first WEA full-time organizer and a man who had at least flirted with the far left, wrote: 'I firmly believe that their opposition gave us something of a backbone and turned out to be a blessing in the end.' The chief institution maintained by the advocates of independent working-class education was the Labour College in Pen-y-wern Road in London's Earl's Court. Financed in the main by the South Wales Miners' Federation, its students included some of the most distinguished of the leaders of the south Wales miners, Aneurin Bevan, James Griffiths and Ness Edwards among them. In 1929, the SWMF, its income much reduced and its leaders dissatisfied with the running of the college and the education it provided, withdrew its £4,500 annual grant and the college closed. In 1953, Thomas recalled with some pleasure that he had been a member of the council of the Federation when the vote was taken. The classes of the IWCE movement in south Wales were at their most numerous in 1926 when they attracted nearly two thousand students, a figure which had halved by the early 1930s. The Rhondda Labour College collapsed in 1933 and that at Merthyr in 1936. There was a revival of activity in 1936 when the Federation began giving direct support to the classes of the Central Council of Labour Colleges but, by the end of the decade, when even the miners were more likely to be found in WEA classes than in those of the advocates of independent working class education, it would seem that victory in the battle between the two traditions had gone to the WEA. The greater resources of the Association – its ability to pay tutors, for example, an issue over which the IWCE movement agonized – was not the only factor in that victory. Equally important were the decline in the millenarian hopes so widespread in the era when coalminers seemed triumphantly indispensable and the emergence of working-class leaders more concerned with practical issues than with immediate revolution – developments which were the direct result of the interwar economic depression.

## The Great Depression

The depression could not but have a massive impact upon the WEA also. There were those who believed that, with a vast pool of unemployed workers, those in enforced idleness would wish to make constructive use of what was euphemistically called 'the new leisure'. There were certainly many who did so, as the intense studies undertaken by Aneurin Bevan and others testify. The experience of idleness could, however, be more enervating than stimulating. As the peace campaigner, Gwilym Davies, put it: 'Many hundreds....who have known no work or useful activity since leaving school....have reached a stage of extreme inertia and devitalization which makes them inaccessible to WEA teaching....We have to deal with many hundreds of young people whose very humanity is threatened.' Those who were fortunate enough to have work frequently had to travel long distances to their employment, a new experience in the south Wales valleys where, in communities which had grown around the pits, a short walk to work had been the norm. Writing of the difficulties of attracting students to classes in Merthyr, John noted in 1930 that 'hundreds of Merthyr workers have to travel to their place of employment leaving at 5 a.m.'

More fundamental, however, was the realization that unemployment undermined the whole rationale of the WEA. Its primary purpose was to equip workers with the skills and the habits of thought which would allow them to give better service to their community and their trade union. Addressing the Barry Unemployed Clubs in 1937, John declared: 'One of the objects of the W.E.A. is to bridge the gulf between the world of work and the world of learning. We assumed that WEA attendants would be involved in work....I have to ask myself: can I, when talking to unemployed men, use the same appeal as I would to men at work? It is no use my urging them to study for the sake of equipping themselves for work in Trade Unions when, for the last ten to fifteen years, they have not belonged to a Trade Union.'

The realization that not all, or even most, of those attending WEA classes would be in a position to give leadership in their place of work, caused much heart searching. (The matter was much more serious for the supporters of the IWCE movement, who were subject to much victimization. By championing independent working-class education they were ensuring, as Richard Lewis put it, 'exclusion from the very movement they aimed to serve'.) The alternative was to consider that the aim of adult education was the maintenance of morale and the encouragement of individual self-development. Despite his central role in the Carnegie Trust's campaign to provide 'works of cheerfulness', John had doubts about such activity. At the 1937 Barry meeting, he referred to the explosive growth of less work-based classes: 'Frankly, I am sceptical as to the value of all this extraordinary activity....I am informed that all this helps to keep up the morale of the unemployed. Speaking as an individual, and not as the secretary of an organization, I have little interest in this aspect of the work….The conditions are such that I, at any rate, would rejoice if there were a good deal more than there is of revolt.' Unemployed clubs were themselves organizations of which he was suspicious, for they 'further segregate [the unemployed] from the rest of the community'. Although he was one of the founders of the Senghennydd settlement and was closely involved with Rhondda settlements – that at Maes-yr-haf in particular – the settlement and the occupational clubs movement also, he believed, offered no solutions. Describing in 1933 the discussions at the Gregynog conference on the future of south Wales, Thomas Jones noted: 'We were all at one in holding that these occupational clubs should not be allowed to mislead the public into thinking that a solution of the unemployed problem had been found….John Davies [was]….emphatic about this and more than once we were on the edge of plunging into a discussion of the Social Revolution.'

Yet, the circumstances of the 1930s obliged adult education enthusiasts to reconsider their priorities. Ben Bowen Thomas, the much admired first warden of Coleg Harlech, argued in 1930 that 'ultimately, the duty of the adult educationalists lies neither towards the industrial worker group nor towards his locality but to the man himself.' In moments of self-reflection, John acknowledged that that was precisely his own experience. Having left school at thirteen, it was self-education which had, as he put it, allowed him to escape 'from the toils of industrialism (in the shape of a shop); [therefore] it is not for me to sit in judgment on….students who also want to escape industrialism'. (Whenever he saw an employee of a draper's shop, Ruby recalled in 1951, he would declare: 'There but for the grace of God goes John Davies.') His post with the WEA had allowed him to join the middle class. His salary of £350 (raised to £400 in 1935) was supplemented by his earnings from *The Daily Herald* and other sources. His house in Wenallt Road, Rhiwbina (which would cost at least £350,000 today), his motor car, his fine collection of Bryn-mawr furniture, his subscription to all the publications of the Gregynog Press, his holidays with Thomas Jones in Denmark and elsewhere and his weekend walking tours in the Mendip Hills placed him in a very different category from most of those he sought to serve. His brother, Daniel, remembered being flummoxed by John's insistence that he, as the secretary of the WEA, was working class, while Daniel, a carpenter employing two men, was a member of the petit bourgeoisie. The contrast in life styles belied the insistence; Daniel lived in a small terraced house in Treorci and his only overseas visit was a malaria-ridden trudge with the South Wales Borderers through the Negev Desert in the campaign to capture Jerusalem.

The implications of his embourgeoisement – an experience he shared with a number of leaders of working-class movements resident in the Rhiwbina of the 1930s – came home to John in 1934 during the controversy over the activities of the Unemployed Assistance Board (the UAB). His mentor, Thomas Jones, accepted one of the five seats on the board. Jones became obsessed with the principle of standardizing payments, a principle which, particularly in south Wales, led to a reduction in the already woefully inadequate relief received by the workless. John was appalled by what he considered to be Jones's harshness and the matter came close to causing a permanent breach between them. 'Ruby and I', he wrote to Thomas Jones in January 1935, 'are wholly in sympathy with the agitation now being carried out in south Wales against the operation of [the UAB]. The last week has been a time of *cyfyng gyngor* [quandary] for us….[We] have had very real searchings of the heart. We have asked ourselves "where did we stand in relation to the working-class movement?" We had become somewhat aloof from it and developed a critical attitude towards some aspects of it, especially its political expression in Parliament and in local bodies. Owing to the administration of the Unemployed Act, we had to face up to things and ask where did we belong. Ruby and I were brought up in the working-class movement. It has been the greatest formative influence in our lives…So we judge all things in relation to this movement. The time of parting has come.'

The worsening conditions of the unemployed in general and the UAB issue in particular caused John to be increasingly radicalized in the last years of his life, a radicalization indicated by his advocacy in 1934 of 'soakings in Economics and History' and his wish in 1937 for 'more revolt'. Yet, during his period as secretary of the WEA in south Wales, the Association became less exclusively a movement for the working class and less involved with subjects considered to be especially relevant to working-class liberation. In 1936–7, the last full year of John's secretaryship, 3,717 students attended the one-year and terminal courses of the south Wales WEA; of these, sixty-eight per cent were manual workers (two-thirds of whom were unemployed), eight per cent housewives, seven per cent professional people (with teachers in the great majority), seven per cent clerical and shop workers, four per cent artisans, three per cent farmers and three per cent uncategorised. The middle-class element was far stronger among the 3,585 attending the tutorial classes arranged in conjunction with the university colleges. In the areas served by Aberystwyth and Swansea, teachers were the largest single group; in the Cardiff area, however, miners and quarrymen constituted twenty-five per cent and teachers sixteen per cent; the equivalent figures in the Bangor area were twenty-six per cent and ten per cent.

In its early years, the WEA had been very much a movement offering a 'soaking in economics and history'. Of the courses offered in 1920–21, two-thirds were concerned with economics and industrial development. In 1936–7, the subject percentages of the 195 tutorial classes held in Wales as a whole were as follows: economics and history 36, Welsh literature and history 16, music 9, English literature 9, religious studies 9, international affairs 9, philosophy and psychology 4, miscellaneous 8. The subject distribution in the 193 courses directly offered by the south Wales WEA was not markedly different: economics and history 44, international affairs 17, philosophy and psychology 12, English literature 10, religious studies 7, Welsh literature and history 6, miscellaneous 4. The most striking development in the 1930s was the increasing prominence of international affairs, a reflection of the deteriorating situation in Europe. The south Wales WEA held four courses on the subject in 1932–3, a figure which would rise to sixty in 1937–8. This was a development which further assisted the WEA in its competition with the IWCE movement; as the Association had close links with the League of Nations Union, it had access to a pool of well informed commentators on world affairs.

Despite his plea for the primacy of economics and history, John could, in some of his many moods, welcome the broadening of the curriculum of the Association. In 1930, he recalled the time when it seemed as if 'the old native culture of south Wales was going to be replaced with another – a culture based on [the worker's] needs as worker....This period has definitely passed....[The worker] is now groping back to his old anchorage and is taking a new interest in Music, in Literature, in Psychology and....in Religion.' He particularly welcomed the increasing demand for classes in Welsh history and literature, for he was as much a Welsh patriot as he was a socialist. Writing to Percy Watkins in 1936, he listed his three abiding concerns: '1. The undividedness of the community. 2. The preservation of the culture and traditions of Wales. 3. The integrity of the working-class movement....I am fully conscious of the contradictions [between them, for] two and three are at war with number one.'

His loyalties were particularly strained following the burning of the bombing school in Llŷn in September 1936 by three prominent members of Plaid Genedlaethol Cymru. Since his Pembrokeshire days, John had been a close friend of one of them, D. J. Williams, and he made a special effort to visit Williams at Fishguard when, as the latter informed Ruby after John's death, 'a dark cloud was hanging over me....Old Jack, as I used to know him, dear old boy, was as brave and challenging as ever.' In his column in *The Daily Herald,* John expressed his 'profound sorrow' regarding the fire, 'but at no time was I prepared to sit in judgment upon these three men….I have lived to see the day when a Conservative prime minister unveiled a memorial to Mrs. Pankhurst….and Miss Mary Allen, who smashed the windows of the Home Office, is now Commandant of the Women Police.' (It may not be without significance that descendants, direct and collateral, of leading figures in the WEA in Wales are now more likely to be found in Plaid Cymru and Cymdeithas yr Iaith Gymraeg than in the Labour Party.)

### 'Education Involves Effort'

The Welsh character of the WEA in Wales has been a matter of some discussion. So embedded was it in Welsh communities by the 1930s that there was a widespread belief that it represented an organic growth springing from the circulating schools of Griffith Jones, the Welsh adult Sunday schools, the traditions of the eisteddfod and the hopes of the more visionary founders of the University of Wales. However, as Richard Lewis has demonstrated and as John Thomas acknowledged, the Welsh district was in fact established by English and Scottish academics. Yet, in the 1920s, the WEA in Wales developed a marked Welsh identity, a government report of 1927 stating that 'in Wales, to a greater extent than perhaps in England, the movement is quickly grasping the community as a whole and is assuming the character of a national movement of enlightenment'. Among the unique features of the work of the Association in Wales was the arrangement with the National Library whereby every class was supplied with a box of at least twenty-five books; in 1929-30, the library distributed 257 boxes containing 6,750 books. John sought to insist that each member of a one-year course should read the entire twenty-five. 'Education', he wrote in 1936, 'involves effort. Some tend to look upon the tutor as the one who does all the work while they are simply passive recipients. A WEA class is not the alternative to spending an idle hour over cards or in gossip….It is a serious affair designed for serious students.'

As the years passed, the WEA in Wales developed a rich mythology. It included stories of attendants collecting candle-ends to illuminate classes in halls lacking gas or electricity, of students dressing in their Sunday best to undergo the quasi-sacred process of education, of farm labourers going straight from the plough to a six-mile walk to a class, of postmen dazzling classes with quotations from Bergson and of train drivers delaying trains so that tutors, held up by the intense debates of their students, could return home. Although such stories could probably have been gathered from any WEA district, they gave rise to a belief in the uniqueness of the Association in Wales. As Percy Watkins put it in 1930: 'Nothing quite like [this activity] goes on in any other country.' In terms of class membership, Wales could certainly claim pre-eminence. It was calculated in 1929 that if the ratio between the population and the membership of WEA classes were considered to be 100 in England, the corresponding figure in Wales would be 232. The Welsh figure was inflated by the extraordinary success of the WEA in Gwynedd (Caernarfonshire 550, Meirionnydd 465) but industrial south Wales provided impressive figures -- Carmarthenshire 279, Monmouthshire 165, Glamorgan 163. Despite the growth in the number of middle-class students in the 1930s, the South Wales

*The location of the classes directly conducted by the South Wales district of the WEA in 1936-7*

District led all districts in its proportion of manual-worker students and in that decade Wales retained and strengthened its position where population/student ratios were concerned.

The geographical distribution of the courses of the south Wales WEA is illuminating. The map of their distribution in 1936–7 shows that where the Association's own courses were concerned, the south Wales WEA was above all a movement of the valleys of the coalfield. Pre-eminent among the valleys was the Rhondda, the location of one fifth of the district's terminal classes. There were concentrations of classes in the upper Taf valley with five courses apiece in Merthyr and Dowlais and a further impressive spread in the Monmouthsire coalfield. Most communities in the more thinly inhabited valleys of mid Glamorgan and of the anthracite coalfield had at least one class, but, bearing in mind their large populations, the Association found less support in the major ports. Newport had one one-year course compared with two in Aberbargoed and three in Trethomas. Cardiff had three one-year courses, a number exceeded by the Brynaman area. It had five terminal courses, well below the number held in the communities around Tonypandy. In Cardiff, complained John, the only successful classes were those addressed by celebrities. The WEA found little support in central Swansea, but there were numerous courses in the surrounding townships, Fforest Fach, Dan-y-graig, Gland□r and Bon-y-maen among them. The Neath area was fertile ground, with Briton Ferry, a place with a deep-rooted tradition of religious and political radicalism, sustaining four one-year courses.

Outside the coalfield and its associated ports, there was a scattering of courses, particularly around Carmarthen. Throughout the interwar years, the Association made virtually no progress in Radnorshire and rural Breconshire; south Pembrokeshire also proved unpromising territory. Cardiganshire's appetite for adult education, manifested in its support for Aberystwyth's tutorial classes, did not extend to the WEA. John ascribed that to the attitude of Herbert Morgan, Aberystwyth's Director of Extramural Studies. 'He has definitely discouraged his tutors from helping us in any way', he wrote in 1932. 'He sits as tightly as he can on what he conceives to be his egg, and the fact is that it is addled.' Morgan, himself a one-time Labour parliamentary candidate, referred to the WEA in 1935 as 'the cuckoo in the nest'. On hearing the comment, John stated that the Aberystwyth courses 'are like the old University Extension courses of Oxford, Cambridge and London where well-to-do retired folk spent a pleasant evening....In the absence of [our] movement, Adult Education will drift from its original purpose of bridging the gap between learning and labour.' But perhaps equally significant was the distance of mid Wales from the Cardiff office and the belief,

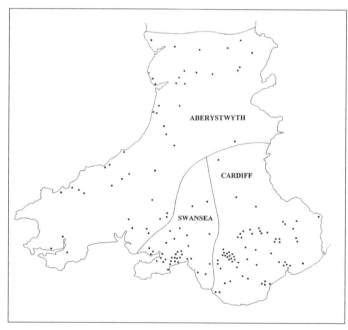

*The location of courses conducted under the auspices of three of the constituent colleges of the University of Wales in 1936-7*

promulgated by Aberystwyth's *Cambrian News,* that the WEA was an industrial movement concerned solely with the teaching of economics. The matter was not seriously taken up until 1954 when a Mid Wales Committee of the W.E.A. was formed. It enjoyed almost immediate success for by 1956 there were 38 classes in Radnorshire and Montgomeryshire.

The distribution of the courses run jointly with the university colleges differed somewhat from that of the Association's own classes. Classes around Aberystwyth were remarkably numerous considering the low density of the population. There was a course in virtually every market town in west and mid Wales, an indication of the fact that tutorial classes had a more middle-class membership than did terminal and one-year courses. Yet the coalfield was well represented, with the Rhondda again pre-eminent. There was an impressive cluster around Swansea, a contrast with the rather lack lustre situation in Cardiff. Reviewing the statistics of 1936-7, John had cause for considerable satisfaction. Under his secretaryship, the number of classes directly run by the WEA had risen from none in 1918–19 to 193 in 1936-7 and the number of tutorial classes in Wales as a whole had increased from 15 to 145.

Yet too much should not be claimed. Although increases in Board of Education grants allowed John to have an office assistant in 1935 and permitted the appointment of seven area tutor/organizers between 1936 and 1938, expenditure on adult education remained low. In the late 1930s, when the annual income of the two Welsh WEA districts was £2,000, and when the Board of Education, the local authorities and the University of Wales contributed between them a further £17,000 towards adult education, £400,000 was spent annually in Wales on tuberculosis prevention, and £600,000 on the care of lunatics. *Cambria* in 1930 pointed out that only five per cent of the population of Wales over fifteen received any form of full-time education. In the late 1930s, when perhaps twelve thousand Welsh people were involved in some form of adult education, the number of adults in the country between the ages of twenty and fifty was well in excess of a million. Thus little more than one person in a hundred was then taking part in activities such as those of the WEA. As the journal *Lleufer* put it in 1947: 'The number we won was small in relation to the population as a whole.' There was much pride in the establishment of Coleg Harlech; yet Denmark had 60 such colleges for a population of three million.

Nevertheless, the impact of an adult education class could reach well beyond those who actually attended it. *The Highway*, the periodical of the WEA as a whole, described in 1938 the impact of the establishment of W.E.A. courses at Tre-fil, a remote limestone- quarrying village north of Tredegar – courses which included A. J. Lush's classes on industrial history and Welsh-medium courses on history and literature. Before the establishment of the class, the village had no water, few other facilities and no road to Tredegar. 'Members of the class were soon leading the local trade union at the quarry. They soon set up an agitation for a village hall, a decent road to Tredegar [and] a water supply. Following this they started an agitation for a Post Office and a Telephone Service[and] a Bus Service....The eagerness of parents for secondary education for their children....[is the] direct result of the propaganda work of the class....Today all these demands have been realized and the village has been transformed into a pleasant community which is alive and sensitive to change.'

In other parts of the United Kingdom, the campaigning work at Tre-fil would have been that of a branch rather than a class, a distinction which, in the view of headquarters, was inexcusably blurred in south Wales. To Ernest Green, the general secretary, the branch was the key to the WEA's activity; its purpose was to heighten public awareness of educational issues – by campaigning for the raising the school-leaving age, for example, or by pressing for improvements in the facilities of local schools. If branches gave rise to classes, all well and good, but, as R. H. Tawney put it in 1936: 'It is not the classes which make the association, but the branches.' John disagreed, as had John Thomas before him. Branch creation presented few problems in areas where there was a substantial socially-conscious middle class, eager to take part in campaigns for educational betterment. John's district did contain some such areas, Cardiff, Newport and Swansea among them, where there were indeed branches. Other places were less promising, particularly in view of the fact that being a branch and a class member was expensive, for branch as well as class fees had to be paid. If a class gave rise to a branch, that was to be welcomed, for John agreed with the comment of his fellow secretary, Silyn Roberts, in 1929: 'Branches that have developed out of classes are always the most vigorous and successful.' As Thomas Jones put it in John's obituary: 'There was, notoriously, hardly a Branch in the whole District and this naturally and properly gave umbrage to Headquarters and begat a litter of letters over months and years.' G. H. Jones, the assistant appointed at Cardiff in 1935, was specifically charged with the duty of establishing branches and in 1936 John acquiesced in the setting up of an organizational sub-committee of which he, significantly perhaps, was not a member.

Believing as he did that 'the only barriers to the New Jerusalem were constitutions, fixed rules and committee meetings', John viewed such developments with foreboding, for they were indicators of what he feared most – that the W.E.A. would become an organization rather than a movement. Remembering John's work at Brynaman, James Griffiths wrote in 1937 of 'those days when it was such a joy to believe in the movement'. That joy, John believed, was ebbing from the Labour Party itself. Instead of the concept of the common weal, he wrote in 1929, 'we now have a strong political party rapidly becoming affected with the defects of the older political parties, becoming sophisticated, losing its pristine innocence – becoming of the world, worldly, getting smart and up-to-date.' Yet despite his suspicions of committees and organizations, he spent two decades deeply enmeshed in them for, apart from his work with the WEA, he was secretary of the Cardiff C.O.P.E.C., a member of the Board of Education's Departmental Committee on Rural Education in Wales, a member of the court of governors of the University Colleges of Cardiff and Aberystwyth, a key figure on the committee which established Coleg Harlech, the co-ordinator of innumerable efforts to ease the path of Welsh migrants to London and the organizer of major protests against government educational policies. (Following that of 1932, John paid the chief speaker, Harold Laski, eight guineas for a half-hour address, over six times the weekly income of an unemployed man.)

Yet, his primary contribution was his passion. 'It might seem to slumber', wrote Thomas Jones, 'under the casual careless surface of his gossip, but it was easily roused and there were moments in a public conference or a private gathering when from the deep would break forth a sudden stream of spontaneous eloquence which made his hearers feel ashamed of their own coldness and slackness.' 'I have often felt gloomy about Adult Education', wrote John Owen of the Monmouthshire Training College in 1937, 'but John never failed to revive my faith….Much of what is best in me I owe to John.' It was this quality which caused John to become the personification of the south Wales WEA. 'One almost felt', wrote Harold Shearman in 1937, 'that in south Wales he *was* the WEA.' 'It may be said' stated D. T. Guy, 'that the WEA. movement in south Wales had grown up around our late Secretary.' His close colleague, David E. Evans, writing of John in 1944 quoted the words of Emerson: 'An institution is the lengthened shadow of a man.'

John died of double pneumonia on 5 December 1937 at his home in Rhiwbina at the age of fifty-five. He was buried at Llangeitho and, in commemoration of his work with the Agricultural Labourers' Union, was carried to his grave by farm workers. The numerous letters of sympathy received by Ruby, his widow, from rank and file members of the WEA are proof of the high regard in which he was held. There were commemorative tributes on the radio and in *The Highway, Y Llenor* and other journals, a memorial service at Gregynog and a memoir published by the Gregynog Press. Plans were drawn up for a commemorative scholarship, and a plaque in the library at Coleg Harlech, but, with the approach of war, the plans were abandoned. In 1936, John had expressed the view that, if anything happened to him, his preferred successor was D. J. Davies, the leading working-class intellectual of Plaid Genedlaethol Cymru and the founder at Gilwern of a folk high school on the Danish model. D. J. Davies's name, however, did not appear in the list of the fifty-five who sought to succeed John as the secretary of the south Wales district of the WEA. The man chosen was D. T. Guy. A Coleg Harlech student with an economics degree from Aberystwyth, his appointment was symbolic of the new direction which the WEA would be taking. Yet, as an ex-miner with a strong chapel background, he shared many of John's values and aspirations.

A few months before his death, John, accompanied by Thomas Jones – with whom he had by then been reconciled – went on a journey through west Wales. Mulling over their travels, John wrote of their time at Llangeitho, where Jones also had family roots. John recalled a visit he had made to the village shortly before he applied for the WEA secretaryship. He had stayed with his mother who, by then, was living in Meidrym Road, a street built on the site of Daniel Rowland's mass open-air communion services. 'My mother', he wrote, 'had learnt to read in the Sunday school. She had had a cwarter o ysgol [three months of schooling] but had not learnt to write….[I] discovered a drawer littered with her attempts to write the name 'John Davies' or 'Dan Davies'. Her desire to be able to write to her sons without the help of others was intense.' It was a defining moment in his life. Thereafter, he devoted his entire energies to ensure that people like his mother, my grandmother, should achieve that fuller literacy which would allow them to enter into their inheritance.

## Bibliography

The sources for the above include *John Davies* (a memoir published by the Gregynog Press for private circulation in 1938), the Thomas Jones Papers (National Library of Wales), National Library Collections ex1586-7 and ex1639 and the archive at the Cardiff office of the WEA. It owes much to Richard Lewis, *Leaders and Teachers: Adult Education and the Challenge of Labour in south Wales, 1906–1940* (1993). There is useful material in the periodicals *Cambria, The Highway, Y Llenor* and *Lleufer*. Memories of conversations with John's wife, Ruby Davies, and his sister-in-law, Mary Davies, have proved to be invaluable. A fully annotated version of this chapter appeared in *Llafur*, Vol. 8, No. 1, (2000).

# ADULT EDUCATION IN NORTH WALES 1908-1945

## RON BROOKS

What legend has brought together let no historian put asunder. Such has been the attitude towards the double first achieved in adult education in north Wales, with the university tutorial class at Wrexham, begun by the Oxford Tutorial Classes Committee almost before the ink had dried on the Oxford Report of 1908 that launched the movement, and the university tutorial class at Blaenau Ffestiniog of 1910-1911, the first to be run by one of the Welsh Colleges, Bangor, in association with the North Wales Quarrymen's Union. These classes were seen to be of impeccable pedigree, combining the best of Welsh educational tradition stretching back through the literary meetings, eisteddfodau, and Sunday Schools to the circulating schools of Griffith Jones of Llanddowror, with the best form of liberal education that Oxford had to offer. The result was that adult education in north Wales, both before the creation of the North Wales District of the WEA in 1925 and after, was perceived not so much as a broad highway but more as a series of A and B roads, with the university tutorial class representing the best to which all other kinds, whether they were single-term, one-day, preparatory, university extension and weekend, should hopefully lead.

That adult education up to 1945 was viewed in the annual reports of the North Wales district in such a hierarchical way is understandable. The university tutorial class movement was first brought to Wales by the WEA's most revered tutor, R.H. Tawney, a Balliol graduate who went on to become President of the association (1928-1944), in whose Wrexham class was A.H. Dodd, a future professor of History at Bangor and WEA tutor. It was extended to north-west Wales by another Balliol graduate and friend of Albert Mansbridge, Sir Harry Reichel, first principal of the University college of North Wales Bangor, who backed the quarrymen's demand for a class under J.F. Rees at Blaenau Ffestiniog. The legend of 'selfless idealists', of Tawney and Oxford, gained such acceptance that it was difficult for adult education to follow any other role-model. Both myth and the control of developments by university academics and like-minded people meant that university tutorial classes became the yardstick by which all others were measured. There were no Central Labour College (CLC) outposts in north Wales to promote discussion of alternative ways forward.

Legend touches history at more points in the case of the Blaenau Ffestiniog class than in that of the Wrexham class. The group which first met in Wrexham's British-Victoria school, with the support of the town's evening classes committee and local education authority on a cold, Monday evening in mid-January 1909, was never to achieve the stature of the classes at Rochdale or Longton and was to be much less successful than its association with Tawney and Dodd have led historians to believe. Dodd, the Wrexham sixth former whose name never appeared on the class register, was the least typical of the thirty-three members who apprehensively completed their applications forms on the first evening, giving their names, addresses, ages and occupations. All were older, mostly aged thirty to forty, and apart from four teachers and the class organiser, William Aston, an auctioneer, few had much background in history. As C.B. Caldecott, a coach builder put it, they did not know whether 'William of Orange, Pitt or Sir Walter Raleigh were primates, pirates, peers or premiers.' Few had the cultural or financial capital on which Dodd could draw, his father being the headmaster of the school in which the class met, but most, like him, lived in Wrexham and worked in the town's shop-based trades, or in printing or book keeping. There were six railway workers but none from the nearby mining communities, which was to be a major political weakness. There were two manual workers who worked in the town, a labourer and a window cleaner. The latter in a letter to Mansbridge, using appropriate imagery, proclaimed: 'Sirs! There are thousands of working men like myself, who are thirsting for a drink at the wells of knowledge.' However, neither when establishing the class, nor a little later, a WEA branch, did Aston seek the help of the North Wales Miners' Association, unlike Reichel in Bangor who cooperated with the North Wales Quarrymen's Union. This was not without its advantages for the class had a broader occupational profile and culture which encouraged women, especially teachers, to join.

But it left the class vulnerable and subject to the political priorities of the Oxford Tutorial Classes Committee: priorities that had nothing to do with Wales and everything to do with its struggle against the Central Labour College in the industrial north. To Mansbridge, the class was not a new venture in Welsh education but the least successful of Tawney's classes, which could be sacrificed to counter the mounting opposition of the CLC in Rochdale under Harold Kershaw, a student the WEA had sponsored at Ruskin College. When the attendance of the members of the Wrexham class flagged, Mansbridge expressed his dissatisfaction with them and took preliminary steps to close the class prematurely and to transfer Tawney to a second Rochdale class. Tawney did not help. His comment to the Oxford Committee that 'the Lancashire people spoil one for any more feeble stock' seemed to hasten the demise of the Wrexham class, even though he recognised that closing the class would hit the 'struggling WEA branch.' Appeals from the class, including one that such a move would gravely affect the working people of Wales, had no effect. Only intervention by the Board of Education enabled Wales's first experiment to last its full three years until 1912. Mansbridge aimed to put any further class under Liverpool and the struggling local WEA branch under the Midland District, now run by Price of Rochdale. It was not until the North Wales Miners' Association joined with the North Wales Quarrymen's Union within the WETUC to help create the North Wales District of the WEA in 1925 that Wrexham was put on a sound footing. Rule from afar, whether from Oxford, London (where the WEA's central office was) or as later from the Welsh District based in South Wales, always involved subservience to the resourcing and political priorities of others. Thus what is hailed by Welsh historians as a major successful educational innovation was seen by Oxford as an unsuccessful experiment not worthy of support.

### Classes in the Quarries

However, that which was to exercise a greater influence on the future pattern of adult education in north Wales was the joint initiative begun in 1910 by the University College at Bangor, whose principal, Sir Harry Reichel, wished to bring a little bit of Balliol (his old college in whose common room the Joint Oxford Tutorial Classes Committee met) to Bangor, and by the North Wales Quarrymen's Union, whose general secretary, R.T. Jones, wished to use university tutorial classes to advance the Independent Labour Party (ILP) educational agenda in Gwynedd. The first step towards setting up the Blaenau Ffestiniog class was taken at the union's May Day rally in Caernarfon, in 1909, when Tom Jones, a former colleague of Tawney at Glasgow, and Philip Snowden pressed their audience to send a deputation to Bangor to persuade the college to establish a Department of Economics. As a step towards its realisation the college agreed in June 1910 that J. Frederick Rees should be appointed to teach industrial history to a tutorial class in Blaenau Ffestiniog. But the collaborative scheme with the quarrymen nearly fell apart when Reichel highhandedly chose one of Jones's predecessors, W.J. Parry, to represent the NWQU on the joint committee. With the mistake quickly rectified, the first Welsh collaborative scheme went ahead. R.T. Jones, a former vice chairman of the ILP branch in Blaenau Ffestiniog, and Silyn Roberts a Methodist minister and keen ILP supporter in Tanygrisiau, ensured that the first class, under J.F. Rees, was established at Ffestiniog; packed with ILP members and quarrymen, including union officials, its success was guaranteed, leaving Robert Richards, Rees's successor from the same Glasgow stable as Tawney and Tom Jones, to expand tutorial work in quarrying areas. Tutorial classes quickly followed at Llanberis, Bethesda and Penygroes. Richards later recalled how each member of the latter class came from all parts of Dyffryn Nantlle in all weathers with a candle to eke out the fitful gaslight if not the heat of the local schoolroom. But the insidious cold and flickering gloom were overcome by the heat and light of the ardent debate which took place once the initial hour's lecture was over. Discussion continued during the days which followed in the *caban*, the dinner-time canteen, which also served as a debating chamber, and on the slate galleries. When Reichel in February 1912, with Mansbridge as his guest of honour, welcomed the quarrymen to the new College buildings as pioneers in a new joint Welsh enterprise between don and worker, his was one of the last expressions of the unbounded, pre-war optimism.

There was one other major development in adult education before 1914 of which Mansbridge did not approve and that was the establishing in 1913 of a summer school at Bangor, which in many ways outrivalled that at Oxford. Students from bench and workshop came to listen to eminent academics, including Unwin, Powicke, Helen Wodehouse and W.J. Roberts of Cardiff and to join in discussion groups. The seven weeks' school had the general advantage to students from the industrial north of shining 'out of the gloom of workaday life like a meteor on a moonless night', as a student from Barrow put it. The two held before the outbreak of war had a particular significance for north Wales in helping to broaden political and curricular horizons. Students from north-east and north-west Wales became increasingly aware of the need for their own district centred around the WEA, the university college and the unions, and for a broader curriculum than the staple diet of economics and economic history of the first tutorial classes. The first world war, which interrupted the 1914 summer school, intended to last from 4 July to 22 August, hastened these changes.

North Wales went more readily to war than did south Wales, with forty per cent of its unemployed quarrymen enlisting by January 1915. The joint committee intended to continue its classes but they were hit by financial difficulties and declining numbers. Nevertheless, as elsewhere in Britain, labour organisations gained increased political confidence. David Thomas, of Talysarn, Caernarfon, a close political associate of Silyn Roberts (who at the time was secretary of the Appointments Board of Wales at the University Registry, Cardiff) anticipating labour's new strength called a conference of north Wales labour organisations in September 1914. The Conference was given publicity in *The Welsh Outlook* by John Thomas, secretary of the Welsh District of the WEA, largely because the promotion of adult education in the area occupied a key position on the conference agenda. The founding of the Workers' Education Trade Union Committee in 1919 helped to ensure that the wartime momentum in education was not lost and its north Wales section headed the demand for a North Wales District of the WEA.

The war also helped to widen the scope of subjects taught in adult education classes. Where they were held in the quarrying areas, Robert Richards continued to teach economic and political theory but the Welsh District based in Cardiff promoted classes which examined the causes of the war by issuing a specimen syllabus which highlighted such issues as the study of nationality. Lleufer Thomas, president of the Welsh District, argued at a meeting of the Cymmrodorion Section of the National Eisteddfod in 1915 that Wales should not slavishly follow the English model. Instead the WEA should become a national institution by studying not only Welsh subjects but other subjects in relation to Welsh life. Silyn Roberts developed this point in his evidence to the Royal Commission which was established in 1916 under Lord Haldane to look into the work of the University of Wales. He argued that 'The subjects taught should include Welsh history, Welsh and English literature ... music, gardening, forestry and in the quarrying districts, geology and mining engineering.' Yet the slate quarrying areas were the last to heed his call and remained steeped in the early tradition of general economic and political theory, though taught in Welsh. The classes on the Llŷn peninsula and in the Wrexham area were the first to break the tutorial mould by studying Welsh literature in the case of the former and music in the latter. However, as Thomas Jones pointed out, science in general was still a neglected discipline, partly because of its dependence on laboratories. The development of new kinds of class, preparatory, one term and one-year, also assisted curricular innovation. Rhosllanerchrugog chose Greek, Pwllheli the scientific study of the Bible and Talysarn, following Silyn's advice, chose geology.

### Silyn and Mary Roberts
However, the administrative structures which had enabled north Wales to play a pioneering role in adult education in the years before 1914 lacked the unity necessary for advance in the post war years. With Wrexham belonging to a WEA

district beyond the borders of Wales, and the rest of north Wales, outside the quarrying areas, largely a forgotten appendage of the Cardiff-based Welsh District (as the annual reports show), adult education in north Wales was in danger of resting on its decaying laurels. The problem was not that of external threat, as with the CLC in south Wales, but administrative disunity and inadequate provision for the five disparate regions of north Wales: the agricultural district of Anglesey and the Llŷn peninsula, the slate-quarrying districts of Snowdonia and Ffestiniog, the central agricultural area consisting of Mynydd Hiraethog and the surrounding lowlands formed by the valleys of the Conwy, Clwyd and the upper Dee and their tributaries, the industrial districts of Flintshire and east Denbighshire, and the market towns and holiday resorts of the north Wales coast. Those who rescued north Wales from becoming an adult education backwater in the interwar years developed their friendships in Barry in the years 1913 to 1916, where the WEA had first taken root in Wales a decade earlier. They were Silyn and Mary Roberts who lived in south Wales from 1913 to 1922 and who went on to play a key role in founding and running the North Wales District, and Tom Jones, treasurer of the WEA in Wales from 1910 to 1917, who a decade after becoming Lloyd George's parliamentary secretary, founded Coleg Harlech.

In 1922 Silyn (the name by which he was always affectionately known) joined the staff of University College, Bangor in place of Robert Richards. With the support of his wife, Mary Silyn Roberts, who was to become joint secretary of the North Wales District with him in 1925 and to be its secretary after his death from 1930 to 1945, and of John Davies the new secretary of the Welsh District, he began the initial planning to combine the six north Wales counties into a WEA District. He wrote a series of articles in *Dinesydd* in March and April 1924 on Undeb Addysg y Gweithwyr (the Workers' Educational Union) as preparation for a conference held in Rhyl in June of that year. His ILP background led him to believe that a new district with branches throughout north Wales would only succeed with union support. Malcolm Hersee, the local secretary of the Union of Post Office Workers, worked closely with him. He had already discussed with John Davies, and the two divisions of the recently formed Workers' Education Trade Union Committee in Wales, the problems of organising classes in the north from Cardiff, Swansea or Newport. The WETUC at its fifteenth meeting in October 1922 suggested that north Wales should hold a conference on the matter. Backed by the miners' union of the north east and the quarrymen's union of the north west and other interested groups, a meeting was held in Rhyl which led to a sub committee being formed, with Silyn as secretary, to press for a separate North Wales District. In February 1925 at a meeting in Colwyn

Bay, chaired by Robert Richards and ably supported by Reichel, John Davies and others, it was agreed to ask the WEA's Central Office in London to approve the creation of such a district. A motion to that effect was proposed in Welsh and English by Thomas Rogers of Wrexham and seconded by Joseph Williams of Blaenau Ffestiniog. The symbolic union of the two movements which history had conspired to keep apart was not lost on the audience. However, the delegates present represented a much broader spectrum of interest, including WEA groups from Shotton to Trevor, university departments, the cooperative movement, trades councils, the Labour Party and several unions including teachers' unions, local education authorities and literary societies. This was an overwhelming display of support, unprecedented in Wales and one which Silyn was careful to nurture in the large, provisional committee.

Yet, as is often the case, behind these momentous events which culminated in the setting up of the new district in June 1915 lies a tale of hand-to-mouth financing, retold by Mary Silyn Roberts shortly after the new district was set up. Silyn was given a room in the university college as a WEA office free of charge. His wife recalled:

> The only worry was from where the money was going to come to pay the small wages of a typist. When one was found, he put her and himself and his notes in a room which belonged to the college's museum, a room which one day he intended to turn into an old Welsh farm kitchen. Two years earlier [at the request of the principal, Harry Reichel] he had taken on a great load of work to be done in his spare time, namely the reorganisation of antiques that had been stowed away in the depths of the college ever since it had moved from its old buildings. He had almost completed the kitchen, and had furnished it with the old cheerful oak pieces, and there was plenty of room to store the literature and the stock of the WEA in the fine cupboards.
> Some furniture had to be bought. He went down to the shop of David Jones, a kindly deacon, and bought: a high stool for the typist, one shilling; a glass-fronted cupboard with a crack in the glass, six shillings. Back he came in high spirits to tell of the bargains – a typewriter from somewhere else, and the whole lot from nine pounds lent and repaid by the WEA during the first year.

Such was the first office of the new District which in its way reflected something of the homely nature of the enterprise and the people it served. The camaraderie or common cause, is also seen in the students' preparation for classes, no matter how humble their backgrounds:

> I can recall how busy it was at home on that evening – everyone offering a hand to help my father to make himself ready for the class. I can see him now – pausing for a minute before setting out, checking the time, putting his left hand inside his coat to make sure that his notebook was there, then using his right hand to hold the pencil to see that it had a good point – and off he went ...
>
> The end of the class for the evening did not mean the end of the discussion. I would see them, about five or six of them, coming down into the road from the school, the discussion still going on. They would reach the road; stop at the corner for a minute or two 'to wind the discussion up' and then separate one by one.
>
> (Moxon in *Lleufer*, Winter, 1954)

Besides his wife, Silyn was fortunate in having the help and guidance of Mary Rathbone, grand niece of the former Caernarfon M.P., William Rathbone. As vice chairman of the North Wales District, one of its representatives on the North Wales WETUC and a member of the College Council, she exercised considerable and, as the College's post war Registrar decorated for valour in battle, soon discovered, formidable power, especially when she advanced towards him across the College lawn to press the new district's cause. She helped to remodel Bangor's joint committee to bring about a more balanced membership, hitherto one quarry representative to five college dons, to ensure full representation of the principal unions in north Wales.

The triumvirate of the WEA, WETUC and the University College gave an unprecedented financial and political stability to adult education in North Wales which continued, despite the untimely deaths of Principal Thomas Rees in 1926 and Silyn Roberts in 1930, until the depression gravely affected classes. The voice of the new district was heard at Central Office in London with W.J. Williams, the most prominent individual subscriber, representing the area on its council. No longer would north Wales be subject to the political impotence from which Wrexham had suffered in the pre-war years or the political marginalisation it experienced as part of the Welsh District. But it would only prove its democratic worth if it established strong branches, was non-political in its appeal, and gave full opportunities to women to participate not just in its classes but in its organization and delivery. Extending the number of classes and branches was to some extent the least of these difficulties. At a time when industrial relations were tense during the events leading to the general strike and during its aftermath, adult education in general and the WEA in particular were accused of 'assisting the Bolshies.' No less a problem was the breaking of the tradition whereby all of the tutors were male. Mary Silyn Roberts and Mary Rathbone had few, if any, counterparts at branch and class level.

The new district's success in expanding its classes was remarkable when set against the backcloth of mounting industrial unrest. In 1924, just before the North Wales District came into being, there were 23 classes in existence; by 1927, the number had nearly trebled, providing for 1250 adults in subjects often taught in Welsh, including the nation's history, geography, geology, literature and music. In the case of the latter, the National Council of Music began to take a pioneering lead. The restraining factor was funding not enthusiasm. The fourth annual report, 1928-29, showed how valued and successful was the work of the new district.

> If the percentage of the population attending adult classes in each county be taken as a basis of comparison the counties of Wales occupy very favourable positions. Taking 100 as the standard average figure for the whole of England, the Welsh counties stand as follows: Caernarvonshire (leading the whole of Great Britain) 550; Merioneth, 463; Carmarthenshire, 279; Montgomery, 275; Anglesey, 268; Cardigan, 228; Denbigh, 224; Monmouth, 165; Glamorgan, 163; Flint, 68; Brecknock, 38; Radnor, nil. The figure for Yorkshire is 140 and for Scotland 23.

Much of this success resulted from the traditional lecture and discussion pattern which in north Wales even the new technologies could not disrupt. The experiment of 'the wireless lecture', with students huddled 'around the loud speakers, followed by group discussion', was not as successful as either Central Office or the District would have liked, if only because students 'can not put questions to a loud speaker.' The expansion in the number of branches was not as swift as that of the number of areas in which classes were held. By the end of the twenties Bangor, Bethesda,

Blaenau Ffestiniog, Carmel, Colwyn Bay, Dolwyddelen, Dyffryn Nantlle, Holyhead, Llanberis, Towyn, Waunfawr and Wrexham had formed branches but the classes in Flintshire were rather slow to do so.

Before his untimely death shortly after he returned from Russia in 1930, Silyn Roberts was to take part in another major educational innovation in the 1920s, the founding of an adult residential college, Coleg Harlech, a new feature of interest in the old outpost of Ardudwy, in addition to its Edwardian castle, golf course and famous marching tune. It was also, like the establishment of the North Wales District of the WEA, a natural evolution in adult education. Just as university tutorial classes had led to a demand for other forms of part-time provision such as preparatory classes and short courses, so residential summer schools, into which these courses fed, helped to fire a demand for lengthier residential study. Yet its future was by no means settled, especially in terms of its relationship with the chief providers of adult education in north Wales, the University College and the WEA. Neither Bangor nor the University of Wales wanted any constitutional links with the new institution and thus Coleg Harlech became an independent provider, looking to the Cassel and Carnegie Trusts and various bodies and individuals for financial support. The opening of Coleg Harlech in 1927 under the wardenship of Ben Bowen Thomas, Silyn having been reluctant to have his name put on the short-list for the post, added a third chief provider of adult education, to the WEA and the joint committee. At a time of social transition and change it offered a unique opportunity for residential study, particularly valuable to unemployed adults who attended Coleg Harlech in relays for a period of a fortnight from various study centres, supported in part by the 'Cofarwydd Silyn' fund raised by the sale of a small booklet of his poems, and later by a donation raised by the Blaenau Ffestiniog branch through a production of Pilgrim's Progress. The 1929 short course intake of unemployed students from WEA branches indicates its immediate success.

| | | | | | | |
|---|---|---|---|---|---|---|
| Abergynolwyn | ... | (6) | Newtown | ... | ... | (2) |
| Blaenau Ffestiniog | ... | (4) | Penmaenmawr | ... | | (4) |
| Brymbo | ... | (6) | Penygroes & Talysarn | | | (6) |
| Cefn Mawr & District | | (3) | Rhos & Ponciau | | | (7) |
| Cesarea, Groeslon | ... | (5) | Talsarnau | ... | ... | (1) |
| Holyhead | ... | (12) | | | | |

On his death, Silyn's position as District Secretary was taken by his wife. As secretary, Mary Silyn Roberts helped to steer the movement through the troubled thirties and the war years. Equally importantly, she acted as a lecturer and class tutor. She held discussion groups with members of the Cooperative Women's Guild and National Council for Women on the major problems of the age, particularly unemployment and the threats to world peace. These were held in both languages and in her introductions she argued that these issues were too important to be just left to politicians and men and should reflect the changing role of women in society. Hers was a rather different contribution to the annual programme than that of other women tutors who were more concerned with the conventional subject areas of art, general history and music.

### Further Expansion

Though the thirties in north Wales were not always the unremitting 'devil's decade' as they are sometimes portrayed, nevertheless agriculture and industry were badly effected by the depression, more so than in many other parts of Britain. The district annual report of 1933 argued that north Wales was an unemployment blackspot with thirty-four per cent out of work compared with a British average of twenty-three per cent. Rural areas of north Wales were severely hit with seventy per cent of the farms under fifty acres and diminishing turnover a cause of great anxiety among farmers. Even worse was the position of farm labourers who, not being insured, were drifting from the land in search of work. The quarrying areas were suffering long term decline. In general, increased unemployment led to increased demand for classes but the district, which had not yet become financially self-supporting, found it difficult to meet the need. With government economies the District Secretary reported that 'an ordered scheme of classes is difficult, nay almost impossible.' However economic adversity was not without its advantages. Unemployed young graduates provided a ready pool of tutors. Furthermore the 'blockage of classes', noted in the annual report of 1932-33, which prevented classes from developing into the three-year tutorial class, did at least raise the question of whether such a system dating back to 1907 was best for the new age.

The tutorial class was not necessarily the best vehicle for missionary work or for enlightening the public on economic, social and educational matters, the dangers of fascism, disarmament and the private traffic in arms, the peace movement and other contemporary issues. Thus through demand, the district helped to organize a series of lectures and short courses in English and Welsh on subjects which were of immediate public interest. In this way, the WEA in north Wales drew public attention to its existence far more effectively than with its rather traditional three-year classes where academic study and essay writing had priority. When Silyn Roberts at the end of the twenties asserted that 'A tutorial class that fails to breed an apostolic spirit in its students is not typical of the movement', he was overlooking the immense practical and propaganda value of less intensive forms of adult education.

Despite the economic downturn, or indeed because of it, there was continued expansion which meant that the WEA began to serve the needs of the whole of north Wales and not just its traditional strongholds. Branches were set up along the North Wales coastal strip and infilling in the more remote parts of Anglesey, Flintshire and Merioneth took place. In 1934-35 the decision was made to shift further powers to the branches and to extend the number of area organisers to include one for Montgomeryshire – what the district executive termed an act of faith. Devolution of power was driven in part by finance, communication in the sparsely populated areas of north Wales being particularly costly, but essentially it reflected and emphasised the democratic character of the movement in an age when fascism appeared threatening and when the diverse needs of the area and its social groups required a tailored response. Such a move appeared more successful in north Wales than in most parts of England. When Tawney in his presidential address was not berating the WEA for 'embalming aged mummies', that is, turning him into a legendary figure in the history of adult education, he was criticising the movement for its failure to attract manual workers, not just from industry but from agriculture. The North Wales District seemed particularly adept at attracting not only manual workers but also that half of the population ignored by Tawney, women. The following figures for 1938 indicate the measure of its success though it provides no precise gender breakdown or reference to the unemployed.

| | |
|---|---|
| Manual Workers | *1442 |
| Clerks, Draughtsmen, Travellers and Foremen | 188 |
| Shop Assistants | 194 |
| Teachers | 308 |
| Civil Servants and Postal Workers | 77 |
| Professional and Social Workers | 76 |
| Home Duties and Nursing | 662 |
| Miscellaneous | 206 |
| *Around 150 of whom were agricultural labourers | 3153 |

As David Thomas, a leading figure in north Wales politics, pointed out in a survey the preceding year, this was no mean achievement given that 'Our population is less than half a million people and that is scattered for the most part over hundreds of square miles of mountainous land.' Though it was beyond the resources of the district to provide a class in each village, nevertheless its twenty branches provided a good network, despite many students, according to David Thomas, 'having to walk several miles over mountain paths every week to a class and walk home afterwards.' Funding for the classes came from the Board of Education (52.5%), local education authorities (18.7%), subscriptions from branches and classes (16.2%) with the remaining 12.6% from a variety of sources, particularly the WETUC and the York Trust. However, though such funding allowed some degree of growth, the movement was still finding it difficult to expand rapidly in the coastal and industrial areas of Flintshire and Denbighshire. Nevertheless, on the eve of war, the district could feel pleased with its achievements in other directions, particularly in the promotion of Welsh-medium teaching, with half of the classes being conducted in Welsh only, and most of the others being provided in parallel classes in English and Welsh.

### The War Years

The second world war was to cause more disruption to the North Wales District than the depression. The first signs of the upheaval to come were evident at the Munich crisis of 1938 when Kenneth Lindsay and W.P. Wheldon, former registrar at Bangor and a founder member of the North Wales District, had hurriedly to decline the invitation to attend the Ffestiniog branch's rally at Coleg Harlech and to return to their posts at the Board of Education to fine tune the evacuation plans. But Munich only provided a breathing space. The following year the Coleg Harlech rally, planned for September 1939 to coincide with the opening of its new library, was cancelled when the war broke out with Germany. The Board's evacuation plans were put into effect and children poured into north Wales from the more vulnerable areas of England. The district's officers gave priority to assisting with the billeting of young evacuees. With restrictions on travel, including blackouts, the branches to which six new ones were added, had to take more responsibility for their classes. It was business but not business as usual, certainly not in the slate quarrying areas, the traditional prop of the movement as their branch secretaries moved to other parts, and as English refugees flowed into these Welsh-speaking areas. Just as the WEA branches helped the newcomers to settle in these and other areas, so Coleg Harlech welcomed staff and students of Liverpool University. The war years were both a time of difficulty and of opportunity. During the war the WEA and the University

College, Bangor, maintained a surprisingly full programme in over 150 villages and towns, particularly with the great demand for one-day schools and special classes dealing with war-related issues. Tutorial classes, the most inflexible of those on offer, had largely dissolved away by 1941. The annual report for that year explained how: 'In the early autumn whole classes of students together with their most experienced secretaries and officers departed,' and it appeared in some areas that adult education would become a war casualty, especially when a few bombs dropped by the Luftwaffe on rural areas on their return journey from Liverpool, left men-folk unwilling to leave their families after dark. However, the erratic ebb and flow of evacuees and war migrants, while absorbing much of the time of WEA members in providing accommodation and other help, led to an increased demand for classes particularly from civilian war workers who were drafted into the area.

Wrexham, under the guidance of its old stalwart, William Aston, opened a WEA Home providing classes and other social gatherings for miners, transport workers and others, with the support of the trade unions. For members of the armed forces, the Bangor Regional committee provided panels of tutors and lecturers to hold classes on international relations and other subjects. But these were shifting populations which helped gradually to move the district away from its over concern with three-year courses and more towards the concept of adult education as a broad highway without A and B roads. This was in part the result of devolution of control to the growing number of branches, over thirty in 1942, who were less dominated by a university outlook and more in contact with wartime needs. While the district annual reports continued to bemoan the weakening of its gold standard, the university tutorial class, the branches recognised the worth of variety without hierarchy, if only because the limited financial resources were best utilised in providing short courses for mobile populations.

However, the adult education movement, and especially the WEA, were not just concerned with immediate needs. Its organization, from its central office under Tawney and Shearman in London to its tutors, students and union-contacts in the field, was well suited to gathering information and providing opinions on reconstruction. Planning for post war Britain had begun as early as 1941 with Herwald Ramsbotham's Green Book on educational reconstruction and the Nuffield College Social Reconstruction Survey. The North Wales District saw the opportunities which involvement in post war planning could bring. It gave its support to Butler's Bill for a unified system of education and also argued strongly for closer ties with the South Wales District to promote Welsh interests in any reconstruction planning. The publication of a new Welsh magazine for the movement, *Lleufer*, by David Thomas, which replaced the north Wales *Atodiad* and which was distributed with *The Highway*, greatly assisted the development of Welsh consciousness, supporting the work done by the WEA through the National Eisteddfod and local eisteddfodau. The use of the new hall of residence, Neuadd Reichel, by the Bangor Summer School Committee was also intended to be a mark of faith in the movement. It was not misplaced, for when Mary Silyn Roberts retired as district secretary in 1945 after fifteen years in office, the North Wales District ran 188 classes (with 3562 students) compared with a total of 126 a decade earlier. The recommendations of the *Survey of Adult Education in Wales*, published in 1940, now became the focus of ideas for the reform for the movement in the post war years.

Thus the history of adult education in north Wales from 1908 to 1945 demonstrated the importance of local control to a healthy, thriving movement. Aston's first university tutorial class in Wales at Wrexham, and the town's WEA branch did not lead immediately to the establishment of classes and branches elsewhere. They were the weakling children of absentee parents, isolated from the local mining union and run from Oxford by its tutorial classes committee which was much more concerned with its battles against the CLC in the north of England than north Wales. While Aston's business interests thrived, his furniture shops becoming a principal feature of most north Wales towns, his educational enterprise failed to haul similar immediate success. It was in north-west Wales, where the university tutorial class movement was not subject to control from London or Oxford, that its first real success was achieved. Organised and run locally by the University College of North Wales and the North Wales Quarrymen's Union, it expanded in the quarrying areas in the years before 1914. However, the joint committee, as constituted, was unable to provide for the whole of north Wales. It was in 1925 with the support of the mining, quarrying and other unions, that the necessary machinery was created by the North Wales District of the WEA to expand adult education through the region. While the new district maintained the old attachment to the university tutorial class as the highest form of adult education, nevertheless progress was made in other directions, particularly by Mary Silyn Roberts and under the pressures of depression and war, in meeting the diverse social and linguistic needs of the area.

## Bibliography

E.L. Ellis, *T.J. A Life of Dr. Thomas Jones, CH* (Cardiff, 1992)

Thomas Jones, *Leeks and Daffodils* (Newton, 1942)

Peter Stead, *Coleg Harlech, The First Fifty Years* (Cardiff, 1977)

University Extension Board, *Survey of Adult Education in Wales* (Cardiff, 1940)

E. White, *Thomas Jones: Founder of Coleg Harlech* (Aberystwyth, undated, but 1977)

J. Gwynn Williams, *The University College of North Wales : Foundations 1884-1927* (Cardiff 1985)

# DAVID THOMAS A'R CYLCHGRAWN
## *LLEUFER*

### ANGHARAD TOMOS

Yr oedd 1943 yn gyfnod mentrus i gychwyn cylchgrawn. Yn wir, dylai fod wedi bod yn amhosibl gan ei bod yn anodd iawn cael papur i argraffu arno heb drafferth difrifol. Ymdrech lew ar ran cylchgronau oedd yn peri eu bod yn gallu dal eu pennau uwchlaw'r dyfroedd yn ystod y rhyfel. Yn ychwanegol at brinder papur, yr oedd dogni petrol a chwtogi ar drafnidiaeth gyhoeddus, a rhaid oedd cael cwpons at bopeth dan haul. Fodd bynnag, penderfynodd y WEA yng Nghymru na fyddent yn aros tan ddiwedd y rhyfel cyn cychwyn cylchgrawn yn yr iaith Gymraeg i Gymdeithas Addysg y Gweithwyr.

Nid yr ymgais ym 1943 oedd yr ymgais gyntaf i gyhoeddi cylchgrawn o'r fath. Mor gynnar â 1922 cyhoeddodd Robert Richards ac Ifor Williams gylchgrawn chwarterol o'r enw *Y Tyddynwr*, ond dim ond am flwyddyn y parhaodd hwn. Ym 1929 awgrymwyd troi *Y Geninen* ar gyfer dosbarthiadau Efrydiau Allanol, ond yr oedd gormod o rwystrau ar y pryd. Llwyddodd Rhanbarth De Cymru o'r WEA i gyhoeddi cylchgrawn dwyieithog rhwng 1930 a 1932 o'r enw *Cambria* gyda David E. Evans, Cwm Rhondda, yn olygydd arno. Yn y 1930au, cafwyd enghraifft o ambell gangen yn cyhoeddi cylchgrawn, megis Cangen Ystumaner dan arweiniad y Parchedig Edward Evans yn cychwyn *Y Droell Fechan* ym 1933, a Changen Uwchaled dan D. Tecwyn Lloyd ac R. Islwyn Pritchard yn cyhoeddi gwaith y dosbarthiadau yn rhifyn cyntaf *Cefn Gwlad*. Yr oedd gan y WEA gylchgrawn Saesneg eisoes o'r enw *The Highway*, ac ym 1937 cafwyd atodiad Cymraeg i hwn. Fodd bynnag, yr oedd nifer yn awyddus i gael cylchgrawn cwbl ar wahân i *Highway* i wasanaethu Cymru.

Ar 15 Mai 1943 trefnodd Rhanbarth Gogledd Cymru o'r WEA gynhadledd yn Gwydir, Llanrwst, ac yno penodwyd is-bwyllgor o bedwar i lunio memorandwm ynglŷn â hanes a gwaith y WEA yn y rhanbarth. Saesneg oedd iaith y gynhadledd gan fod llawer o gynrychiolwyr o Fflint a Maelor yno. Ond un o'r pedwar ar yr is-bwyllgor oedd D. Tecwyn Lloyd, a'i syniad ef oedd cyhoeddi cylchgrawn. Chwe mlynedd ynghynt, yr oedd Tecwyn Lloyd wedi cyhoeddi *Cefn Gwlad* ac yr oedd yn awyddus i ganghennau eraill ddilyn ei esiampl gan gyhoeddi gwaith creadigol aelodau dosbarthiadau mewn blwyddolyn. Ei syniad ef oedd y gallai ardaloedd gwledig gyhoeddi eu gwaith yn ystod y gaeaf a changhennau trefol yn yr haf. Syniad arall ganddo mewn memorandwm oedd y dylid cyhoeddi deunydd nad oedd yn llenyddol. Credai y gallai Rhanbarth De a Gogledd Cymru ddod at ei gilydd i gyhoeddi cylchgrawn ar faterion technegol addysg; dyma yn wir oedd deunydd *Highway*.

Yr hyn ddigwyddodd yn y diwedd oedd i'r ddau syniad yma gan Tecwyn Lloyd ddod ynghyd, a dyma gofnododd hwnnw:

> Ymhlith y pwysicaf [o benderfyniadau cynhadledd Llanrwst] ydoedd argymell cael cylchgrawn chwarterol i Ranbarth y Gogledd a'r De hefyd. 'Dwn i ddim a oedd pawb yno yn sylweddoli'n hollol beth a olyga mewn gwaith, ond nid oedd neb yn amau nad oedd eisiau un.

Sefydlwyd pwyllgor ac aelodau'r pwyllgor cyntaf oedd D. Tecwyn Lloyd, Emrys Jenkins, Caradog Jones, Dylan Pritchard, O. Llew Rowlands, a Mrs Alma Evans. Gwahoddwyd Owen Parry a David Thomas hefyd a chyfarfu'r pwyllgor ar 11 Rhagfyr 1943 gyda D. Tecwyn Lloyd yn gadeirydd. *Gwerin* oedd y teitl cyntaf ond fe'i newidwyd yn fuan i *Lleufer*. Awgrym David Thomas a Mrs Silyn Roberts oedd y teitl *Lleufer* fel 'cyfuniad hapus o enw Syr Daniel Lleufer Thomas a'r hyn ydoedd y gŵr da hwnnw i'w wlad a'i bobl'. Y cyfeiriad cyntaf yn nyddiaduron David Thomas at y gwaith fyddai'n dod yn gymaint rhan o'i fywyd oedd: 'Fy mhenodi yn Olygydd *Y Werin*'. Fel *Y Werin* y cyfeiriodd y *Western Mail* at y cylchgrawn ym 1944. Pan geisiodd y *Daily Post* egluro ystyr y gair 'lleufer' yn Saesneg, eu cynnig hwy oedd 'bobbing up with brightness'

Er ei bod yn gwbl amhosibl cychwyn cylchgrawn newydd yn ystod y rhyfel oherwydd dogni papur, yr oedd modd cyhoeddi llyfr, detholiad o lyfr neu gyfres. Y gwahaniaeth rhwng cylchgrawn a chyfres oedd fod cylchgrawn yn cael ei ddyddio ond cyfres yn cael ei rhifo. Penderfynwyd galw rhifyn cyntaf *Lleufer* yn gasgliad annibynnol o ysgrifau, ac ar y clawr fe'i disgrifwyd fel 'Atodiad i'r Highway'. Yn y golygyddol cyntaf fe'i disgrifwyd fel 'dolen gydio rhwng yr hen Atodiad a'r Cylchgrawn newydd sydd i ddod'. Cafwyd y casgliad cyntaf yn gyfrol ym 1944 a'r ail a'r trydydd casgliad ym 1945. Cychwynnodd fel cylchgrawn gyda'r pedwerydd rhifyn, a nodwyd fel 'Cyfres Un, Rhif 4. Gaeaf 1945'. Nododd Tecwyn Lloyd na chododd y cwestiwn iaith o gwbl: 'Cymraeg fu hi o'r cychwyn', a'r gred oedd na fyddai cylchgrawn dwyieithog yn llwyddo o gwbl o safbwynt marchnad. Meddai Tecwyn Lloyd: 'Nid oedd unrhyw amheuaeth ychwaith pwy oedd i fod yn Olygydd. David Thomas oedd hwnnw, ar bob cyfri, ym marn pawb.'

Er fod David Thomas yn 64 oed ac ar fin ymddeol, ymroddodd i'r gwaith o olygu *Lleufer* gyda sêl. Fe'i ganed i'r gwaith. Yr oedd yn waith a oedd yn cyfuno ei ddiddordeb mewn addysg, llenyddiaeth a materion cyfoes ac, yn goron ar bopeth, câi wasanaethu'r achos oedd agosaf at ei galon – addysg pobl mewn oed.

Mewn ysgrif, myfyriodd Tecwyn Lloyd yn ddifyr ar y gwahaniaeth rhwng agwedd Saeson at addysg ac agwedd y Cymry. Yn ei farn ef, 'method' oedd addysg i Sais. 'Technegau ac allanolion yw eu byd,' meddai, ac adlewyrchwyd hyn yn eu cylchgronau a oedd yn ymwneud â sefydliadau, trefn a gweithredu trefn. Ond yng Nghymru, credai fod y pwyslais ar 'ansawdd yn hytrach na dulliau', ar y celfyddydau dyniaethol a darddodd o'r Dadeni Dysg yn hytrach na'r diddordeb mewn gwyddoniaeth a ddatblygodd yn ddiweddarach. Cyfaddefodd fod perygl mewn gorgyffredinoli, ond honnodd na allai'r Cymro oedd yn ymwybodol o'i etifeddiaeth 'ysgaru gwybodaeth dechnolegol a gwyddonol oddi wrth gyfrifoldeb moesol a chymdeithasol'. Beirniadodd Tecwyn Lloyd yr *Highway* yn llym iawn gan ddweud mai hwn oedd y sychaf o gyfnodolion, y mwyaf 'sefydliadol', gan nodi ei fod yn llawn 'jargon' am addysg oedolion. Yr oedd *Lleufer* yn wrthbwynt llwyr i hyn yn ei farn ef, gan sôn am David Thomas fel 'gŵr na ddewisodd olygu cylchgrawn sefydliad mewn modd sefydliadol'.

Yn y rhifyn cyntaf, amlinellodd David Thomas amcanion y cylchgrawn, sef bod yn ddolen gyswllt rhwng canghennau'r WEA yng Nghymru ac adrodd eu hanes; egluro gwaith y WEA i bobl o'r tu allan; darparu deunydd fyddai o wasanaeth i aelodau dosbarthiadau ac 'ymdrin ag Addysg yn ei holl agweddau, yn enwedig yng Nghymru, a goleuo barn y wlad arnynt'. Ni ellir cael gwell crynhoad o faes gwaith y cylchgrawn. O'r cychwyn yr oedd cydbwysedd rhwng y deunydd ffeithiol a'r deunydd llenyddol a chreadigol. Byddai erthyglau ar Ddeddf Addysg Butler

1944 yn amlinellu ei hamcanion, ac erthyglau ar ymladd diweithdra a'r mater o hawl i streicio. Ni chyfyngwyd y trafod i Gymru; cafwyd erthygl megis 'Cyflwr Economaidd y Byd' oedd yn edrych ymhell y tu hwnt i Glawdd Offa. Ymdriniwyd â datblygiadau cyfoes megis y syniad o gylchoedd gwrando ar gyfer y radio. Ym mhob rhifyn yr oedd erthygl am berson arbennig, megis Thomas Edward Ellis wedi i'w gofiant gael ei gyhoeddi, neu Mary Silyn Roberts ar achlysur ei hymddeoliad. Ochr yn ochr â hyn, cafwyd erthyglau ar lenyddiaeth megis 'Barddoniaeth T. Gwynn Jones', neu 'ganmlwyddiant y Traethodydd', ambell gerdd a stori fer, ac, unwaith eto, yr oedd yr olwg yn un eang. Cafwyd cerdd wedi ei chyfieithu o'r Sbaeneg ac erthygl ar gwrs Cymraeg ar lenyddiaeth Rwsia. Ym mhob rhifyn yr oedd adolygiadau o lyfrau newydd. O'r rhifyn cyntaf, cafwyd erthygl reolaidd hynod fuddiol ar 'Pa Beth i'w Ddarllen' – ar hanes Cymru, ar lenyddiaeth Gymraeg, ar bynciau'r dydd gartref, a diau fod y rhain o gymorth mawr i athrawon dosbarth. Yn y pedwerydd rhifyn, cychwynnwyd cyfres boblogaidd 'Mae Mwy Nag Un' yn trafod enw cyffredin megis 'Ifor Evans' neu 'John Jones' ac yn rhestru tri neu bedwar person oedd yn rhannu'r enw hwnnw gan nodi pwy oedd pwy. Pethau bach fel hyn a wnâi'r cylchgrawn yn un difyr, yn ogystal â'r pytiau bach o wybodaeth neu ddyfyniadau ddaeth yn nodwedd o *Lleufer*. Yn aml iawn yr oedd yna elfen o hiwmor yn perthyn i'r rhain. Meddai Tecwyn Lloyd:

> Lawer tro, er mwyn llenwi ambell arffed go anhwylus ar waelod dalen, dewisodd [David Thomas] stori neu englyn neu ddyfyniad ac mae'n syn gymaint ohonynt sy'n ddarnau doniol, ysgafn. Byddwn i, a llawer o'm cydnabod yn blasu'r tameidiau hyn bob amser; a dewiswyd hwy bob tro yn ofalus.

Wedi'r erthyglau ffeithiol a'r cyfraniadau llenyddol, trydedd rhan y cylchgrawn oedd y wybodaeth am sefyllfa'r WEA yng Nghymru. Dan y pennawd 'Yma a Thraw' rhoddwyd gwybodaeth gyffredinol am bobl yn ymddeol neu yn cychwyn swyddi newydd gyda'r mudiad. Ysgrifennwyd erthygl reolaidd ar 'Y Mudiad yn y De' (a roddai'r argraff bendant mai cylchgrawn y Gogledd ydoedd) ac ysgrifennai ysgrifenyddion gwahanol ganghennau yn rhoi newyddion o'u cylch hwy. Cafwyd adroddiadau am ysgolion haf ac yn ystod y 1940au yr oedd yn amlwg fod materion rhyngwladol yn ennyn llawer o ddiddordeb. Cynhaliwyd ysgolion haf a rhai undydd ar faterion megis 'Rwsia a'r Crisis', 'Problemau Cydwladol', 'Cyfraniad y Gwledydd Bychain at Wareiddiad' a'r 'Safle Gydwladol Heddiw'. Yn y rhifyn cyntaf, soniwyd am alwedigaethau myfyrwyr y dosbarth. Pobl yn gweithio â'u dwylo oedd y mwyafrif, yn chwarelwyr, peirianwyr, gweithwyr haearn a dur a gweision ffermydd, ond yn ogystal â hyn, yr oedd cryn dipyn o athrawon, gweithwyr siopau a'r post, masnachwyr a merched yn gweithio gartref.

O ran hysbysebion, yr oedd casgliad reit amrywiol. Hysbysebwyd cyhoeddiadau'r WEA, y *Highway*, tynnwyd sylw at y WETUC a byddai gweisg fel Gwasg Gee, a gyhoeddai'r *Faner*, a Gwasg Gomer yn prynu gofod yn ogystal â Llyfrau Pawb a Nelson Discussion Books. Pris *Lleufer* bob chwarter oedd chwe cheiniog. Yr oedd ymateb y wasg i'r cylchgrawn yn ffafriol ac fe'i disgrifiwyd fel cylchgrawn difyr. Rhoddodd adolygwyr groeso cynnes iddo gan dynnu sylw fod Nodiadau'r Golygydd yn dangos ei fod a'i fys ar byls materion cyfoes. Meddai'r *Tyst*, 'Nid oes nemor ddim sydd o bwys i'r werin, yn feddyliol, cymdeithasol, gwladwriaethol, heb ei fynegi yn glir ac yn goeth'. Gwerthfawrogwyd amrywiaeth y testunau a'r ymdriniaeth o bynciau nad oedd yn arfer cael eu trin yn Gymraeg, megis materion economaidd a diwydiannol. Yr oedd cael erthyglau ar gyflwr economaidd y byd ochr yn ochr â thrafod gwaith Dafydd ap Gwilym o fewn cloriau'r un cylchgrawn yn beth gwbl newydd yn Gymraeg ac yr oedd y cyfranwyr yn bobl amlwg ym mywyd Cymru. Dywedodd y *Daily Post* yn Hydref 1946 fod y cylchgrawn yn 'giving us without fail the best sixpennyworth in our language'. Cyfeirir yma hefyd at y dyfyniadau bachog: ' One of the delights of *Lleufer* are those little page-end pieces of information and snatches of philosophy.'

Mae'n amlwg fod David Thomas ei hun â chryn feddwl ohonynt gan iddo eu torri yn ddefosiynol o'r cylchgrawn a'u gosod mewn llyfr.

Yr oedd *Lleufer* yn llwyfan hwylus i David Thomas gael mynegi ei syniadau drwy gyfrwng y 'Nodiadau Golygyddol', ac yr oedd ganddo weledigaeth bendant iawn. Dywedodd Kate Roberts, 'Mae nodion y Golygydd . . . yn batrwm o ran eu barn ddoeth ac ysbryd eang.' Yn yr ail rifyn, rhestrodd David Thomas yr ystod eang o bynciau y gobeithiai ymdrin â hwy gan ddweud y carai gael hanes y canghennau a gofynnodd i'r darllenwyr beth yr hoffent ei weld. Dywedodd fod yn rhaid i addysg gymhwyso pobl ar gyfer bywoliaeth, ond rhaid oedd meddwl yn ehangach na hynny: '. . . fe erys yr angen am wneud rhywbeth mwy . . . sef, darparu cyfleusterau i'r bersonoliaeth dyfu'n rhydd yn ôl ei elfen. Dyma bwrpas uchaf addysg.'

Yr oedd yn dal i ddal gafael ar y delfrydau oedd ganddo yn ugain oed. Mewn un erthygl olygyddol, ceir golwg ar y modd arbennig yr ystyriai David Thomas y natur ddynol, a'i gred mai dim ond rhan ohono'i hun a ddefnyddiai dyn i wneud ei waith:

Yn ei oriau hamdden y caiff gyfle i feithrin y rhannau eraill o'i bersonoliaeth, a thyfu'n ddyn crwn; . . . chwarae peldroed, neu ddal brithyll, neu ddiwyllio'i feddwl . . . Caiff ymuno â chôr . . . canu'r ffidil . . . drio'i law ar gyfansoddi . . . Caiff ddysgu caru prydferthwch yn ei holl ffurfiau – sonedau Shakespeare . . . gywyddau Dafydd Nanmor . . . Beethoven a Mozart. Caiff ymuno â'i gyd-fyfyrwyr i chwilio am y gwirionedd mewn athroniaeth neu ddiwinyddiaeth, neu economeg , neu hanes . . . Caiff balu'r ardd a gwylied rhyfeddodau'r coed a'r adar a'r pryfed, neu ddilyn y gwyddorydd i mewn i gyfrinion dirgelaf mater, neu chwilio'r ehangderau, i fyd y sêr a'r heuliau, ac ymgolli mewn syndod uwchben eu harddwch a'u mawredd.

Ni ellir meddwl am well darn i grynhoi maniffesto *Lleufer*. Wedi darllen y darn hwn, fe sylweddolir nad oedd dim y tu hwnt i ffiniau'r cylchgrawn. Magu'r 'dyn crwn' oedd y bwriad, gydag ymdeimlad o ryfeddod sy'n perthyn i blentyn. Mae'r darn yn cloi fel hyn:

Yn ôl fy nghred i, nid oes un diben arall sydd yn werth aberthu dyn er ei fwyn. Dyn ei hun yw'r diben, ac nid moddion mohono; a darparu cyfleusterau i feibion a merched i ddilyn eu helfen a thyfu'n ddynion cyflawn, dyna ydyw swydd uchaf pob cymdeithas addysg.

Wedi deall pwysigrwydd hyn i David Thomas, gellir gweld mai cenhadaeth oedd ganddo, a sêl cenhadwr a'i gyrrai ymlaen. Dyma pam yr oedd golygu *Lleufer* nid yn unig yn llafur cariad ond yn fraint i'w thrysori.

Rhoddwyd pwyslais cyson hefyd ar Gymru a'r iaith Gymraeg. Tua diwedd y Rhyfel, yr oedd David Thomas yn falch o weld Deddf Addysg 1944 yn rhoi hawliau arbennig i Gymru i drefnu ei haddysg ei hun. Meddai:

Rhaid cynllunio cwrs ein haddysg i feithrin ein nodweddion cenedlaethol ein hunain, ac ar yr un pryd gymhwyso ein bechgyn a'n merched i fod yn ddinasyddion y byd, a chymhwyso cenedl y Cymry i fod yn aelod cyflawn o frawdoliaeth y cenhedloedd.

Yr oedd cenedlaetholdeb David Thomas bob tro yn pwysleisio Cymru fel rhan o 'frawdoliaeth y cenhedloedd'.

Rhoddodd Tecwyn Lloyd gynnig ar wneud arolwg empeiraidd o gynnwys *Lleufer* yn ystod y blynyddoedd cynnar. Nododd fod David Thomas, yn wahanol i olygydd yr *Highway*, wedi dewis peidio cynnwys unrhyw adroddiadau am gyrsiau penwythnos nac unrhyw gofnodion am siarad siop, gan wahardd unrhyw jargon yn gyfangwbl. Meddai: 'Nid pethau ynglŷn ag Addysg Rhai Mewn Oed ydynt ond y peth hwnnw ei hun; ei briod ddeunydd, y porthiant hanfodol yn y rhesel. Neu fel y dywedodd f'ewyth Bob, 'Y Pethe', 'ngwas i'.'

Pan ddaeth *Lleufer* yn gylchgrawn swyddogol yng ngwanwyn 1946, cyhoeddodd David Thomas mai'r bwriad oedd ei gyhoeddi yn rheolaidd bob chwarter blwyddyn ym Mawrth, Mehefin, Medi a Rhagfyr, a chadwyd at y cynllun hwnnw. Ar ddechrau 1946, mynegodd ei awydd i weld rhagor o gynnyrch aelodau'r dosbarthiadau ac yr oedd hefyd yn awyddus i gael hanesion canghennau. Yn y man fe ddaeth cynnyrch o'r dosbarthiadau ac o 1948, neilltuwyd dwy dudalen yr un (a dim rhagor) i adroddiadau gan ysgrifenyddion Rhanbarthau'r Gogledd a'r De a dwy dudalen ar gyfer hanes Coleg Harlech wedi i hwnnw ailagor ym 1946.

Argraffwyd y ddau rifyn cyntaf o'r cylchgrawn gan Gwenlyn Evans a'i Fab yng Nghaernarfon a'r trydydd a'r pedwerydd rhifyn gan Priory Press, Caerdydd, ond pan ddaeth yn gylchgrawn daeth yn gyfrifoldeb R. Evans a'i Fab yng Ngwasg y Bala. Cafwyd cryn dipyn o newidiadau ym 1948. Cododd y pris o chwe cheiniog i swllt a chafwyd 52 tudalen yn lle 36, gyda'r print yn fwy bras. Tan hynny, trwy ganghennau yn unig y'i gwerthwyd, ond wedi 1948 yr oedd ar werth mewn siopau yn ogystal. Yng ngwanwyn 1948 hefyd y gwelwyd cynllun clawr trawiadol Ivor Owen, Llanuwchllyn am y tro cyntaf mewn oren a du gyda'r oren yn cynrychioli 'goleuni'. Y flwyddyn ganlynol cafwyd amrywiaeth mewn lliwiau gyda gwyrdd ar glawr rhifyn y gwanwyn, coch i rifyn yr haf, brown i'r hydref a du i'r gaeaf. Yr oedd hyn yn eu gwneud yn hawdd i'w didoli pan oeddynt ar silff. O ddiwedd y 1940au ymlaen cafwyd nifer helaeth o adolygiadau, a daeth hyn yn rhan bwysig o'r cylchgrawn. Nid adolygu beirniadol oedd David Thomas ei eisiau, ond 'adolygu addysgiadol'. Meddai: '. . . fel athro'n cyflwyno llyfrau i'w ddosbarth – sôn wrthynt am eu cynnwys, a'u safonau a'u gwerth, a'r rhesymau paham y talai iddynt eu prynu.'

Yr oedd pwyslais *Lleufer* ar y cyfoes – yng Nghymru ac yn rhyngwladol. Pan fyddai Mudiad Rhyngwladol Llafur (yr ILO) yn cyhoeddi llyfr amserol megis *Co-operative Organisation and Post War Relief*, byddai adolygiad yn ymddangos yn *Lleufer*. Wrth i Amgueddfa Werin Sain Ffagan gael ei sefydlu, cafwyd Iorwerth Peate ei hun

71

i gyfrannu erthygl ar 'Gwerth Amgueddfa'. 'Olew a Heddwch Byd' oedd y pwnc amserol ymddangosodd ddiwedd 1947. Rhai byr a bachog oedd yr ysgrifau. O dro i dro byddai un o erthyglau *Lleufer* yn ennyn ymateb. Pan ysgrifennodd Cynan i *Lleufer* ar 'Yr Allwedd i Awdl Hedd Wyn', cychwynnodd trafodaeth yn *Y Faner* gyda Mignedd yn cwestiynu rhai o osodiadau Cynan a J. R. Morris yn ychwanegu ei bwysau yn ddiweddarach, a pharhaodd y drafodaeth ynglŷn â dylanwad Shelley ar Hedd Wyn. Er mai dim ond bob chwarter yr ymddangosai *Lleufer*, gallai fwydo papurau a ymddangosai yn amlach. Weithiau, cafwyd erthygl megis 'Y Gymdeithas Fechan' gan George M. Ll. Davies yn trafod y duedd sydd tuag at y personol a'r cartrefol ymysg y Cymry, a byddai un o adolygwyr y wasg yn cymryd erthygl fel hon i fachu sylwadau arni. Un o'r storiau a enynnodd yr ymateb mwyaf oedd yr un gan Ernest Roberts ar 'Neli Dywyll'. Honiad yr awdur oedd mai gŵr y delynores Neli Dywyll, Huw Cocos o Landygái, oedd y sail i gymeriad 'Wandering Willie' yn nofelau Walter Scott.

Yr oedd ymateb da yn gyson yn y wasg i erthyglau *Lleufer*. Wedi rhifyn y Gwanwyn 1947, disgrifiwyd y cynnwys fel 'the cream of literary studies'. Yr un flwyddyn meddai'r *Daily Post*:

> Luckiest of Welsh editors is Mr David Thomas, Bangor . . . The fount of his contributors never seems to run dry . . . he has marshalled his usual eminent parade of writers and subjects which are too broad in aspect to be confined within the Welsh borders.

Nid lwc mohono, ond gwaith caled, a dwyn cryn berswâd ar eraill, fel y tystia'r llu gohebiaeth sydd yn archifau *Lleufer*. Yr oedd ganddo drefn fanwl a rota o ysgrifenwyr, ac mewn llyfr nodiadau, cadwai gyfrif o pa bryd y gofynnai i rywun am erthygl, dyddiad ei derbyn a pryd y byddai yn ei chywiro. Dim ond trwy gadw cofnod manwl fel hyn y gallai sicrhau nad oedd yn mynd ar ofyn neb yn rhy aml. Nododd Tecwyn Lloyd mai cryn gamp yng Nghymru oedd cadw cyfranwyr i gylchgrawn, fel y dangosodd hanes *Y Llenor*. Yr oedd yr ystod eang o gyfranwyr yn rhyfeddol. Llwyddodd David Thomas i gymell a derbyn gwaith gan 'bron bob llenor Cymraeg o 1944 [hyd 1965]'. Yr oedd o fantais ei fod yn adnabod llawer yn bersonol. Yn ôl Tecwyn Lloyd, y gyfrinach oedd peidio gadael i *Lleufer* fynd yn gylchgrawn clic a phlaid a sect a'i gadw allan o bob grŵp felly. Meddai:

> Er dyddiau Cymru (O. M. Edwards), ni wn am gylchgrawn na golygu mwy goddefgar a bonheddig; parod bob amser i gyflwyno dadl a gwrthddadl ond nid i gymell dadlau a checru er mwyn i hynny chwyddo'r cylchrediad . . . Pwrpas dadl i David Thomas yw goleuo a dehongli, nid arddangos myfiaeth a hollwybodaeth.

Y cydbwysedd hwn yn *Lleufer* a dynnodd sylw Kate Roberts, er ei bod yn gresynu na fyddai mwy o ddeunydd creadigol yn cael ei gynnwys. Parhau i fod yn ffafriol wnai y *Daily Post* gan ddweud fod *Lleufer* yn dal ei 'front rank position among Welsh periodicals'.

Cyn diwedd y 1940au, yr oedd *Lleufer* wedi ymdrin â sawl pwnc cyfoes gwyddonol megis yr Atom, Plastics, Radar, Meicroffilmio a'r Teledu. Nid yn unig oeddynt yn bynciau cyfoes ond yr oedd ymdrin â hwy trwy gyfrwng y Gymraeg yn newydd, ac yn ôl Kate Roberts, yr oedd hyn yn dangos mor bwysig oedd cael geirfa i wyddoniaeth yn Gymraeg. Cafwyd ambell erthygl ym maes bioleg. O bryd i'w gilydd, cafwyd ysgrif brin ar gelf (trafod y llun 'Salem') neu gerddoriaeth (hwiangerdd ar Lanofer) neu'r theatr (yn Oes Elisabeth). Cafwyd nifer o erthyglau ar hanes, a mwy nag un gyfres ddifyr gan Bob Owen Croesor – pedair erthygl ar sut i astudio hanes plwyfi a phedair erthygl ar hen ewyllysiau. Y gobaith gan David Thomas wrth gynnwys cyfres oedd gwella'r gwerthiant wrth i ddarllenwyr brynu rhifynnau er mwyn cael cyfres gyflawn.

O'r cychwyn, yr oedd golygon *Lleufer* yn eang iawn. Cafwyd gwybod am ddatblygiadau yng Ngholeg y Bobl, Elsinor yn Nenmarc. Adroddwyd hanes dathlu Dydd Gŵyl Dewi yn Hong Kong a hanes teithiwr fu'n ymweld â Pharis. Ni chyfyngwyd llenyddiaeth i lên Cymru: cafwyd cyfieithiadau o Tolstoy, Twrgenieff, a cherdd gan fardd o Sgandinafia. Ond yr oedd crynswth y cyfraniadau ar lenyddiaeth yn dod o Gymru, boed hwy'n storïau byrion, yn gerddi neu'n ymdrin â'r grefft o lenydda. Ysgrifennodd Kate Roberts erthygl fuddiol ar 'Sut i Ysgrifennu Stori Fer', cafwyd erthygl gan Pennar Davies ar waith Gwenallt, cafwyd ysgrif ar 'Frawdoliaeth yr Emyn' ac erthygl ddifyr ar 'Amodau Cymdeithasegol Llenyddiaeth' gan J. E. Caerwyn Williams pan nad oedd astudiaethau cymdeithasegol yng Nghymru ond megis dechrau.

Neilltuwyd cryn ofod yn *Lleufer* i bwnc oedd o ddiddordeb mawr i David Thomas, sef materion cymdeithasol a rhyngwladol. Rhoddodd gryn ofod i Gwilym Davies i sôn am ddatblygiad y mudiad newydd, UNESCO, ac yn wir neilltuwyd rhifyn Haf 1948 yn 'Rhifyn UNESCO'. Yn y 1950au cafwyd erthyglau ar Dde-Ddwyrain Asia, yr Israel fodern a Phalestina, Deddf Addysg y Bantw ac India Gandhi dan Nehru. Cafwyd erthyglau cyfoes ar bynciau'r dydd megis tai, yr hyn oedd gan ABCA (Biwro y Fyddin ar Faterion y Dydd) i'w ddysgu i bobl, ysgrif ar etholiadau, trethi lleol, Keynes, hawliau dynol, democratiaeth a chytundeb megis un Bretton Woods, oedd yn ymgais i roi trefn ar fasnach arian y byd. Ym marn David Thomas, nid oedd yr un pwnc uwchlaw sylw'r gweithwyr a chynigiai tudalennau *Lleufer* wybodaeth amserol a difyr am bynciau pwysig yr oes.

Un o nodweddion David Thomas, yn ôl Tecwyn Lloyd, oedd ei obaith: 'Bu'n annog a chynghori ei ddarllenwyr i weld fod dynion a'r byd yn gwella'n araf, ar y cyfan, er gwaethaf ei holl golliadau'. Meddai David Thomas yn ei nodiadau golygyddol yn rhifyn Gaeaf 1946:

> Rhaid i mi ddatgan fy argyhoeddiad fod yr ewyllys i wneuthur daioni yn cryfhau yn y byd, a bod mwy o ewyllys da rhwng pobl a'i gilydd heddiw nag oedd gan mlynedd yn ôl, dywedwch . . . Y mae ein safonau wedi codi.

Yr oedd hyn yn rhywbeth y credai'n gryf ynddo.

Erbyn hanner cyntaf y 1950au, yr oedd llai o erthyglau ar wyddoniaeth a materion cymdeithasol, a dros hanner y cylchgrawn yn cynnwys erthyglau naill ai ar yr iaith a llenyddiaeth Gymraeg neu ar wahanol agweddau o hanes. Yr oedd llawer o erthyglau wedi eu seilio ar adolygiad o lyfr oedd newydd ei gyhoeddi. Yn hyn o beth yr oedd *Lleufer* yn gyfrwng i dynnu sylw pobl at ystod eang iawn o lyfrau. Yr oedd David Thomas yn ddarllenwr heb ei ail, ac anaml y gwelid ef yn unman heb lyfr. Byddai'n darllen yn gyson ac yr oedd ei chwaeth yn eang iawn. Cadwodd gofnod o bob llyfr a ddarllenai a llwyddai i ddarllen nifer dda yn wythnosol. O ganlyniad, yr oedd y wybodaeth am y cyhoeddiadau diweddaraf mewn sawl maes ar flaenau ei fysedd. Un o'i brif ddyletswyddau gyda *Lleufer* oedd canfod pobl i adolygu'r cyfrolau hyn.

Y gyfres hwyaf i ymddangos yn *Lleufer* oedd y gyfres 'Yr Arloeswyr'. O gychwyn 1951, byddai ffotograff yn ymddangos ar dudalen gyntaf y cylchgrawn a byddai ysgrif am un o sylfaenwyr y WEA. Os oeddynt yn dal yn fyw, byddai'r arloeswyr eu hunain yn rhannu eu hatgofion. Ymysg yr arloeswyr yr oedd John Morgan Jones, Percy Watkins, Henry Jones, Thomas Jones, O. M. Edwards, Robert Owen a'u tebyg ac yr oedd y gyfres hon yn gyfraniad gwerthfawr i addysgu aelodau am dwf a datblygiad Mudiad Addysg y Gweithwyr. Parodd y gyfres hon tan 1954. Yn ogystal â hanes yr arloeswyr, trafodwyd pethau'n ymwneud â'r mudiad: erthyglau ar 'Yr Athro a'i Ddosbarth' ac 'Oedran Myfyriwr' ac yn aml cafwyd atgofion pobl am ddosbarthiadau cynnar mewn gwahanol rannau o Gymru. Rhoddwyd pwyslais ar hanes Cymru a hanes lleol. Ochr yn ochr ag erthyglau ar lenyddiaeth Gymraeg, trafodwyd yr iaith Gymraeg ei hun wrth i ymwybyddiaeth amdani dyfu yng Nghymru'r 1950au. Cafwyd mwy nag un erthygl ar ddysgu Cymraeg mewn ysgolion ac erthyglau ar faes newydd dysgu Cymraeg – ar y gramoffon a'r radio.

Ym maes gwyddoniaeth, cyhoeddwyd erthyglau ar Ymladd Malaria, Meddyginiaeth Atomig ac ymdriniaeth wyddonol o'r Dilyw ochr yn ochr ag ysgrifau ar flodau gwyllt. Cyfunai ambell erthygl hanes a gwyddoniaeth, er enghraifft 'Byddin Harri VII a'r Clefyd Chwysu' gan Glyn Penrhyn Jones oedd yn Gofrestrydd Meddygol yn Ysbyty Môn ac Arfon. Pan drafodwyd y pynciau hyn, byddai'r awduron yn arbenigwyr yn eu maes. Cafwyd pennaeth yr NPL (National Physical Laboratory), a oedd yn awdurdod ar hanes gwyddorwyr Cymreig, i gyfrannu. Cafwyd Dr Gwilym Peredur Jones, darlithydd Economeg yn Sheffield i drafod Sir Gaernarfon ar drothwy'r bedwaredd ganrif ar bymtheg. Ambell waith, cyfieithai David Thomas erthygl a glywodd ar y radio, megis yr erthygl ar y Dilyw a ddarlledwyd gan Syr Leonard Woolley, awdur ac archeolegydd. I gael gwybodaeth am y sipsiwn, cafodd David Thomas gyfieithiad o ysgrif gan wraig oedd yn ysgrifennydd y Gipsy Lore Society yn Lerpwl. Diau fod cael gafael ar ysgrifenwyr addas fel hyn neu gyfieithwyr yn golygu cryn dipyn o ymchwil i David Thomas. Ond dibynnai yn drwm ar ddarlithwyr prifysgolion, Bangor yn enwedig, a'r rhai a oedd ar garreg ei ddrws, ac yn aml cyfrannai prifathrawon ac athrawon. Cafwyd cyfraniadau gan arolygwyr ysgolion, gweision sifil, enillwyr eisteddfodau a nifer helaeth o athrawon y WEA eu hunain. Cynhwyswyd deunydd gan aelodau dosbarthiadau. Mewn rhifyn nodweddiadol megis un Gwanwyn 1954, yr oedd darlithydd Anianeg Prifysgol Bangor (a oedd hefyd yn gadeirydd Rhanbarth y Gogledd o'r WEA) yn cyfrannu ochr yn ochr â gorsaf-feistr Afonwen (a oedd yn aelod o ddosbarth yng Nghricieth). Yn y modd hwn, yr oedd y WEA yn dod ag amrywiaeth cyfoethog o bobl at ei gilydd ac yr oedd *Lleufer* yn ddolen gyswllt bwysig rhyngddynt.

Ymhell cyn i astudiaethau 'traws-gwricwlaidd' ddod yn bwysig, yr oedd *Lleufer* wedi deall yr egwyddor hon. Nid oedd rhaid i bopeth ffitio'n ddestlus dan bynciau. Cafwyd erthygl ar agweddau gwahanol ar berson, megis 'Hywel Harris y Ffermwr' neu 'R. Williams Parry yn yr Oes Atomig' yn yr un rhifyn. Aethpwyd ymhellach na thrafod hanes yn y modd confensiynol pan gafwyd ysgrif ar 'Mesur Amser Pell' a oedd yn trafod gwyddor yr archeolegydd. Yn lle rhoi sylw i enillwyr dragwyddol, cyfrannodd Cynan ysgrif hynod ddifyr ar 'Ail Gafodd O' yn trafod pobl a gafodd yr ail wobr mewn eisteddfodau. Llwyddwyd i gael testunau gwahanol, megis 'Y Faled Daflennol yng Nghymru', a rhestrwyd y cynnwys ar y clawr i ennyn darllenwyr i brynu.

Yr oedd pwyslais cyson ar fod yn ymwybodol o safon addysg ac i ba gyfeiriad yr oedd yr addysg hwnnw yn mynd. Teitl un bennod oedd 'Lle Ymchwil Wyddonol Mewn Prifysgol', ac yn amlwg teimlai David Thomas fod hyn o ddiddordeb i bobl y tu allan i gylch cyfyng prifysgol. Mor gynnar â 1953, yr oedd ysgrif dan y pennawd, 'A All Peiriant Feddwl?' pan oedd cyfrifiaduron ond megis dechrau. Dan y pennawd 'Siarad a Gwrando', trafodwyd beth a ddigwyddai yn wyddonol wrth i bobl ddefnyddio eu clustiau a'u tafodau. Yr oedd ymwybyddiaeth o'r dulliau diweddaraf o ddysgu, ac ym 1953 trafodwyd 'Y Ffilm a'r Athro' pan oedd ffilm yn dal yn gyfrwng arloesol i'w ddefnyddio mewn dosbarth.

Yr argraff a rydd yr ystod eang hwn o bynciau yw fod David Thomas o'r farn fod popeth o ddiddordeb i ddarllenwyr ac nad oedd dim byd 'y tu hwnt' iddynt. Ar y trywydd hwn yr aeth Tecwyn Lloyd mewn ysgrif ddadlennol a difyr ar 'Yr Athro a'i Ddosbarth' lle'r ymdriniodd â sut y dylid trafod dosbarth o oedolion. Yr oedd yn grefft gwbl wahanol i'r un o ddysgu plant. Meddai:

> ei ystyr [addysg oedolion] . . . yw eich bod yn delio â dynion a merched sydd a hawl gyflawn a rhydd ganddynt i'ch cywiro a'ch gwrthwynebu hyd yn oed ar fater o farn a gweithred, trwy air a gweithred. Yn wir, y mae ganddynt ryddid hollol i ddweud wrth un athro 'Dos' ac wrth un arall 'Tyred', . . . [a] dyma un arwydd o ffyniant yn y dull hwn o addysgu.

Mae hyn yn datgelu llawer inni am natur credo y WEA, yr un gredo ag yr ymarferai David Thomas ar ddalennau *Lleufer*. 'Cyfarteiliaeth' rhwng athro a disgybl oedd yn holl bwysig. Dywedodd Tecwyn Lloyd:

Sylfaen y berthynas rhwng athro ac unrhyw ddisgybl . . . yw hon, sef
bod yr athro – a'r disgybl hefyd – yn sylweddoli petai pwnc y
dosbarth yn newid o fod yn Athroniaeth Groeg i rywbeth fel
Elfennau Naddu Cerrig mewn Chwareli, y byddai'r disgybl a'r athro
yn newid lle ar unwaith.

Yr oedd y cydraddoldeb hwn rhwng dynion yn rhan o gred wleidyddol David
Thomas, ond cafodd gyfle i'w hymarfer mewn modd ymarferol iawn fel golygydd
*Lleufer*. Addysg dda oedd addysg glir, ddealladwy, ddifyr, ac yr oedd modd trafod
unrhyw bwnc dan haul yn y modd hwn. Yr oedd gan David Thomas ei hun
ddiddordeb byw ym mhob peth ac adlewyrchwyd hyn yn y pytiau a gyfrannodd ef
ei hun i'r cylchgrawn. Nid oedd y cyfraniadau yn fwy na thudalen o hyd. Un tro,
yr oedd yn trafod y gair 'peilat' yn un o emynau Ann Griffiths, dro arall yr oedd yn
ysgrifennu ar 'Ddirgelwch y Marie Celeste'. Un waith, canfu fod dau fesur
poblogaidd mewn barddoniaeth Gymraeg yn tarddu o'r un hen rigwm werin
Saesneg, 'Three Blind Mice'. Ni fyddai'r rhan fwyaf o bobl yn trafferthu â hyn, ond
cyhoeddodd David Thomas y stori dan y pennawd 'Darganfyddiad Pwysig' a
gorffennodd gyda'i dafod yn ei foch: 'Onid ydyw hyn yn ddarganfyddiad pwysig
a chwyldroadol? Disgwyl am Wobr Nobel fydd hi bellach.'

Y mae rhyw naws agos-atoch-chi yn y pytiau hyn, a oedd yn fodd i ysgafnhau'r
cynnwys. Dangosai hefyd fod yna ochr ysgafnach i gymeriad David Thomas. Nid
oedd pendraw ar amrywiaeth y pynciau a gâi eu trin a'u trafod yn *Lleufer*. Dan y
pennawd 'Deryn To', cynhwysodd David Thomas araith Robert Richards o Hansard
pan siaradodd hwnnw dros Fesur Diogelu Adar Gwylltion yn y Senedd. Ym marn
y golygydd, byddai rhywrai o'r darllenwyr yn sicr o fod â diddordeb yn hyn.

Ceisiodd Tecwyn Lloyd ddisgrifio'r amrywiaeth hwn oedd yn nodweddu *Lleufer.*

cyfres o erthyglau gan yr Athro Caerwyn Williams ar yr Hengerdd
Gymraeg – Taliesin, Llywarch Hen, Aneirin. Fedrwch chi
ddychmygu gweld *Highway* neu *Adult Education* yn cyhoeddi
cyfres o erthyglau ar 'Beowulf' neu Chaucer . . . i'r aelod dosbarth o
Sais? Glyn Ashton yn trafod cynghanedd Caradog Prichard, Cynan
yn sôn am ddysgu barddoni, Eic Davies ar un o ddramau Saunders
Lewis, O. E. Roberts yn trafod llyfr Eirwen Gwynn ar deithio i'r
lleuad, Bobi Jones yn gweld swrealaeth Ceiriog, ysgrif gynnar gan R.
Williams Parry …

O edrych ar gynnwys *Lleufer* o ganol y 1950au i ganol y 1960au, pan ddaeth golygyddiaeth David Thomas i ben, gwelwn nifer yr ysgrifau gwyddonol yn aros yn gyson, a'r nifer o ysgrifau ar lenyddiaeth yn cynyddu. Achlysurol oedd yr erthyglau ar yr economi a materion cymdeithasol. Yr oedd erthygl yn ymddangos ar wyddoniaeth a bioleg unwaith y flwyddyn, yn amrywio o erthyglau ar fitaminau, problemau ffermio, plannu coed ac astudio'r môr i bynciau mwy cyfoes megis egwyddorion etifeddeg, hyfforddi technolegol, bwyd tun, a theithio i'r lleuad. Ryw ddwywaith y flwyddyn ceid erthyglau ar bobl amlwg a phytiau o hanes yn ymwneud â'r WEA, Jiwbili'r Ysgol Haf a gwibdeithiau gwahanol ddosbarthiadau. Dyry'r argraff fod y WEA yn fudiad bywiog iawn yng Nghymru. Parhaodd yr adroddiadau o'r gogledd, y de a Choleg Harlech yn gyson drwy'r blynyddoedd. Yn yr un modd parhaodd golwg eang *Lleufer* ar y byd gan drafod materion y tu allan i Gymru, ond deunydd llenyddol oedd hwn gan mwyaf. Efallai ei bod yn syndod fod y cylchgrawn wedi taro ar batrwm llwyddiannus reit ar y cychwyn ac na newidiwyd mohono. Y newid mwyaf oedd y canran uchel o'r cynnwys erbyn canol y 1950au a neilltuwyd i adolygu llyfrau a thrafod llenyddiaeth Gymraeg.

Erbyn y 1950au, yr oedd y Gymru Gymraeg wedi gweld adfywiad mewn llenyddiaeth a barddoniaeth. Ni thrafodwyd llenyddiaeth y Gymru ddi-Gymraeg o gwbl o fewn cloriau *Lleufer*. Cododd to o feirdd a llenorion ifanc a chynhyrchiol, a naturiol oedd i *Lleufer* adlewyrchu hynny. Yr oedd *Y Llenor* wedi dod i ben ym 1955, ond yn rhifyn Hydref 1961 o *Lleufer*, rhoddwyd croeso i gylchgrawn newydd yr Academi Gymraeg, *Taliesin*, a byddai hwn yn ei dro yn dod yn un o brif gylchgronau trafod llenyddiaeth Gymraeg. Ond nes gweld dyfodiad hwnnw, yr oedd *Lleufer* yn gwneud cymwynas fawr â'r dadeni llenyddol yng Nghymru.

Wedi naw mlynedd gyda Gwasg y Bala, cymerodd Gwasg Gee y gwaith o argraffu *Lleufer*. Llwyddodd David Thomas i gael myfyrwyr addawol megis Meredydd Evans, R. Tudur Jones a Pennar Davies, gwŷr a ddaeth yn ddisglair yn eu meysydd wedi iddynt ddod i oed, i gyfrannu erthyglau. Gwelwyd enwau megis Jâms Nicholas, Gwyn Erfyl ac Eirwen Gwynn yn cael eu cynnwys ymhlith y cyfranwyr ac yr oedd lle amlwg yn cael ei roi i ddoniau newydd. Ym 1957, cafwyd ymdriniaeth o waith dau fardd, Euros Bowen ac Alun Llywelyn Williams a thraethodd Waldo ar ganu Bobi Jones, a oedd yn llais newydd trefol mewn barddoniaeth Gymraeg. Bobi Jones ac Euros Bowen oedd y 'beirdd tywyll' i fod, ond trodd Bobi Jones y cysyniad hwn wyneb i waered drwy gyfrannu ysgrif i *Lleufer* yn Haf 1958 ar y testun 'Ceiriog – y Bardd Di-Synnwyr'. Cymerai David Thomas ddiddordeb byw mewn canu newydd a neilltuodd ei golofn olygyddol yn Hydref 1952 i feirniadaeth lenyddol am y tro cyntaf. Amddiffynnodd bryddest anfuddugol yr Eisteddfod y flwyddyn honno gan Harri Gwynn, 'Y Creadur'. Neilltuodd saith tudalen o *Lleufer* i amlinellu ei resymau yn ofalus pam y credai yn rhinweddau'r bryddest hon gan egluro pam y credai ei bod yn gyfraniad i lenyddiaeth Gymraeg.

Yn ogystal ag ymdrin â darnau clasurol o lenyddiaeth Gymraeg, cafwyd ymdriniaeth fywiog o lenorion cyfoes – Kate Roberts, D. J. Williams, T. Rowland Hughes, Caradog Prichard a stori fer gan Saunders Lewis. Ysgrifennodd John Gwilym Jones ar sut i ysgrifennu drama a chyfrannodd Gwenallt a Waldo ill dau, yr olaf ar 'Awen Euros a Pennar'. Yr oedd Cynan yn un o'r cyfranwyr mwyaf cyson i'r cylchgrawn a chafwyd ysgrif ddiddorol ganddo yn egluro'r cefndir i'w gerdd enwog 'Anfon y Nico'. Yr oedd lleisiau newydd i'w clywed, megis Emyr Humphreys a ysgrifennodd am y nofel a'r ddrama gyfoes yng Nghymru. Byddai cyfeillion Wesleaidd megis Tilsley a Tegla yn cyfrannu hefyd. Ym 1963, ac yntau yn ei wythdegau, yr oedd Tegla yn dal yn ffyddlon i'w hen ffrind. Bob blwyddyn, o 1959 ymlaen, cafwyd cyfraniad gan aelod o staff y Llyfrgell Genedlaethol yn rhoi rhestr o'r ysgrifau yn ymwneud â Chymru a'r Gymraeg gan nodi ym mha gylchgronau y cyhoeddwyd hwy; ac yr oedd hyn o gymorth mawr i ymchwilwyr. Syniadau David Thomas oedd y mwyafrif o'r deunydd a gynhwyswyd. Anfonai gopi cyfarch i bob un a gyfrannodd at bob rhifyn a gwneud yn siwr ei fod yn cynnwys nodyn bach o ddiolch personol. Meddai Tecwyn Lloyd: 'Cwrteisi amheuthun oedd hyn a golygai gryn dipyn o drafferth ychwanegol i'r Golygydd; yr oedd hefyd . . . yn rhan o fwynder ac ewyllys traddodiadol Maldwyn a Phowys.' Nid oedd ganddo ysgrifennydd i'w gynorthwyo, felly ef a fyddai'n anfon at bawb yn gofyn iddynt gyfrannu, yn gohebu â hwy ac yn diolch iddynt ar y diwedd.

Yn ogystal ag ysgrifennu'r golygyddol, parhaodd David Thomas i gyfrannu ei bytiau bach ei hun. Ambell dro, byddai yn ysgrifennu ar bwnc digon ysgafn megis pwt o gerdd a gofiai yn blentyn am 'Y Bastai Fawr', dro arall byddai ar bwnc dipyn mwy astrus, megis y ddwy ysgrif ar 'Y Pedwerydd Dimensiwn'. Yn yr ysgrif hon, soniodd fel yr oedd pobl yn gallu gweld pethau mewn tri dimensiwn, ond o ystyried hanes, yr oedd hyn yn ein galluogi i weld pethau mewn pedwar dimensiwn. Wrth ymdrin â phynciau fel hyn, yn wahanol i'r arddull a ddefnyddiai yn y golygyddol, ysgrifennai fel pe bai'n siarad â'r darllenydd:

> Rwan, meddyliwch am ddigwyddiadau heddiw – mewn tri
> dimensiwn debyg iawn – y rheiny ydy'r wal ffrynt inni mewn amser,
> rheini sy agosa atom-ni. Ond mae amser yn dryloyw i'r cof, on 'tydy-o?

79

Yr oedd ysgrifennu mewn dull mor llafar yn beth weddol newydd yn Gymraeg nes i Caradog Prichard dorri'r tresi gyda *Un Nos Ola Leuad* ddechrau'r 1960au.

Er gwaetha'r ffaith ei fod yn ffafrio ysgrifennu fel hyn ambell waith, yr oedd gan David Thomas y parch mwyaf at gystrawen iaith. Am flynyddoedd bu ganddo golofn yn *Y Faner* ar 'Glendid Iaith', ac yr oedd yn berffeithydd wrth ymwneud â gramadeg. Ambell waith byddai'n ysgrifennu pwt i *Lleufer* dan y pennawd 'Dad-Ddysgu ac Ail-Ddysgu' gan drafod pwyntiau gramadeg penodol. Un waith, rhoddodd gynnig ar lunio soned ei hun – nid oedd dim byd na fyddai yn fodlon rhoi cynnig arni.

Ym 1960, bu raid codi pris y cylchgrawn o swllt i swllt a chwe cheiniog. Dewiswyd gwneud hyn yn hytrach na lleihau nifer y tudalennau. Gofidiai David Thomas yn arw fod yn rhaid codi'r pris, ond yr oedd 'Lleufer mewn argyfwng' ac yr oedd codiad sylweddol wedi bod ym mhris argraffu. Hwn oedd y codiad cyntaf ers 1948, ac ni dderbyniai'r cylchgrawn geiniog o nawdd. Hyd yn oed petai nawdd ar gael, mae'n gwestiwn a fyddai David Thomas wedi cytuno i'w dderbyn. Ei safbwynt ar nawdd oedd 'Os gallwch wneud hebddo, derbyniwch o, ond os na fedrwch, da chi, gwrthodwch o'. Y perygl o fod yn ddibynnol ar nawdd oedd y gallai atal y nawdd hwnnw fod yn gyfrifol am ladd menter. Yr oedd y WEA mewn trafferthion ariannol cyson.

Yr oedd y nodiadau golygyddol i bob rhifyn yn sylwadau oedd yn werth cnoi cil arnynt. Meddai Tecwyn Lloyd am y darnau hyn:

> Yn y paragraffau hyn y gwelir rhai o'i nodweddion eraill, sef tegwch barn ac, uwchlaw pob dim, ei ymwrthod bwriadus ag eithafion pesimyddol wrth drafod Cymru a'r byd . . . Nid oedd gan David Thomas amynedd gyda phrudd-der escatolegol diffrwyth . . .

Yn nodion golygyddol Haf 1961, mae David Thomas yn sôn am ei fwriadau pan sefydlwyd *Lleufer*. Un ohonynt oedd cyhoeddi mwy o waith creadigol ynddo nag a lwyddodd i wneud cyn hynny, a gresynai o'r herwydd. Peth arall oedd 'edrych ymlaen yn fwy nag yn ôl'. Ni theimlodd iddo lwyddo'n hollol gyda hyn ychwaith, gan fod mwy i'w weld o edrych yn ôl. O daflu cipolwg ar gyfrolau *Lleufer*, cydnabyddodd fod gormod o ysgrifau ar hanes a llenyddiaeth a dim digon ar bynciau'r dydd a gwyddoniaeth.

Pan oedd *Lleufer* yn gylchgrawn ifanc, yr oedd cryn dipyn o'r nodion golygyddol yn ymdrin ag addysg, ac yr oedd hyn yn naturiol gyda Deddf Addysg Butler 1944 yn garreg filltir bwysig. Ond yn ogystal â thrafod y mesur ei hun, byddai David Thomas yn myfyrio ar gwestiwn megis ai peth da neu beth drwg oedd gwybodaeth yn ei hanfod? Yr oedd modd defnyddio gwybodaeth i bwrpas dieflig iawn, megis y bom atomig, ond credai David Thomas fod yr ewyllys i wneuthur daioni yn cryfhau yn y byd, er gwaethaf popeth. Parhaodd y gobaith hwn ynddo hyd y diwedd; er enghraifft, yr oedd dau olygyddol yn y 1960au yn nodi fel y gwellodd amodau byw pobl a sut yr oedd dyn yn gwella. Ym maes addysg, croesawodd ddyfodiad Cyd-Bwyllgor Addysg Cymru fel corff a sefydlwyd yn benodol er mwyn delio â Chymru. Ond bu'n llym ei feirniadaeth o'r Llywodraeth pan gwtogwyd ar addysg gyda swllt yn llai ymhob punt.

Drwy gydol ei gyfnod fel golygydd, bu Democratiaeth yn destun sawl un o'i nodion golygyddol, ac ambell waith bu'n pledio achos go ddadleuol. Un o gerrig sylfaen ei gred oedd fod gan bawb hawl i'w farn, hyd yn oed Ffasgwyr. Gan ddyfynnu Morgan John Rhys a Milton, a gan adleisio geiriau Chomsky yn ddiweddarach, meddai:

> Os na fedrwn ni wrthbrofi syniadau'r Ffasistiaid trwy ddadleuon teg, yna dadleuon gwael ydyw carchar a phlismon a hwliganiaeth y dorf .
> . . O dan wirddemocratiaeth, fe fydd rhyddid i ddadlau yn erbyn democratiaeth, fe fydd rhyddid llafar yn cynnwys rhyddid i lefaru yn erbyn rhyddid llafar.

Safbwynt go fentrus i'w gymryd oedd hwn dim ond blwyddyn wedi buddugoliaeth sawl gwlad yn erbyn Natsïaeth. Yn yr erthygl, gwthiodd yr un egwyddor i fyd darlledu gan ddweud nad oedd anffyddwyr yn cael unrhyw amser gan y Gorfforaeth Ddarlledu Brydeinig i ddadlau eu safbwynt hwy:

> Ymha le y buasent hwy [aelodau'r eglwysi rhyddion] heddiw tybed, oni bai am yr hawl i fod yn anuniongred, mewn crefydd a gwleidyddiaeth? Fe ddylai pawb sy'n hawlio rhyddid iddo'i hun ei hawlio i bawb arall yr un modd. Os gofynnwn am ryddid yn unig i bobl y byddwn yn cytuno â hwynt, pa ragoriaeth sydd i ni? Onid ydyw'r Natsïaid a'r Ffasistiaid hefyd yn gwneuthur felly?

Gan ddilyn yr egwyddor hon i wleidyddiaeth Cymru, dadleuodd dros hawl Plaid Genedlaethol Cymru i ddadlau ei hachos ar donfeddi'r Gorfforaeth Ddarlledu Brydeinig.

Ddiwedd y 1940au, amlinellodd David Thomas y pynciau y dylai llywodraeth a'i phobl fod yn eu trafod – hanfod democratiaeth, natur Comiwnyddiaeth, faint o hawl gorfodi dylai Llywodraeth ei gael, a sut i ateb anghenion cenedlaethol Cymru. I ymdrin yn llawn â'r materion hyn, rhaid oedd cael mwy o wybodaeth nag oedd mewn papurau newydd, ac atseiniodd y ddadl a oedd mor bwysig iddo pan oedd yn ugain oed – fod yn rhaid i bobl feddu ar wybodaeth i osod trefn ar eu meddyliau. Gallai astudio pethau yng ngoleuni hanes hefyd eu gwneud yn gliriach.

Yr oedd canol y 1950au yn gyfnod cythryblus yn y byd a rhoddodd hyn ddigon o ddeunydd trafod i David Thomas, yn enwedig ar fater lledaeniad Comiwnyddiaeth. Darllenodd erthyglau Walter Lippmann o'r *New York Herald Tribune* a'r *Guardian* a ddaliai fod Stalin wedi aberthu un genhedlaeth o bobl yr Undeb Sofietaidd er mwyn llusgo gwlad amaethyddol i'r ugeinfed ganrif. Nododd David Thomas fod yr Undeb Sofietaidd wedi bod yn obaith i Tseina, a bod perygl i'r Dwyrain Pell a'r Dwyrain Canol ddilyn esiampl yr Undeb Sofietaidd. O gadw hyn mewn cof, yr oedd ymdrech Nehru yn India yn un 'anhraethol bwysig'. Ceisiai Nehru arwain y wlad 'nid drwy dotalitariaeth ormesol a chreulon, ond trwy ddulliau democrataidd a dyngarol'. India yn y cyd-destun hwn oedd 'gobaith y byd'.

Materion rhyngwladol fyddai'n mynd â bryd David Thomas yn aml yn ei nodion golygyddol, er y cyffyrddai ar faterion cartref megis hawl i streicio a dileu Tŷ'r Arglwyddi. Ond ar ddiwedd 1949, y modd yr oedd y byd wedi ymrannu'n ddau gyda bygythiad y bom atomig fel cwmwl uwch eu pennau oedd yn pryderu pawb. Gwnaeth David Thomas ymdrech lew i ddeall yr anghydfod oedd rhwng y ddwy ochr a rôl y Cenhedloedd Unedig newydd yn hyn i gyd.

'Beth . . . sydd wrth wraidd yr elyniaeth hon rhwng Rwsia a gwledydd y gorllewin? 'Rwy'n methu'n lân â chael esboniad sydd yn ddigon mawr i 'modloni,' meddai yn onest, gan geisio cychwyn ymchwil am ateb digonol drwy gyfrwng y nodion golygyddol. Dadleuodd fod gwahaniaeth rhwng Comiwnyddiaeth a Sosialaeth:

> Cred Sosialaeth democrataidd fod y rhyddid i dorri llwybr newydd
> iddo'i hun . . . yn rhan o'r rhyddid personol y cais Sosialaeth ei ennill
> i bob dyn. Y mae'n amheus gennyf a fyddai Comiwnyddiaeth yn
> goddef y rhyddid hwnnw.

Ni ddadleuodd fod pethau'n berffaith ym Mhrydain o bell ffordd, a gallai Prydain ddysgu cryn dipyn gan Rwsia ynghylch rhoi mwy o lais i'r gweithwyr i reoli eu hamgylchiadau gwaith. Ar y llaw arall, deallai mai ychydig iawn o ryddid mynegiant oedd gan ddinasyddion Rwsia, er na wyddai faint o bropaganda gwrth-Sofietaidd oedd hyn. Seiliai ei ddadleuon ar wahanol lyfrau a ddarllenodd, ac yr oedd y llyfrau hyn yn mynegi mwy nag un safbwynt. Megis ustus heddwch, cyflwynai David Thomas un ddadl yn erbyn y llall, eu pwyso'n ofalus a cheisio dod i gasgliad. Wedi edrych ar bethau o safbwynt Rwsia yn rhifyn Haf 1949, edrychodd ar y ddadl o safbwynt America yn rhifyn Hydref 1949. Credai fod mwy o ddeunydd rhyddid yn America na Rwsia, er yn cydnabod fod ei wybodaeth o Rwsia – a gwybodaeth pawb arall am y wlad – yn anghyflawn. Ni chredai, fodd bynnag, mewn gwyngalchu'r Undeb Sofietaidd. Bu'n ddarllenydd cyson o'r *Daily Worker* ac nid oedd awgrym ar ei dudalennau fod Rwsia yn ddiffygiol ar unrhyw fater.

'Lle y ceir rhyddid barn a llafar, a llywodraeth werinol,' meddai David Thomas, 'bydd gobaith am ddiwygiad.' Ychwanegodd, 'A ddaw'r diwygiad mewn pryd cyn iddi fynd yn wrthdaro, dyna gwestiwn sydd yn peri llawer o bryder.' Yn hyn o beth, yr oedd y bys cyhuddgar yn cael ei bwyntio tuag at America oherwydd ei hymdriniaeth o bobl dduon, a chyfeiriodd David Thomas at frwydr y dyn du yn gyson yn ei erthyglau. Credai fod llawer o'r ofn o Gomiwnyddiaeth yn America yn 'codi o gydwybod euog' a'r ofn y byddai Comiwnyddiaeth yn gafael yn nychymyg y bobl dduon. Yr oedd wedi cael Esgob Bangor i drafod nofel Alan Paton am dduon De Affrica, *Cry, The Beloved Country*. Chwe blynedd yn ddiweddarach, darllenodd David Thomas lyfr gan Walter White, ysgrifennydd yr NAACP (National Association for the Advancement of Coloured People), a gododd ei galon yn fawr, a dywedodd iddo gymryd diddordeb yn hynt y bobl dduon ers darllen *Uncle Tom's Cabin* yn blentyn. Croesawodd y ffaith fod Uchel Lys yr Unol Daleithiau wedi datgan fod gan blant duon hawl i fynychu rhai ysgolion i blant gwynion gan ei ddisgrifio fel 'un o ddigwyddiadau mawr yn hanes America'. Cyfeiriodd yn gyson at frwydr y dyn du ar ddechrau'r 1960au, a rhagwelodd yr hyn fyddai'n digwydd yn y 1990au:

Nid tynged y dynion duon sy'n peri'r pryder – fe ddont hwy drwodd i'r goleuni rywbryd – ond druain o'r bobl wynion pan ddaw'r farn sydd yn eu haros ar eu gwarthaf.

Yn ogystal â champwaith Beecher Stowe a ddarllenodd yn blentyn, llyfr arall wnaeth argraff ar y David Thomas ifanc mor gynnar â 1910 oedd *The Souls of the Black Folk* gan Du Bois. Cyfeiriodd at farwolaeth yr awdur hwn ym 1963, gŵr a oedd yn un o sylfaenwyr yr NAACP. Yn ystod blwyddyn olaf ei olygyddiaeth, soniodd David Thomas fel y defnyddiai Prydain yr esgus na allai'r duon reoli eu hunain fel rheswm pam eu bod yn gorfod parhau i gynnal presenoldeb yng ngwledydd Affrica. Bu'n ddeifiol ei feirniadaeth o 'wareiddiad' y dyn gwyn:

> . . . o 1939 hyd 1945, buont [y gwynion] yn ymladd yn ffyrnicach nag o'r blaen, ag arfau mwy dinistriol a marwol nag erioed, arfau tu hwnt i ddychymyg 'anwariaid' duon Affrica. Os ydyw rhyfeloedd yr Affrica yn brawf o anghymwyster y bobl dduon i lywodraethu, beth raid fod ein barn am 'wareiddiad' y bobl wynion yng ngoleuni'r ddau Ryfel Mawr?

Oedd, yr oedd David Thomas yn 85 oed yn gallu bod yr un mor frathog â'r gŵr ifanc tanbaid hanner can mlynedd ynghynt.

Parhaodd ei ymlyniad at heddychiaeth. Bu'n edmygydd o waith George M. Ll. Davies ar hyd ei oes. Tynnodd sylw at ddatganiad Iawnderau Dynol y Cenhedloedd Unedig ddiwedd y 1940au a'r cyfieithiad Cymraeg ohono, a chroesawodd Neges Ewyllys Da gan blant Cymru. Wrth i'r rhyfel yn erbyn Corea ddirwyn i ben ganol y 1950au, neilltuodd ei golofn olygyddol i drafod y Cenhedloedd Unedig. Cyfaddefodd ei bod yn syrthio'n fyr o'r ddelfryd ac mai 'sefydliad ffaeledig, amherffaith' ydoedd fel Cymdeithas y Cenhedloedd hithau. Yr oedd sawl gwlad dan fawd America a gorfodwyd y gwledydd Comiwnyddol i fod yn ffyddlon i Rwsia. Fodd bynnag, tra oedd y gwledydd hyn yn cynnal deialog gyda'i gilydd, yr oedd gwell siawns am heddwch, a 'rhaid oedd cadw ffydd yng ngrym ein delfrydau'. Ym 1956, pryderai fod yr Americanwyr yn rhy barod i ddefnyddio'r bom atomig fel bygythiad yn erbyn gwledydd eraill, y 'bomb-rattling' chwedl yr *Observer*. Nid America yn unig oedd dan y lach, ond Prydain hefyd am y modd yr oedd yn trin gwledydd gwannach megis Cyprus, Cenya, Tanganica a Rhodesia. Erbyn 1962, wedi 17 mlynedd o'r 'rhyfel oer', yr oedd David Thomas yn fwy gobeithiol. Yr oedd sawl gwlad yn Affrica ac Asia wedi ennill ei hannibyniaeth a heb droi at Gomiwnyddiaeth, ac nid oedd cyfalafiaeth yn rym mor hollalluog yng ngwledydd y Gorllewin ag y bu:

> Sylweddola pob gwlad heddiw na ellir ei ennill [y frwydr am oruchafiaeth] heb i'r gost fod yn anhraethol fwy na'i werth. Y mae heddwch yn beth mor anhepgorol erbyn hyn nes bod Krushchev, fel pawb arall, yn dyheu amdano drwy gyd-ddealltwriaeth ag America.

Yn ei erthyglau golygyddol nid oedd gan David Thomas ofn mynd ar drywydd mater dadleuol. Ym 1956, yr oedd Camlas Suez yn y newyddion a David Thomas yn achub ar y cyfle i dynnu sylw at y deffroad mawr ymysg Arabiaid y Dwyrain Canol. Yr oedd yn bryderus ynglŷn â'r ffaith fod yr Arabiaid eisiau cadw eu gafael ar olew a'r Eifftiaid am gadw rheolaeth ar Gamlas Suez. Gofynnodd i'r cenhedloedd hyn ymarfer pwyll ac amynedd:

> Gwin go gryf ydyw gwin rhyddid, ac yn y dechrau y mae perygl iddo godi i ben pobl nad ydynt yn gynefin ag ef; y mae hyn yr un mor wir am genedlaetholwyr y gwledydd newydd ag ydyw am ddosbarth y gweithwyr yn y Wladwriaeth Les.

Mae rhybudd slei yma hefyd i weithwyr Prydain i beidio cymryd gormod o raff gyda'u rhyddid newydd. Yr oedd llais y David Thomas cymhedrol a gofalus yn dal i'w glywed. Tan ddiwedd ei oes, parhaodd David Thomas i gymryd diddordeb byw yn y sefyllfa ryngwladol.

Er iddo barhau'n aelod triw o'r Blaid Lafur hyd ddiwedd ei oes, bu ganddo gydymdeimlad dwfn ag achos Plaid Genedlaethol Cymru. Byddai wedi ymaelodi â hi pe na bai'n blaid wleidyddol, ac yr oedd ganddo gydymdeimlad mawr â'i hamcanion:

> Mae arna i eisiau hunan lywodraeth i Gymru – yr un fath â Gogledd Iwerddon . . . ond 'rwy'n methu gweld fod gobaith byth am ei chael hi drwy blaid wleidyddol i'r pwrpas hwnnw'n unig . . . fydd ganddi hi ddim hawl i lefaru yn Nhŷ'r Cyffredin yn enw Cymru heb fod ganddi fwyafrif o aelodau yno, sef 19, a wela'i ddim gobaith am gael hynny byth.

Dim ond trwy'r Blaid Lafur y gwelai obaith o gael mesur o ymreolaeth, a chredai petai'r holl ymdrech a wnaed gan Blaid Cymru yn cael ei wneud y tu mewn i'r Blaid Lafur y byddai hunanlywodraeth wedi cyrraedd cymaint â hynny'n gynt. Er hynny, ystyriai ei hun yn genedlaetholwr:

> Dyna ystyriaeth y talai inni Genedlaetholwyr oll, i ba blaid bynnag y perthynom, feddwl yn ddwys uwch ei phen [y dylid llunio polisïau fyddai yn gymeradwy gan fwyafrif pobl Cymru a chofio mai lleiafrif oedd y Cymry Cymraeg].

Ym 1950, neilltuodd ddwbwl y gofod arferol yn *Lleufer* i drafod y mater hwn o Gymry Cymraeg a Chymry di-Gymraeg. Yn Eisteddddfod Caerffili y flwyddyn honno, yr oedd Ness Edwards wedi sôn am y 'llen haearn' yr oedd y Cymry Cymraeg wedi ei chodi rhyngddynt a'r Cymry Saesneg eu hiaith, ac anghytunai David Thomas yn chwyrn â hyn:

> ...ond am y llen sydd rhwng y Cymry a'r Saeson, fe dorrodd y Cymry drwyddi'n ddigon rhwydd drwy ddysgu Saesneg, a gallai'r Saeson dorri drwodd yr un mor rhwydd drwy ddysgu Cymraeg.

Ar fater Senedd i Gymru, rhaid oedd ei chael, neu ddewis y ffordd i Gors Anobaith, ond sylweddolai mai Senedd Saesneg ei hiaith fyddai hon oherwydd statws y Gymraeg a'r mwyafrif helaeth o bobl Cymru a siaradai Saesneg. Dadleuai rhai na fyddai hyn o fantais o gwbl i'r diwylliant Cymraeg, ond mynnai David Thomas mai haws oedd lefeinio Cymru na lefeinio Prydain. Aeth rhagddo:

> Mwy na hynny, y mae lle i obeithio y bydd cydweithredu'n feunyddiol ar les Cymru, a meddwl am bopeth o fewn terfynau Cymru, yn dyfnhau yn y Cymry di-Gymraeg yr ymwybyddiaeth o'u dinasyddiaeth Gymreig.

Erbyn canol y 1950au, yr oedd ymgyrch o blaid Senedd i Gymru, a chafwyd barn David Thomas ar bwysigrwydd pleidiau gwleidyddol o'i gymharu â phwysigrwydd diogelu iaith a diwylliant. Credai mai *moddion* yn unig oedd y Blaid Lafur neu Blaid Cymru – a Senedd Gymreig – er mwyn y dibenion y gobeithiai'r aelodau eu cyrraedd drwyddynt. Ond yr oedd iaith a diwylliant yn ddiben 'am fod iddynt hwy werth ynddynt eu hunain'. Rhybuddiodd bobl rhag peidio cael eu rheoli gan y moddion.

Erbyn 1955 yr oedd yr ymgyrch o blaid Senedd i Gymru wedi casglu 240,000 o enwau ar ddeiseb, ac yr oedd yn destun trafod gan bawb. Er pwysiced y mater yng ngolwg eraill, cyfeirio ato wrth basio wnaeth David Thomas, er mwyn cynhyrfu'r dyfroedd ar fater arall. Cafodd yr ymgyrchwyr dros agor tafarnau ar y Sul bron i hanner cymaint o enwau ag a gafodd yr ymgyrch Senedd i Gymru, ond gwrthododd pob aelod seneddol Cymreig gyflwyno'r mater yn Nhŷ'r Cyffredin. Llwyrymwrthodwr rhonc oedd David Thomas na chyffyrddodd ddiferyn o alcohol ac anghytunai ag agor tafarnau ar y Sul, ond credai'n angerddol yn hawl dinasyddion i gael gwasanaeth eu haelodau seneddol. Ehangodd y ddadl hon i amddiffyn democratiaeth.

Yr oedd nodiadau golygyddol *Lleufer* yn gyfoes yn y 1960au wrth i David Thomas drafod y mewnlifiad a cholli tir Cymru i gorfforaeth ddŵr Lerpwl. Mor gynnar â 1955 yr oedd trafod bwriad corfforaeth Lerpwl i foddi cwm yng Nghymru ac yr oedd Dolanog dan ystyriaeth, man agos iawn at galon David Thomas gan mai yno y magwyd ei dad a'i gyndeidiau. 'Ni charwn weld dim yn digwydd a amharai ar Gymreictod y fro annwyl hon. Nac ar yr un fro Gymraeg arall,' meddai, gan fod ymysg y rhai cyntaf, mae'n siwr, i ddefnyddio'r ymadrodd y 'fro Gymraeg'. Erbyn 1956, yr oedd ysgrifennydd Pwyllgor Amddiffyn Capel Celyn, Elizabeth Watkin Jones, wedi ysgrifennu ato gan ei ddisgrifio fel 'champion of your cause' i ofyn a wyddai am unrhyw fudiad a fyddai'n fodlon protestio ar ran ymgyrch Capel Celyn. Tynnodd David Thomas sylw at ddeuoliaeth a welodd ymysg y Cymry. Pan wnaed apêl i achub capel Ann Griffiths yn ardal Dolanog dair blynedd ynghynt, ni chafwyd dim ymateb. Ond pan soniwyd am foddi capel neu fro, yr oedd helynt mawr yn codi drwy'r wlad. Nid adeiladau oedd yn bwysig, dadleuodd, ond pobl. Colli cymuned oedd y golled wirioneddol, ac meddai: 'Y mae corff y gymdeithas sy'n siarad Cymraeg wedi lleihau cymaint yn barod, ni allwn fforddio goddef i ddarnau cyfan ohono gael eu di-Gymreigio heb geisio eu hachub.'

Ysgrifennodd hyn saith mlynedd cyn i Saunders Lewis draddodi ei ddarlith 'Tynged yr Iaith'. O fewn degawd, yr oedd y mater o Seisnigo ardaloedd o Gymru drwy gyfrwng mewnlifiad yn destun trafod ac yn pwyso'n drwm ar feddwl David Thomas, yn enwedig y bygythiad i sefydlu tref newydd yng nghanol Sir Drefaldwyn a'i llenwi â Saeson o Ganolbarth Lloegr. Yr oedd bai hefyd ar Gymry a fyddai'n troi i'r Saesneg ac yn magu eu plant yn ddi-Gymraeg. Soniodd fel yr oedd ei ardal ef wedi ei Seisnigo yn ddifrifol. Lle y deuai'r dylanwadau Seisnig i mewn yn raddol, yr oedd gobaith i ardaloedd Cymraeg eu cymathu. Ond pan fyddai gallu cryf o'r tu allan, megis y wladwriaeth, yn plannu cymdeithas gref o Saeson mewn ardal wan ei Chymraeg, yr oedd yn gwbl anobeithiol cadw'r diwylliant cynhenid yn fyw. Mewn amser, byddai'r neges hon yn dod yn bregeth gyfarwydd, ond yr oedd David Thomas ymysg y rhai cyntaf i'w lleisio.

O'r 1950au ymlaen, gwelir pryder cynyddol David Thomas ynglŷn â sefyllfa'r iaith Gymraeg. Yn aml iawn, codai'r sylwadau hyn wrth iddo wneud sylwadau golygyddol am yr Eisteddfod Genedlaethol, sefydliad oedd yn agos iawn at ei galon. Mynychai'r Eisteddfod yn gyson ac yr oedd yn aelod o'r Orsedd, dan yr enw Dewi o Fechain. Eisteddfod Pen-y-bont, 1948 oedd y gyntaf i gael sylw ganddo yn *Lleufer*, pan ymosododd ar ei Seisnigrwydd. Ymdriniodd â'r cwestiwn a ddylai'r Eisteddfod ymseisnigo er mwyn y Cymry di-Gymraeg, yn enwedig yn yr ardaloedd Saesneg. Fe'i câi yn anodd penderfynu ar y mater a chredai mai'r rhai ddylai benderfynu oedd yr athrawon a frwydrai dros y Gymraeg mewn ardaloedd Saesneg. Erbyn Eisteddfod Caerffili ym 1950, teimlai fod yr awyrgylch yn Seisnig a daeth i gasgliad pendant: 'Byddai aberthu Cymreigrwydd yr Eisteddfod Genedlaethol yn golygu aberthu darnau helaeth iawn o'r feri diwylliant Cymraeg yr ymdrechwn mor galed i'w gadw. Allwn ni ddim fforddio'r golled.'

Yr unig gyfaddawd yr oedd yn fodlon ei gynnig oedd neilltuo un diwrnod o'r ŵyl yn 'Ŵyl Gyfeillgarwch y Cymry a'r Saeson yng Nghymru', lle byddai mwy o Saesneg yn cael ei ddefnyddio er mwyn i'r di-Gymraeg allu dilyn y gweithgareddau'n well. Hyd yn oed pe câi'r awgrym hwn ei fabwysiadau, yr oedd y cwestiwn mawr yn aros, 'Sut y gallwn hyrwyddo orau gyfeillgarwch a chymdogaeth dda yng Nghymru rhwng y Cymry Cymraeg a'r Cymry na fedrant Gymraeg?' Daeth yn ôl at y testun hwn wedi Eisteddfod 1959 gan fynnu fod yn rhaid i'r Eisteddfod lynu at y rheol Gymraeg: 'Pan geir y ddwy iaith gyda'i gilydd, ni all yr iaith Gymraeg gystadlu â Saesneg y Saeson uniaith.' Datganodd yn groyw mai meithrin yr iaith Gymraeg a'r diwylliant oedd pwrpas yr Eisteddfod Genedlaethol.

Nid â iaith yr Eisteddfod yn unig y byddai'n ymdrin. Croesawodd y modd y magodd yr Orsedd lawer mwy o urddas wedi gwelliannau Cynan a chymerai ddiddordeb byw yn y cystadlu. Ym 1953, bu'n llym ei feirniadaeth am na chadwodd yr awdl fuddugol at y mesur y gofynnwyd amdano. Neilltuodd ei sylwadau golygyddol mewn un rhifyn ym 1958 yn unswydd er mwyn mynegi ei farn ar y mesur y canwyd yr awdl arno. Datguddiodd ei natur obsesiynol bron gyda rheolau a threfn: 'Pan osoder amodau, swydd beirniad ydyw barnu yn unol â hwynt.'

*Top:*   'Dip. Day' at Coleg Harlech 1993.
Can you spot the future MP?

*Above:*   Annie Williams: Principal Coleg
Harlech/WEA North Wales

*Above:* Tutor-oganizers.
Back: Robin Cain and
Gareth Morris.
Front: Lyn Hurley,
Terry Burns, Sharon
Reader, John Morris,
Lynne Hayes

*Left:* Graham Price: General
Secretary South Wales,
1998-2007

*Above:* Art Class at Harlech

*Below:* WEA Students in South Wales

© South Wales Argus

© South Wales Argus

*Top:* Certificate presentation Maesglas, Newport, 1996

*Above:* Risca delegates, International Women's Day, 1996

*Left:* Risca ceramics class 1997

Yn y 1950au gwelwyd agor drysau ysgolion swyddogol Cymraeg am y tro cyntaf yn ogystal â chylchoedd meithrin Cymraeg. Gan A. O. H. Jarman, un o gyfranwyr *Lleufer*, y clywodd gyntaf am yr arbrawf yn y Barri i sefydlu cylch meithrin Cymraeg gan rieni a oedd yn ddi-Gymraeg eu hunain. Cadwodd gysylltiad â Phwyllgor Rhieni Ysgolion Cymraeg y Barri. Rhybuddiodd yr ysgolion hyn, fodd bynnag, rhag magu 'garrison mentality' tuag at yr iaith, ac atgoffodd ei ddarllenwyr mai 'ymosod, nid amddiffyn, ydyw'r unig bolisi a lwydda'. Unwaith eto, yr oedd agwedd filwriaethus fel hyn ar ran y Gymraeg yn rhywbeth newydd ac yr oedd David Thomas i raddau o flaen ei oes. Byddai'n llawenhau dros bob ymdrech dros y Gymraeg, ond cwyn gyson ganddo oedd nad oedd y Cymry yn prynu papurau a llyfrau Cymraeg. Nid oedd yn hapus ychwaith fod Cymru yn hyfforddi digon o athrawon ond bod y Weinyddiaeth Addysg yn eu gorfodi i ddysgu yn Lloegr. Golygai hyn fod prinder athrawon i ddysgu Cymraeg yng Nghymru.

Erbyn diwedd y 1950au yr oedd mater sicrhau dyfodol i'r Gymraeg yn uwch ar yr agenda wleidyddol yng Nghymru a neilltuodd David Thomas ddau olygyddol i drafod y pwnc. Unwaith yn rhagor, pwysleisio pwysigrwydd cael trefn a wnâi. Rhestrodd yr achosion oedd yn milwrio yn erbyn y Gymraeg a'r galluoedd oedd yn gweithio o'i phlaid. O roi trefn ar y galluoedd oedd yn gweithio ar y ddwy ochr, credai y byddai hynny'n help 'i drefnu ein hymdrechion i'w rheoli'. Ei hen fformiwla ydoedd o adnabod y gelyn a threfnu ymgyrch i ymladd yn ei erbyn. Y ffactorau a welai oedd yn bygwth yr iaith oedd addysg Saesneg, y Saesneg fel iaith swyddogol, y mewnlifiad, priodi rhwng Cymry a Saeson a magu plant yn Saesneg, cyfryngau torfol Saesneg a 'thrais' megis 'rheibio' Mynydd Epynt a Chwm Tryweryn. Y ffactorau oedd yn gweithio o'i phlaid oedd yr Ysgol Sul, colegau'r Brifysgol, Yr Urdd, Ysgolion Cymraeg a Meithrin, ysgolheictod Cymraeg, cyhoeddwyr, y tipyn Cymraeg gan y BBC, yr Eisteddfod Genedlaethol, dysgwyr a'r myrdd o fudiadau oedd yn cael eu sefydlu er mwyn hyrwyddo'r Gymraeg. Yn ddiweddarach yn y 1960au a'r 1970au, byddai cytundeb ymysg cymdeithasegwyr iaith mai'r rhain oedd y prif achosion oedd yn bygwth ac yn diogelu'r Gymraeg. Teimlai David Thomas fod arwyddion gobaith, ond yr oedd ganddo rybudd clir:

> Nid marw y mae'r iaith Gymraeg – y mae digon o arwyddion bywyd ynddi – ond mae perygl iddi gael ei lladd os na allwn ni orchfygu'r galluoedd sydd yn gweithio i'w herbyn. Cawn weld a ydyw ewyllys cenedl y Cymry yn ddigon cryf i wrthsefyll y peryglon hyn i gyd.

Dyma oedd ei rybudd amserol ddwy flynedd cyn araith fawr Saunders Lewis.

Dysgu Cymraeg fel ail iaith yn effeithiol oedd yn gonsŷrn mawr iddo ym 1961, gan borthi pregeth y dydd gan Bobi Jones. Ym 1962, haerai mai yn nwylo'r bobl gyffredin yr oedd tynged yr iaith. Hwy yn unig allai gadw'r Gymraeg yn fyw, faint bynnag o waith a wnâi'r ysgolheigion. Heb wneud y Gymraeg yn 'ddigon diddorol a phwysig i'r bobl gyffredin ddal gafael ynddi', nid oedd gobaith ei chadw'n fyw. Mae'n ddadlennol ei fod wedi dod yn ôl i'r pwyslais hwn. Drigain mlynedd ynghynt, byddai wedi defnyddio'r term 'y werin'; ddeugain mlynedd ynghynt, mae'n ddigon posib mai'r 'dosbarth gweithiol' fyddai'r disgrifiad; erbyn 1960 'y bobl gyffredin' ydoedd. Ond yr un oedd ei bwynt: pobl gyffredin oedd y ffactor fyddai'n penderfynu tueed hanes yn y pendraw. Yn y cyswllt hwn, nid oedd ei ddadl mor boblogaidd. Credai sawl un mai yn nwylo'r dosbarth canol a'r bobl ddysgedig yr oedd dyfodol y Gymraeg; dadleuai eraill mai cyfryngau torfol a'u heffaith fyddai'r ffactor hollbwysig.

Er mai ei fwriad wrth gychwyn cyhoeddi *Lleufer* oedd edrych ymlaen yn fwy nag edrych yn ôl, gwelwyd tueed naturiol i edrych i'r gorffennol wrth i David Thomas heneiddio. Pan oedd yn 75 oed, collodd un o gyfeillion ei lencyndod, Robert Richards, a chyfaddefodd mai tristwch tyfu'n hen oedd gweld cyfeillion yn mynd o'i flaen. Erbyn y 1960au, yr oedd mwy a mwy o'i nodiadau golygyddol yn edrych yn ôl er na olygai hyn eu bod yn lleddf bob tro. Yn aml iawn, rhyfeddai at y cynnydd a wnaed mewn amodau cymdeithasol ers dyddiau ei blentyndod. Yn Hydref 1958 ceir sylwadau diddorol ganddo am ei lyfrgell. Edrychodd 'yn foddhaus' ar ei silffoedd gan ddweud sut y cafodd afael ar ambell gyfrol, a sut y difarai beidio prynu rhai eraill. Dyn yn byw er mwyn ei lyfrau ydoedd. Wedi darllen yr ysgrif hon, gellir deall ei ysgrif chwe blynedd yn ddiweddarach pan hiraethai am ei lyfrgell: 'Rwy'n digwydd bod ymhell oddi wrthynt [y llyfrau], i lawr yn y De yma, ac efallai fod tipyn o hiraeth arnaf.' Byddai'n byw am gyfnodau yn ne Cymru tua diwedd ei oes er mwyn i'w ferch allu gofalu amdano. Yn tynnu am ei benblwydd yn 83 oed, rhestrodd y cyfeillion a gollodd yn ddiweddar, llawer ohonynt yn bobl fu'n ymwneud â'r WEA. Meddai am farwolaeth: 'Gwell gennyf edrych ar farw yn syml fel y peth ydyw – i'r marw, cysgu a pheidio a bod; ac i'r byw, colli a hiraethu. Teimlo'r colli y byddaf i.'

Darluniodd y teimlad hwn o golled yn fwy graffig yn ddiweddarach pan gyffelybodd marw i'r profiad o ymgolli mewn stori gyffrous, a chanfod erbyn y diwedd fod y dalennau olaf ar goll ac nad oedd modd gwybod beth oedd diwedd y stori. I rywun a garai fywyd gymaint â David Thomas, nid syndod yw teimlo'r rhwystredigaeth hon o beidio cael bod yn rhan o'r byd a'i ddatblygiadau. Ni fyddai byth yn cael gwybod a fyddai'r iaith Gymraeg yn fyw yn y flwyddyn 2000, er enghraifft. Ond ymgadwai rhag suddo i felancoli: ' 'Rwy'n dal i gael blas o hyd ar y storïau cyfoethog sy'n digwydd yn y byd o 'nghwmpas i, er i mi wybod yn iawn na cha i byth gyrraedd diwedd y llyfr.'

Rhaid oedd gadael ar eu hanner y storïau am ddeffroad y dyn du ar gyfandir Affrica a'r Arabiaid yn y Dwyrain Canol. Dywedodd Tecwyn Lloyd y câi'r erthygl hon y lle blaenaf petai'n gwneud blodeugerdd o ddoethineb y Cymry ar hyd yr oesau.

Yn wir, gŵr cyndyn i fynd i'w fedd oedd David Thomas ac roedd ganddo hiraeth am yfory. Yn 83 oed, yr oedd yn dal i ddarllen yn helaeth ac yn dal i gael ei gynhyrfu gan syniadau modern. Petai'n cael ei brofi fod bywyd ar blanedau eraill, yr oedd ganddo gant a mil o gwestiynau i'w gofyn i'r bodau eraill. Mae hyn yn adlais o ysgrif a gyfansoddodd ym 1904 pan ddychmygodd ymwelydd o blaned Mawrth yn dod i'r ddaear i weld amodau byw y blaned hon. Dyma'r cwestiynau yr hoffai fod wedi eu gofyn i fodau arallfydol ym 1963:

> A oes ganddynt lenyddiaeth? … A allai ein clustiau ni fwynhau cynghanedd eu cerddoriaeth hwy? A oes ganddynt grefydd neu grefyddau? A fyddant yn pechu? A ddaeth Mab Duw i'w byd hwythau i farw drostynt? A oes ganddynt fomiau niwcliar? A fedrant fynegi eu meddyliau i'w gilydd heb gyfrwng geiriau? A oes ganddynt beiriannau i deithio yn ôl ac ymlaen mewn amser?

Un peth fyddai'n aros yn ddirgelwch iddo fyddai sut y gallai un anfon neges yn gynt na chyflymder goleuni. Meddai ar ddiwedd yr ysgrif hon, 'Bydd y cyfanfyd yma yn lle diddorol dros ben i'r bobl a gaiff ddyfod iddo ymhen dwy fil o flynyddoedd.' Dengys ei gwestiynau feddwl wedi dotio at ryfeddodau gwyddoniaeth a dyn oedd yn meddu ar wreiddioldeb anghyffredin.

Unwaith yn unig y bu *Lleufer* yn hwyr yn ymddangos. Y frawddeg gyntaf yn rhifyn Gaeaf 1964 yw ymddiheuriadau am yr oedi. Bu David Thomas yn ei wely dan orchymyn doctor, 'dim byd gwaeth nag effaith gor-weithio', a chwynodd fod ei ddiwrnod gwaith 'yn mynd yn fyrrach o flwyddyn i flwyddyn'. Yr oedd yn tynnu at ei 85 ar y pryd. Pan orfodwyd ef i roi'r gorau i'r olygyddiaeth y flwyddyn ganlynol, cyfaddefodd mai braint fu'r gwaith ac 'ni fuaswn yn rhoi'r gorau iddo yn awr oni bai fod fy nerth yn pallu.' Cafodd flas arbennig ar y gwaith. Yr oedd yn waith a gâi ei werthfawrogi hefyd, ac a gyflawnai swyddogaeth bwysig yng Nghymru. Yn gynnar yn hanes y cylchgrawn, yr oedd un o'r darllenwyr yn awyddus i weld *Lleufer* yn dod yn 'faes trafod ar addysg yng Nghymru'. Yr oedd Kate Roberts yn gyson ei gwerthfawrogiad, a mynegodd D. J. Williams ei farn o'r golygydd: 'O weld gwerth 'Y Lleufer' . . . a'ch cael chwithau'n ŵr mor serchog o gwrdd â chwi . . . yn yr Eisteddfod, nid oes dim amdani ond mynd ynghyd â hi gynted ag yr oedd modd [i gyfrannu erthygl].'

Nid pawb oedd mor deg ei dafod, er enghraifft J. Glyn Davies pan feiddiodd David Thomas olygu testun o'i eiddo: 'Be yn enw Satan a wnaeth i chwi newid fy ysgrif?' gofynnodd mewn llythyr at ei ffrind cyn ei rybuddio rhag newid dim mwy. Ond prin oedd beirniadaeth fel hyn ac yr oedd David Thomas wedi hen arfer â llythyrau brathog J. Glyn Davies.

O edrych yn ôl ar y rhifynnau a ymddangosodd yn ystod un mlynedd ar hugain ei olygyddiaeth, gellir dweud mai *Lleufer* oedd uchafbwynt gyrfa David Thomas. Cysegrodd ei hun yn llwyr i'r gwaith a hynny gyda mwynhad aruthrol. Bu'n gyfraniad pwysig i gylchgronau'r iaith Gymraeg a thrwy gydol y cyfnod mae yna gysondeb gweledigaeth a chysondeb safon. Fel y nododd Tecwyn Lloyd am ei gyfaill agos, ffydd mewn cyd-ddyn oedd y peth pwysicaf i David Thomas: 'Heb ffydd, nid oes ddim diben i unrhyw addysg. I David Thomas, y ffydd hon yw'r echel sy'n cynnal popeth, a'i cholli, mewn unrhyw fodd, yw'r pechod yn erbyn yr Ysbryd Glân . . . Ei waith yw ei ffydd.'

# 'MIRACULOUSLY UNFOLDING POSSIBILITIES': COLEG HARLECH AND RESIDENTIAL ADULT EDUCATION, 1927-2007

## NEIL EVANS

In 1932, the English writer, H. V. Morton, went *In Search of Wales*. His quest took him to Harlech, where he detected a kind of microcosm of Welsh history. His conception of this was rather like that of the Welsh educationalist, Owen M. Edwards, who argued that there were two great ages in Welsh history, the age of the princes and the age of the people. The old Wales was represented by the castle: little could express better the ending of the age of the princes than the massive southern anchor point of Edward I's 'ring of iron'. But he also found there evidence of the modern Wales, the age of the people. That was Coleg Harlech, though Morton couldn't manage the Welsh name, which had been opened five years previously. This was the Wales of opportunity and social mobility:

> Harlech College is typical of modern Wales as the castle is of medieval Wales, for Wales resembles Scotland in its passion for knowledge. ... The self-sacrifice of the older generation who slaved to educate their children, just as the Scottish farmer slaved, has given the world many great scholars. Most of the celebrated Welsh preachers of the past century were born in the small farms or in workmen's dwellings. Men like Sir O. M. Edwards, Sir John Rhys, Sir Henry Jones, and Mr. Lloyd George, were sons of the people who seized the opportunities for which their fathers strove so wisely and so well. (p. 157)

*Thomas Jones*

Coleg Harlech owed its existence to two features of the modern history of Wales and to one man who brought them together. The first was the railway system which brought in tourists and settlers. Many of these were intellectuals. Barmouth had attracted Fanny Talbot who tried to implement the ideas of John Ruskin on its precipitous heights. A generation or so on, Clough Williams Ellis offered retreats to intellectuals and writers who needed the space to be creative at Portmeirion. In between, geographically and chronologically, was Harlech where around the turn of the century a closely-connected group of incomers created a distinctive society. Prominent amongst them was George Davison, British director of Kodak, who built in the Edwardian period, on a barren outcrop, a house he called Wern Fawr.

The other prominent feature of modern Wales was, of course, industrialisation which concentrated the hugely expanded population of the country in geographically small areas. Two thirds were in the two southern counties of

Glamorgan and Monmouthshire. They were raw, turbulent places, turning to social protest of an increasingly polarising tendency. Out of this society had come the man who would connect the two features - Thomas Jones, born in Rhymney in Monmouthshire in 1870, but travelling an unconventional educational route out of the Valleys via Aberystwyth, Glasgow and Belfast into public service. By the First World War he had became the most powerful political fixer in Wales, with the ear of Lloyd George, the coalowner David Davies, and many others of power and influence. His meandering but untempestuous journey had taken him to Harlech and Davison's opulent arts and crafts outpost on many occasions. He had found Fabian socialism to be the best guide to the future and had a constant concern for leadership. Davison found Tolstoy's anarchism to be a better guide to action and his connection with south Wales had led him to sponsor the White House in Ammanford, where men like Jim Griffiths had learned of socialism, syndicalism and other creeds rather more adventurous than Jones's belief in quiet progress.

By the mid 1920s Davison was tiring of Harlech and wanting to sell up. TJ sensed the opportunity to promote adult education in some way and begged him to sell it at a knock-down price. He found an old-school friend, Henry Gethin Lewis, prepared to buy the building and give it for educational uses. TJ's intentions were far from clear – even to himself, it seems – and one letter suggests that the building should be an outpost of the WEA. But he had in mind the Fabian summer schools which he had attended in north-west Wales, the combination of relaxation in beautiful surroundings with strenuous intellectual effort. Out of this vision, Coleg Harlech was born.

The creation of the college took place against an industrial crisis. In 1925 a national coal strike was averted only at the cost of a nine month government subsidy to miners' wages. When this ran out in the spring of 1926, there followed a nine day General Strike in support of the miners and a six month lockout of the miners. By the end of the year the miners had returned to work in utter defeat. Fragile markets had been shattered by the conflict and afterwards there was no disguising the collapse of the South Wales Coalfield. One of the consequences of this was the closure of the Central Labour College in London, which had been supported by the south Wales miners and the railwaymen. A college aimed at workers in Wales but which was more circumspect than the doctrinaire Marxism of the CLC (or the syndicalism of the White House) must have seemed to have better prospects than a few years before. TJ had always wanted moderate leadership derived from the ranks. Years before he had criticised the miners for employing injured men as caretakers of their institutes. Pay decently for a man with a love of books, he pleaded, and let him spread the word through the district. In a sense he was now trying to do this on a bigger scale, and the attraction of the emotion of conflict recollected in the relative tranquillity of rural Wales and placed in context by bright young minds must have seemed a cause worthy of promotion.

The brightest of those young minds was Ben Bowen Thomas appointed as warden at the age of 27 – so impressive in interview for the vice-warden's position that he was given the top job. Coming from the Rhondda, and unusually a card-carrying Welsh nationalist, he proved to be a charismatic and eminently suitable figurehead of an institution which saw itself as an addition to Welsh nation-building, and would draw most of its students from the South Wales Coalfield.

### A Welsh Institution

If TJ seemed to lack a clear purpose for Wern Fawr in the mid 20s, this had been rectified by the time the college opened in September 1927. It was to be an addition to the Welsh system of education built up in the nineteenth century which had provided well for professional training and been complemented by a network of adult educational institutions. The new college was to cap this system by providing an opportunity for sustained study for those who did not wish to proceed to higher education but return to their former occupations. Ruskin College was available for those who wanted a trade union style education and when the college opened it was still possible to go to the Central Labour College in London as many prominent leaders of the south Wales miners did. But Coleg Harlech appealed as a distinctively Welsh institution – as one student put it in a letter of application:

> I am anxious to be admitted, otherwise I shall be obliged to apply to English colleges, where it will be more difficult for me to keep up my Welsh and religious associations, and in my quest for wider educational facilities I desire, above all, to retain my familiarity and affection towards all things Welsh.

Sir Harry Reichel, the principal of the University College of North Wales, Bangor, expressed forcefully what TJ and his acolytes saw as the role of the college in an address in 1929: '…if Wales can claim to be regarded as the home of adult education, Harlech may boast itself as, from this point of view, the capital of Wales.'

As well as the full time courses the college provided short courses, mainly in the form of summer schools and a meeting place for conferences and non-political bodies in Wales. It also had an impact in the locality with the tutors conducting tutorial classes in their subjects in Harlech and its surrounding villages.

The key feature of the early years was the smallness of the college. At the start in 1927 there were a mere six students, a position which made for intimacy between staff and students and clearly influenced the approach to teaching. Ben Bowen Thomas described the ethos in an early report to the executive committee:

> Every effort has been made, not to utilise the men as receptacles of knowledge, to be passively received and contained, but, on the contrary, to train them as confident and self-reliant students. Each 'class' has commenced with an essay from one student; this has been followed by a discussion, and the so-called 'lecture' has resolved itself into an attempted criticism and synthesis of the views elicited.

Such smallness made for something like a total institution with leisure not being clearly distinguished from work. The staff was resident in the college as well as the students and in the early thirties when resources were under pressure money was spent on an architect-designed house for the warden, to ensure his proximity. Personal relationships were close and often sustained by correspondence once students had left the college. There were formal morning assemblies with choral singing and readings and discussions. Each student did two afternoons a week in the college's extensive gardens. To counter the isolation of Harlech from the cultural life of urban communities, which had been the background of most students, visiting speakers were invited, mainly at the weekend. They discussed their topics in formal sessions and as one telling remark in an annual report put it 'around the fireside'. As soon as numbers of students allowed they formed societies for debates, discussing politics and economics, tramped (what would now be called rambling) the surrounding area and visited places of interest. They read plays aloud and performed them. They read books in a location with several thousand volumes right from the beginning, not exactly unprecedented for those who came from the south Wales valleys, but now with direction and discussion to supplement them, as well as more time to consume them.

What did they study? The interests of the students and the college were formed in the earliest years. Literature (both Welsh and English), history, political science and economics, philosophy and psychology were the central concerns and would remain so until the millennium. Students had predictable problems with written work and equally a commitment to their studies which arose from their efforts to understand the society from which they came. The depression ensured that the college could secure the services of well-qualified and committed tutors. D. James Jones who was vice-warden from the beginning taught philosophy and psychology, writing a Welsh-language philosophy text while on the staff and then moving on to Bangor as professor of philosophy. Wallis Evans, from Aberdare, who was recruited to teach literature, and allow the warden to teach history, had been a fellow of the University of Wales. Ieuan Jeffereys-Jones, from Ystrad Mynach, came with three degrees – in economics, history and an MA in economic history -- taught political science and economics. Another fellow of the University was T. Rowland Hughes who also taught literature in the period and went on to become a radio producer and then a prominent Welsh-language novelist.

Most students came from the South Wales Coalfield. Rural Wales provided relatively few, despite the location of the college, because of the population distribution of Wales and the differences in social structures. Such reliance on the southern coalfield meant that the college shared in the inter-war crisis of the Valleys. The 'Barry-Cardiff coterie' of which TJ was the leading member had been formed in the final years of the expansion of the coalfield. Their plans for the future had assumed that the expansion would continue. The Welsh Housing and Development Association, another creation of the group, had produced visions of a remodeled urban society and the word 'development' in its title was a clear indication of its aspirations for the future. Coleg Harlech was similarly aimed at a society which was expanding – and certainly not at the catastrophic decline which characterized south Wales in the inter-war period, particularly after the defeat of the General Strike. This produced problems of sustaining the institution and its students.

### The Response to Unemployment

Fund raising to sustain the staff and fabric was paralleled by the efforts to support students almost none of whom had resources of their own. They often had family responsibilities – especially in the days of the household means test - and could be reluctant to leave a job, even temporarily, when gaining another could be a virtual impossibility. The annual reports of the 1930s are filled with poignant observations on students' struggles to come to Harlech and to survive once there. If the college often seemed to have the atmosphere of a country house – and clearly had the facilities of one – its students had this tempered by the continuing experience of poverty and the awareness that their time in Harlech was for many simply a privileged interlude in a life which offered little more than the experience of the dole and the means test.

By the early thirties student numbers had climbed to around thirty a year. Yet TJ in particular felt that much more had to be done to address the desperate plight of the unemployed. Changes several years in the making became apparent in 1934 when extensive short courses were added to the long-term provision. It can be seen as a major effort to retain Harlech's position at the top of the Welsh adult educational hierarchy when the nature of provision had been changed by the depression. Unemployed clubs and occupational centres had sprung up in response to structural, long term unemployment and in 1934 the creation of the Welsh Council of Social Service offered an opportunity to expand the college's work. In 1933 grants and reserve funds were used to create accommodation in semi-permanent wooden buildings (apparently **not** Nissen huts, despite appearances to the contrary!). At the same time the gym was built, with the aid of the National Council of Social Service. The old dining room in the college was turned into a class room. This process meant that two new appointments were made in handcrafts and physical training. The Ministry of Labour supported the scheme by allowing the transfer of benefits from home areas.

The need which was being addressed was to provide leaders for the unemployed clubs and the curriculum included intensive courses in crafts in addition to some exposure to the college's normal provision. There was much concern about whether this work and the rather older, less academically inclined, students it attracted challenged the fundamental purposes of the college. What has to be stressed is that not only were the short-term students exposed to the ordinary teaching of the college but also that the emphasis on craftsmanship was an implicit critique of the soulessness of industrial work. This was the ethos that would be expressed in the documentary film *Eastern Valley*, documenting community work in Brynmawr, a few years later. The craft work shared many of the characteristics of the ordinary study in providing a critical stance on industrial society. It was entered into in the spirit of William Morris. The sessional and the short-term students were integrated and shared facilities and were regarded as being in positions of complete equality.

This went well beyond the approach of much of the provision of unemployed clubs and in bringing together people from many depressed parts of Wales experience could be pooled, and what is now known as 'best practice' diffused.

The new direction attracted much interest – it was this which induced the Prince of Wales, a keen advocate of voluntary action, to visit in 1934. The college was able to claim a much wider influence in Wales than its still tiny band of sessional students could claim. In 1935 the thirty-five sessional students were supplemented by eleven terminal students in music and a total of 164 on the monthly courses. At any one time there were sixty students and 700 being influenced by the college if summer schools were included. The scale of the economic and social crisis of the era must have meant a particular keenness to emphasise the numbers. By the late 1930s there were around 280 of the short-term students a year, necessarily a small proportion of the 25,000 members of unemployed clubs in Wales but an important leaven of their work. They were meant to be leaders of the broader movement and perhaps as many as a thousand had passed through the college by the outbreak of war.

The integration of the college into the life of Wales continued with the use of old students as publicists, recruiters and supporters. Already by 1932 there were a hundred of these and they were being organised in branches. Many old students remained in touch through letters and many went on to work in settlements and educational ventures throughout Wales. Ieuan Gwynedd Jones, who attended a summer school in 1942, remained in contact with James Jones for years afterwards by letter, and he remembers warmly the effort which a distinguished academic was prepared to expend on a young student. A growing number of Harlech students went on to university – far more than the founders had intended but economic circumstances seemed to encourage this - as returning to industrial depression was a miserable prospect. By the early 1930s the college was also making some play of the academic standing of its staff and their role in Welsh public life, including in publication. They were also sent out to have contact with the settlements in south Wales. Coleg Harlech was something of a hothouse, intense and isolated: – 'The whole atmosphere, mental as well as physical, vibrates with a glorious healthy life.' remarked a student in 1931. Less kindly, H. V. Morton thought they were rather too monastic for a Protestant country! But it operated as something of a neighbourhood heating scheme for the whole of Wales, though its impact on the overall temperature was limited by its size.

Not was it isolated in the wider sense. From the beginning there had been overseas students and at the end of the first year the warden had taken a group of students to a League of Nations Summer School in Geneva. Such traditions were maintained and supplemented by the close links established with Danish Folk High Schools, particularly Elsinore, which would continue into the 1960s. But by the end of the 1930s the outside world had become more of a threat than an opportunity. The 1939 report looked forward to the opening of the new library scheduled for 30 September but was written in the context of the gathering storm. The Library would not be opened until 1946, after war had scattered the students and staff 'through six unparalleled years and five continents.'

Despite the upheaval the college maintained at least a skeleton existence throughout and one which connected it with higher and adult education. Liverpool University was evacuated to the buildings at the beginning of the war and remained until 1942. It was replaced by Army Bureau of Current Affairs, the forces' adult education arm which the Tories blamed for the Labour victory in 1945. In fact the forces' vote for Labour was not sufficient for ABCA to take the credit. One of those who passed through was Jim Dyos, later to be Professor of Urban History at the University of Leicester, who was beginning his journey into education. TJ himself came into residence, with the offices of the Pilgrim Trust. His personal library was placed in the college library as a major addition to its resources. While these uses of college facilities were in line with the objectives of Coleg Harlech its own provision did not cease. The series of *Pamffledi Harlech* (Harlech Pamphlets) offered appraisals of the international situation in Welsh by staff and people closely associated with the college. The war made a slow start – 'sitz krieg' according to comment of the time - and this allowed some of those students who had been selected for entry in 1939 to come in for a truncated course, apparently in two houses in Bronwen Terrace. Summer schools were held until 1942 and non-residential summer schools in many parts of Wales throughout the war. It meant that at the end of hostilities the college could look forward to regaining its position within Wales – but in a much changed world.

In many ways the college saw its role after the war as a continuation of what had been established in the depression – and with little hope that circumstances had improved; 'All the signs show that we are entering an era of peace beset by extraordinary difficulties at home and abroad.' But there was still a role for the college and one which was much like its pre-war one, as Ieuan Jeffries-Jones observed in 1946:

We need a better ladder of Adult Education, from the Tutorial Class to the Community Centre Short Course, and from the Short Course to Coleg Harlech. There should be but one Coleg Harlech in Wales, but the tributaries should be broadened and multiplied.

### A Slow Revival

Ben Bowen Thomas had moved on to be director of extra mural studies at Aberystwyth, and later into the civil service, in the war. He was replaced as warden by Dan Harry who had been a conscientious objector in the First World War and had subsequently been a school teacher and adult tutor in south Wales. Ieuan Jeffries-Jones returned from the pre-war staff as senior tutor and the college was quickly functioning in its old areas of economics, history, Welsh and social studies. The major new departure and a gesture to the new world was the admission of women on terms of equality. From the beginning there had been a desire to admit women which initially was frustrated by the small size of the college and a feeling that a group of women was needed rather than just one. Women had, of course, been admitted to the summer schools and played a large role in these. Now, a house in Harlech, 'Islwyn' – soon renamed 'Llys Branwen', was bought for women students with Nancy Jeffries-Jones installed as its supervisor. This was quickly superseded by Crown Lodge and 'Llys Branwen' became staff accommodation.

But the college found it difficult to fill the accommodation it had provided for women, particularly with Welsh women. This was clearly a reflection of the occupational structure of Wales which still provided few opportunities for waged work for women – and that was the major route into adult education. Women had not been able to fill many places in adult classes and were largely excluded from the educational opportunities offered by the miners' institutes in south Wales. The gap had to be filled with Danish and, increasingly, English women. The college could not resist blaming Welsh women for their plight, a reflection of just how weak was the understanding of women's position in the post-war world:

> Our women must be brought to realise that this is the era of equal
> rights and opportunities in adult education and it is their responsibility
> to show Wales that the College in opening its doors to women in
> October 1947 was not indulging in an idle gesture.

But the college was resolute in rejecting suggestions that women could be attracted by courses in housewifery and similar subjects. It clearly wanted them on terms of intellectual equality. One clear consequence of women's admission was a steady stream of romances and marriages. Amongst these were Eddie Jenkins and Gwen Lawrence, the first two students to gain state scholarships for university admission in 1950.

The accommodation provided for short term students in the mid 1930s now allowed the college to expand its long-term provision. But it struggled to survive at least as much as it had in the pre-war era. The membership of the college had declined and it raised less money in Wales than in the past. Some of the gap was filled with trade union scholarships, and with local authority grants and fees. But both were limited in number and the college could always find more suitable students than there were grants available. Many of those who received grants found them inadequate for their support and student life, as well as college finances, remained precarious.

Many efforts were made to attract students – a film was made, radio and TV publicity sought. Student life remained much what it had been before the war – intense and with little separation of work and leisure, more societies than might be thought possible in a tiny institution, and close relations with staff. There was still much of an international atmosphere with students from Europe – especially Denmark – in evidence. In 1956 several refugees were taken in from the Hungarian uprising. One was Miklos Pronay who came speaking no English. John Selwyn Davies, the English tutor, taught him English through the medium of Latin, the only language they had in common. Nicholas Pronay, as he became, went on to gain a first in History in Cardiff as a medieval historian before becoming more famous as a pioneering film historian at the University of Leeds.

The curriculum also remained much the same as in the past, though with something of a shift in numbers towards literature as opposed to economics and history. Many adult tutors were hostile to this trend, but Coleg Harlech had always, and wisely, taught a wider range of subjects and could accommodate the shift in interests. D. O. Thomas was appointed tutor in philosophy and psychology in 1955 and received his doctorate the following year for his study of the political philosophy of Richard Price. More students were going on to higher education than in the past and now there was a pride in this, rather than the apology of pre-war days. Indeed, there was a growing pride in the post-Coleg Harlech careers of students, as when Eddie Jenkins became one of the pioneers of trade union education in south Wales. Post war Britain had opportunities for social mobility and an occupational structure which was shifting from manual work to white collar and professional jobs. Coleg

Harlech was playing a role in this process and supplying teachers, social workers and administrators who brought diverse backgrounds and an intense educational experience to their new professions.

*The Common Room: early 1960s*

By 1960 the number of students had clawed its way up to seventy – about twice the number of pre-war days – though the position was far from secure. Financial crisis was always on the horizon or even crossing it. But by 1960 it was possible to look ahead with more optimism. This was not the result of a single development but of a number of simultaneous ones. The college finances were overhauled by the industry and skill of Gordon Calvert, appointed bursar in 1955. Even an illiterate in accountancy is impressed by the business-like presentation of the accounts under his direction. At the end of 1958 Llewelyn Heycock became the president. He had long been an active supporter of the college, an enthusiast for providing the opportunities he had not received in his time on the railways in south Wales, and determined to provide them in Coleg Harlech. The folklore of the college is that his support and the generosity of the scholarships from Glamorgan (whose political boss, in the full American sense, he had become) saved the college from extinction. There is no reason to doubt this. Whatever else Lord Heycock is remembered for, Coleg Harlech has much for which to thank him. Then, in 1960, Ieuan Jeffries-Jones became warden and there is a palpable sense of energy and vision in the reports. To say this is not to criticise Dan Harry but simply to indicate that there was a sense, now, of what was needed to develop the college for the post-war world. This was made possible by the more expansive economy and aura of the sixties. Between 1955 and 1960 the college moved from a desperate rearguard to hold on in a surprisingly hostile environment to having the opportunity to shape its own future.

### Years of Growth

More women came in now, though many were from England rather than Wales, which the college still saw as its major constituency. By 1961 there had been 1000 students admitted and a milestone had been passed. There were still few from north Wales, a reflection of population size, and often of meanness on the part of local authorities. But generally applications were booming and rigorous interviewing had to be done to sift them. Arthur Chisnall, the social entrepreneur, encouraged applicants from Eel Pie Island. The advent of full employment made it easier for people to leave jobs for education. There was now little fear that it would be hard to find another. Indeed there was optimism that it would be easy to find a better one once qualified.

The college had two real needs. One was for better accommodation: the semi-permanent buildings of 1934 were reaching the end of their life and there was enough prosperity in the post-war world for students to expect better facilities. The second was for a means of gaining qualifications which reflected the fact that most students now were seeking to advance themselves. One student from the era has described the college's approach to this in the period as fundamentally hypocritical. Curricula were adjusted to A-level syllabuses but students sat the exams in the comprehensive school in Harlech as external students. The college encouraged them to do this but played no official role in the process. A-level syllabuses were a poor fit for many of the traditional subjects of adult education – philosophy, psychology, even history.

Jeffries Jones cut the Gordian knot by going to the University of Wales to negotiate a two-year diploma course which would be validated by the university, and assessed by external examiners, but have its subjects and curriculum decided by the college in consultation with the university. What came out of this process was almost an honours degree. Students would end up sitting six examination papers and writing a 10,000 word dissertation. It was nothing if not thorough. Indeed many students in the diploma era would feel that they regressed in the first year in university after the second in Coleg Harlech, when most were working at honours level, rather than first year university level. The accommodation issue was resolved with the first capital grants given to the college by central government and duly the ten storey hall of residence was erected. Ieuan Jeffries-Jones had been instrumental in these changes and slaved to push them through. Those who knew him claim he drove himself to death in pursuit of the advancement of Coleg Harlech, where he had worked since the 1930s, apart from the war years. When he died in January 1967 the most tangible link remaining in the college with its founders had been snapped.

The late 1960s marked a turning point in the college's history, the result of Jeffries-Jones innovations. In 1968 the University of Wales Diploma course started, marking a distinctive approach and curriculum for adults. The new hall of residence provided decent accommodation for students for the first time and opened the same year, while the fire in the Great Hall was a crisis which ultimately led to the building of Theatr Ardudwy and provided the college with an arts centre which would play an important role in its life thereafter. Overseeing, all this was a new Warden, Ieuan Williams-Hughes. By then he had twenty years experience in adult education, teaching in Manchester Extra-Mural Department and being director of adult education in East Africa and in Hong Kong. Public money was more available than in the past and prospects seemed fair.

And so they were, in many ways. It was a time of great change. Students were now present for two years, in almost all cases. The Diploma offered a preparation for University which was thorough and effective. Most were supported by local authority grants and within a few years they would get mandatory grants from central government. The precariousness of student life of only ten years before had ended. Many of the students gave up secure and quite well paid jobs to further their education and change their life patterns. Students were drawn from throughout England and Wales and the closeness of the connection with south Wales slipped. There were still many miners, though now more from Yorkshire, directed by Michael Barratt-Brown's extra mural courses. Economic changes were producing more white collar and professional jobs and Coleg Harlech was facilitating the mobility of students into the new opportunities.

The changes were shown in the turn-over of staff as much as in anything else. The expansion of higher education in the period offered new opportunities to the existing staff and all moved on. The core of the staff for the next twenty years was recruited on the cusp of the changes of the late 60s. The new tutors were often recent graduates with little teaching experience, though the staff was leavened by some with varied experience, two of whom, Allan Parfitt and Jim Yuill, brought the insight of being former students of the college to their other talents, which in Allan's case included skills on the football field to which everyone in the college interested in the sport deferred. Mike Jenkins had a background in social work, and had also been a mature student, though not at Coleg Harlech. He combined psychology with all-round cricket talent, and was perhaps the wisest and most approachable of tutors. Graham Allen, vice-warden from 1971 taught literature and became well-known as a poet and playwright, while his colleague Richard Poole combined poetry with acclaimed criticism on English-language Welsh writers. Dafydd Elis Thomas briefly taught Welsh in the early 1970s while establishing his position in Welsh politics. Lewis Lloyd, a polymath, whose abiding love was local and especially maritime history, taught politics. Dave Wiltshire combined an Oxford D. Phil, with goalkeeping, wicket keeping, drumming and the guitar. Dai Michael taught sociology but had an encyclopaedic knowledge; there is only one recorded case of him being defeated by a question and everyone has now forgotten what it was. All were committed to a sense of adult education as something different and exciting, though clearly the academic threshold had risen. Appointments had to be approved by the University of Wales and some approaches to teaching could be overly academic. But generally tutors learned their skills on the job and from the influence of older colleagues. The blend was effective.

Part of the expansion of the period was in the subjects taught. Social Studies had had a single tutor for sociology and psychology in 1971. Within a few years there were two tutors in each subject. The Welsh Office now funded the college on a deficit basis, which meant that approval had to be sought for new appointments but in the early 1970s this could still be obtained, in many instances. Literature, in both languages had always been central to the college and it was the subjects available which ensured that Coleg Harlech had a substantial proportion of women amongst its students. This meant that that the college had to take fewer specific measures to redress the gender balance than Ruskin and Northern College. Their much stronger emphasis on politics and industrial relations made them less friendly places for many female applicants. Coleg Harlech achieved a steadily increasing proportion of women students without special efforts at recruitment, apart from some positive discrimination at the margins, though much effort was put into trying to provide a crèche to ease the path of women students. Funding agencies proved highly resistant to this provision. There was a massive gender imbalance in the staff and before the

1990s there were only two full time female tutors- Maureen Power appointed to teach economics in 1949 who was in the college for a few years and Marie-Louise Schalken who taught psychology in the mid 1970s, until her tragic death in a road accident outside the college. Women's studies did not appear until the gender balance of staff changed in the 1990s with Sue Chamberlain and Clare Hodgson playing pioneering roles.

However, adult education was undergoing many changes in the period and the college did not fit easily into the new pattern. On the one hand there was a development of a broader range of courses, in areas like local history, literature, art and languages, few of which involved students in written work and the kind of development which Coleg Harlech's students were expected to show. On the other hand there was a great deal of development of trade union education, especially after the TUC took over responsibility for the old National Council of Labour Colleges courses in 1964. Coleg Harlech's approach was more theoretical, purposely building on the practical foundations of shop steward training. In a sense it was more in line with the radical approach which was coming out of some universities and polytechnics in subjects like history and sociology – which were often sympathetic to adult students -- rather than to the new styles of adult education. But it still aimed at the same broad goals as in the past. The growth of trade union membership in the 1970s and the expansion of educational services by the TUC and individual unions brought many students with trade union backgrounds to the college. Courses on industrial relations, labour history and the industrial and social history of Wales benefited as a result. These developments offset the lack of contact which new tutors had with grass roots adult education. This apartness was emphasised by the ending of the links between extra-mural and WEA courses in summer schools. It had been the pattern for tutors with sessional classes to bring groups of students to Coleg Harlech for summer schools. Ieuan Hughes ended this by adopting the Manchester pattern of general advertising and recruiting and, inadvertently, a major connection was severed.

### The Restless Seventies

In the 1970s there was some disquiet amongst students and some of the staff about the direction which the college was taking. Some felt that the more academic atmosphere and the emphasis on the route to university and professional jobs was a breach with the original purposes of the institution. The links with other adult education bodies in Wales had become rather tenuous and those with universities closer. What about the students who had in former times returned to their communities to become leaders in politics and trade unions? In fact, most students continued to serve their communities after they had graduated and become teachers and social workers, both in their places of work and outside them. This was confirmed by a survey of students who had studied at the college undertaken by Ieuan Hughes in his final (and sabbatical year) in 1980-1. A questionnaire elicited replies from 165 students from 1967 to 1978. Of those in employment twenty-nine per cent were teachers of some kind and another seven per cent were working in adult education. Social workers were sixteen per cent of the total and overall some sixty per cent were in caring professions. Four percent of these students were full time trade union officials, but many more were part time activists in unions and political parties. Attending university had not really diminished the students' social and political concern.

Nor were relationships between the Warden and staff always harmonious. Ieuan Hughes' teaching experience was from a more relaxed and less rigorously academic background, more suited to some of the extra mural work which was now being done. The staff felt that the administration of the college was suffering from a lack of direction and leadership. After a series of confrontations the college established rather top-heavy formal committees in order to establish clearer lines of responsibility. By the mid 1970s the staff had withdrawn from any serious effort to shape the direction of the college and gave all their attention to teaching.

Tutors had close relationships with students but in some respects the nature of the college was changing. The common room, which had been a central venue for staff and students alike was turned into offices in 1971 and something of a divide opened up. In one of the disputes which affected all educational institutions in the period, a student said it was like having the proletariat in the block (the appropriately unlovely name given to the Hall of Residence) and the bourgeoisie in Wern Fawr. The divide was much more one which affected the administration than the teaching staff but there could be a sense of confrontation. It was a time in which Marxism was the common currency of many in adult and higher education and analogies of class division came easily. But there were plenty of uniting factors. Some of the staff took part in the regular Wednesday afternoon football matches and participated in student societies which were open to all, like the Socialist Society and the Film Society (a student society which had staff as officers after a financial crisis). Ieuan Hughes decreed that all students and staff should be known by their first names, though he was often still addressed as 'Warden'. Friday night lectures on general subjects, bringing in often distinguished visiting speakers were well attended and discussions continued long afterwards in the pubs and in student rooms. Classes were generally quite small, at least in seminars, the staple of teaching and there was much individual tuition, whether timetabled in classes or more informally. There was certainly no sense of having the 'office hours' which are prominent on university lecturers' doors these days. In 1999 a consultant with little sense of the traditions of adult education would mock this as 'open all hours.' The staff preferred to think of it as caring for their students. Perhaps the greatest expression of the community ethos of the college in this period was 'dip day' – the summer day on which students got the results of the diploma examinations. Staff and students joined in the celebrations and many old students returned giving it the air of a reunion and keeping the college in touch with previous generations of students.

Under Jeffries Jones the college had been tightly controlled and work discipline enforced, including regular ringing around the pubs in the afternoons asking landlords to enject any students! Collective activities like Friday night lectures, Saturday morning science lectures and morning assemblies had structured the week. Male and female students were segregated at night. This situation was never going to survive the social and cultural changes of the sixties and seventies. Morning assembly was ended in 1971 when Ieuan Hughes was on extended leave after a heart attack. The gender segregation by floor broke down as students made their own room sharing arrangements. In the early 1970s the resident tutor deliberately turned a blind eye to this, while assuring horrified cleaners that he would deal with the matter. After long-term temperance and sabbatarian attitudes on the college council gave way, as the generations changed, a student bar was opened in the mid seventies.

It was a time of student politics and Coleg Harlech students played their part. At times in the 1970s ten per cent of the student body were members of the Communist Party, though Trotskyists were much rarer. Student politics were often infused with a sense of realism – the real struggle was in the workplace – an attitude fostered by the CP. But there were conflicts and student occupations with a fair degree of regularity. These almost always affected the administration, and teaching often continued throughout. Students gave support to far-away causes – Chile was the Spain of the seventies – but this meant meetings and fund raising and securing places in the college for refuges from Pinochet's brutal regime. But so much of the history of the British left in the twentieth century was of solidarity with far away places of which we knew a little.

By the end of the 1970s things were changing again. The optimism and expansion of the previous decades had been undermined by the oil crisis, stagflation and industrial crises from 1973. Margaret Thatcher came to power in 1979 with a government notably unsympathetic to Coleg Harlech and all that it stood for. This is not to say that Thatcher was unprecedented. Heath's 'Selsdon man' of 1970-2 had tried a similar approach until derailed by trade union and other opposition. As Dave Wiltshire memorably concluded in a seminar in the British Labour History course which he, Joe England and I taught in the period: 'Thatcher was Heath with balls.' Student militancy persisted into the early 1980s but died a death in 1984, that year of Orwell's predicted dystopia.

### Difficult Years

Joe England had arrived as the new warden in 1981, revitalising the administration, though he was always faced with trying to hold on to what the college had rather than being able to expand and develop. His first communication from the Welsh Office informed him that the college was in a 'no growth' position. The underlying trends were hostile indeed. The return of mass unemployment, actively promoted by the Thatcher government, made people less likely to leave jobs with any kind of security for an uncertain future. Trade unions lost members and mining suffered a terminal crisis in 1984-5 in some ways more severe than that which had marked the birth of the college in the twenties. Adult education was undergoing changes, most of which were hostile to the college's position. Essentially adult education had been aligned with universities from its nineteenth-century origins. By the end of the 1980s this was changing in a variety of ways. Many universities closed their adult education departments and deployed staff into internal teaching departments. Others rejected the idea of subject tutors and opted for staff who organised part-time tutors and themselves did research in adult education. It became increasingly rare to find someone who worked in an adult education department who actually seemed to teach adults. Meanwhile the drop in the number of young people as the post-war bulge subsidised sent further education colleges in search of students and produced a sudden conversion to adult students. Out of this were born 'Access' courses run in most FE colleges and offering entry to university in one year and with courses taught close to home, without the disruption of family life and relationships which often characterised residential education. These courses came out of the very different traditions of FE and varied enormously in quality. But they offered to government a much cheaper form of adult education than residential colleges. These had often been seen by civil servants as being more expensive per student than Eton. Somehow the political situation never allowed the colleges to ask 'why not?' and observe how much more useful than Eton they were.

Government interest in the colleges now increased. In 1988 the Scottish Office withdrew funding from Newbattle Abbey, the Scottish college which had been modelled on Coleg Harlech. The future of all the others was under review. The basis of funding had changed. In the palmy days of the 1970s the Welsh Office had supplied deficit funding. That is, after general prescription of staffing levels and many other features, central government met the deficit on running the college. There could be difficulties in this situation but they were often resolved by negotiation with the civil servants. Eirene White, the daughter of TJ, and a good friend to the college over many years, continuing her father's role, was particularly adept at these situations, drawing on her formidable experience as a civil servant, her authority as a former government minister and her position in the House of Lords to which she had been elevated as Baroness White of Rhymney after her retirement as a Labour MP in 1970. It was Lady White, for instance, who had the idea of securing sabbatical leave for tutors and drove this through the Welsh Office in 1979.

This position changed with the coming of the funding councils in 1993. No longer was it possible for the college to apply political and personal pressure within the Welsh Office and stringent requirements were being imposed to make the college conform to the norms of FE. The two funding councils had a single chief executive but this did not allow for any of the flexibility that might have been expected in administration between the two sectors. Indeed, people involved in Coleg Harlech often felt that there was a particular animus towards the institution. It needed to float between the sectors and clearly its ethos had always been more Higher than Further education. This was not allowed as stringent financial restraints were imposed. At the same time the length of the Diploma course was reduced from two years to one, starting in 1993, by the simple expedient of refusing to provide students with grants for more than one year. Efforts to retain students for two years through franchising arrangements with universities, allowing the first year of a degree course to be taught in Harlech, were blocked by the Founding Council, despite initial encouragement for the process. The English residential colleges were treated much better as there were six of them and they had their own category in the English Funding Council's accounts. By the end of the 1990s the tiny Fircroft College in Birmingham was getting a government grant almost the equal of Coleg Harlech's for under half the number of students.

In some respects the college adapted well to this position. A one year course meant doubling the student intake overnight, in an era where there was competition from Access courses and universities were becoming less interested in formal qualifications than they had been in the past and were often admitting adults directly. The increase in recruitment was achieved, though it reinforced a trend which had been emerging: the college was becoming more orientated to Gwynedd and Merseyside as its recruitment base. Historically this had not been the case. In the 1930s, and subsequently, most of the students came from south Wales. By the 1970s they were drawn from the whole of Britain, but with few from the local area. This changed when central government bursaries became available in 1974. Student numbers from north Wales had been restricted by cheeseparing local authorities until centralisation of funding made this irrelevant. One year courses meant the contact between tutors and students became more fleeting and certainly did not allow for the depth of interest which two year courses had provided. Yet it was still a small college and relationships were very close, if somewhat reduced by comparison with the recent past. By the 1990s much of the wider educational experience of the college had dropped away and the focus was very much on immediate course requirements. Science lectures, a relic of the early commitment to broad education, had died in the early 1970s. More general lectures by visiting speakers – that effort between the wars to counter isolation – had only a tenuous existence.

Something might have been expected from a Labour government in 1997 but it only piled on the misery. Its hostility to non vocational degrees and commitment to student fees combined to undercut student numbers in subjects which had been the basis of the college since its foundation. A consultant ended history in 1999, just ten years after Fukuyama had, along with English literature. Social sciences only barely survived in the rush to go for information technology and drama/media. It is pleasing to report that social sciences are once again the college's mainstay.

### Student Voices

Much has changed in Coleg Harlech and the wider world in the past eighty years. The devastation of the industrial working class by de-industrialisation was bound to imply vast changes for an institution which had been founded upon that class. Much of what H. V. Morton had meant by 'modern Wales' was bound up with the working class and industrial society. Post-modern Wales is something different and one of its features is a deep division between those in secure employment and those struggling to survive. The college now draws its students not from the solid working class looking for advancement but from those who have a more precarious position and are looking for a start on the ladder. It is indicative of the change that there is now a pre-nursing course, whereas in the past qualified nurses were occasionally admitted as students. But undeniably there is a need for nurses and preparing people for a caring profession is in the best traditions of the college. As I was writing this essay I was teaching a group of students an introductory course in political philosophy, with a syllabus not far removed from that of the first year of the college (though it was called political science in those days). Something survived of the old ethos in a changed situation. The context was very different: in the past tutors worried about the intense political commitment of students and the way that this might interfere with studies. My main concern – with some, at least –was how to counter political indifference, apathy and ignorance. When I confided this to Professor Ieuan Gwynedd Jones, whose own career was influenced by Coleg Harlech, he told me – rightly – that it was important to try. And that was what tutors had been doing for eighty years, whatever the changing circumstances.

Some sense of continuity is provided by students' experiences over the years. Perhaps the most important theme of students' appreciation of Coleg Harlech is that it was much more than a routine educational experience but something that altered the whole tenor of their lives. The annual report of 1932 expressed this by observing that: 'for each new group of students the year is one of miraculously unfolding possibilities.' There is a consistency in recorded student views over the decades, rooted in small group teaching and close personal relationships between tutors and students. Even though the college grew in size, to up to 150 or so students in the 1980s, which meant that there were now formal lectures unlike in the early years, the core values of teaching and learning remained and remain. It was characteristic that the word 'tutor' was used and not 'lecturer' as descriptions of the teaching staff.

The opinions of students spanning the period from the two year diploma to the shift to one year are remarkably similar. Ken Davies, a student from 1972, remembers:

> It is only really with the retrospective knowledge of the subsequent university experience that a true appreciation of the quality of tutors at Harlech emerged
> ... the lectures, seminars and tutorials given by Neil Evans, Dafydd Elis Thomas, Richard Poole, Brian Anderson and Mike Jenkins really do live on within me today, even the lessons of the brief period I worked with Alan Parfitt and Jim Yuill (who once explained human jealousy to me in terms of a theory about currency - but that was in a pub)

His comments are echoed by Graham Frewell, a student from 1995-96:

> The skilful counselling of the tutors at Harlech was vital to all of us.
> We saw only mountains to climb. The lecturers saw real potential and
> despite our pessimism encouraged us to take that big step into higher
> education ... I can still remember some of the long conversations I had
> with Neil Evans and Richard Poole, both had that precious love of their
> subject. That love came over in their lectures, seminars and tutorials.
> My own success is due directly to their enthusiasm and knowledge.

More recent students make similar points:

> I always wanted to go to college: at 16 I found myself pregnant so I
> started bringing up a family. I worked for the same firm for 23 years
> and my job came to an end and I thought 'what am I going to do now?'
> my children encouraged me to go back to education "its your turn
> now" they said.

> I think when you've been a mother and brought your children up you
> tend to lose something of yourself. It's helped me think, yes, I am an
> OK person and that people value my opinion its good for your self
> esteem. (Susan Rowlands)

> Before I came to Coleg Harlech I was under a mental health team
> getting through the after effects of post traumatic stress disorder and
> addiction. It was pointed out that although I've had a lot of bad
> experiences I could now look to using them in a positive way. I realised
> I couldn't get any paid work or I couldn't advance because I didn't
> have any education I only had army education

> Coming to Coleg Harlech has totally changed my life, it's not just an
> education it's a life changing experience.

> Learning again that what I have to say is important, that I'm not stupid,
> its confidence building, at the same time its not excessively scary it's in
> a small atmosphere. (Mark Squires)

This is not to say that all students found the experience to be the same. That is not
the case in any institution. Some did not stay the course, others found little to interest
them. Ron Berry, one of the major novelists produced by south Wales in the post-war

era is on record as finding the experience 'bizarre'. Anyone who has read those novels can imagine that writer's confrontation with any disciplined environment. But for many students the experience was one that made them different people, or was at least a catalyst in the journey of rediscovery that they had begun to undertake for themselves.

Coleg Harlech changed the lives of thousands of people and gave Britain, and Wales in particular, some of its cadre of committed social workers, teachers, politicians, trade union officials and social entrepreneurs. They worked like yeast in society, helping to raise its ideals and aspirations. It still plays a role in that process. Its place in modern Wales is undeniable. Its place in post-modern Wales can be won.

## Bibliography

Peter Stead, *Coleg Harlech: the First Fifty Years,* (Cardiff, 1977), the official history is readable and stakes out the ground. The standard work on the town is Lewis W. Lloyd, *The Book of Harlech,* (Buckingham, 1987). Oliver Wynne Hughes, *Everyday was Summer,* (Llandybie, 1989) is a vivid evocation of the town in the Edwardian era, based on oral evidence. Harold Watkins, *Life has Kept me Young,* (London, 1951) includes an affectionate portrait of the college in the immediate post-war period. Rufus Adams and Geoff Powell offer their reminiscences of teaching there in the sixties in *Planet* 2005-6. For Eirene White's career, see Joe England, 'White, Eirene Lloyd, Baroness White (1909-1999)', *Oxford Dictionary of National Biography* (Oxford, 2004).

The basic sources are the annual reports and other material in Coleg Harlech and the TJ papers in the National Library. However I have often relied on my memory as a full-time tutor 1971-2000 and a part-time one since. I have also spoken to many people over the years with memories stretching back to the origins of the college. I encountered every Warden apart from Ieuan Jeffries-Jones, and many old students and tutors. I have drawn more directly on the memories of Tudor Bowen-Jones who is probably the last-surviving pre-war student, and those of Glenys and Allan Parfitt who were students under Jeffries Jones. Dai Michael provided some valuable material on the 1930s and I hope he will find the time to harness his vast knowledge of the history of adult education in Wales. I have also drawn on a questionnaire sent to former students in 1997. I am grateful to Joe England for letting me use this material and for helpful comments on a draft. But my view is essentially personal, rather than a product of exhaustive research.

# WORKING WITH THE UNIONS
## 1945-1975

JOE ENGLAND

*The SCW day-release course was magnificent.*

Garfield Davies (Lord Davies of Coity), former general secretary of the Union of Shop and Distributive Allied Workers.

*The courses at Port Talbot gave us a good grounding and background for achievement in the union.*

Tom Fellows and Lyndon James, former Presidents of the Iron and Steel Trades Confederation.

For some twenty years from the mid-1950s workers' education took an exciting and fresh direction that energized the whole South Wales District. New students, new tutors, new sources of income, and new methods of teaching all came from a WEA commitment to work closer with active trade unionists.

## The Background

In 1945 trade unions emerged from the war with enhanced prestige and restored vigour. They were seen to have a larger role and greater responsibilities than ever before in the context of a Labour government, full employment, nationalized industries, and a developing welfare state. In the phrase of the time, 'a new social order' required the participation of trade unions and their members in a more democratic Britain that was trying to rebuild its economy. Yet full employment also gave greater bargaining power to trade unionists in the factories and enabled them to push up wages. By 1948 the government was urging 'pay restraint' and by the end of the fifties 'the trade union question' had moved to the centre of British politics. It was to dominate the domestic agenda for the next thirty years. It was in these circumstances that the WEA nationally became increasingly aware of the arguments from both left and right that there was a job of work to be done to meet the educational needs of trade unionists in a situation very different from the Depression years. A heady mixture of motives coalesced. Here was an opportunity to grapple with the political and economic conundrums of the post-war world, to prepare trade unionists for new challenges and, by extension, to become enlightened civic activists. At the same time here was an opportunity for the WEA to reconnect with its traditional target, the working class. Furthermore, if the WEA did not act there were other bodies that would do so. There was always the old enemy the NCLC but, much more significantly, from 1946 the TUC began to provide courses of its own devising and individual trade unions began to increase their educational work and designate education officers.

In Wales there were additional factors. The economy was being rebuilt by deliberate state action. By vigorous use of the Distribution of Industry Act, 1945, expanding firms were steered into Wales. The wartime ordnance factories at Hirwaun, Bridgend, and Pembrey were transformed into trading estates similar to the one set up at Treforest in 1936, and another added at Fforestfach near Swansea. In addition, over 400 new industrial buildings were put up in Wales between 1945 and 1952. There followed an influx of major employers into the trading estates and other locations around the periphery of the coalfield — Ystradgynlais, Merthyr Tydfil, Brynmawr and Pontypool — or on the coast at Swansea, Baglan and Barry. At the same time old pits were being closed, new ones opened up and the steel industry was being revolutionized through the opening in 1951 of the Abbey works at Margam, Port Talbot. The recession of 1958-59 and the accelerated closure of the old tinplate and sheet works of west Wales as the new works at Trostre, Velindre and Margam got into their stride instigated another burst of government activity in the early sixties. A £2 million factory was built at Swansea for Prestcold refrigerators, Revlon opened a cosmetics factory at Maesteg, Rover began to build Landrovers at Cardiff, and Fisher and Ludlow opened a new body-building car plant at Llanelli where Morris Motors was already expanding. At Llanwern, near Newport, the Spencer steelworks was built on a green field site.

These developments were a social as well as an industrial revolution, creating new relationships between work, home and leisure and between workers with different skills. With most new jobs located on the coast or around the fringes of the coalfield commuting became a way of life for many. Time for leisure pursuits, including evening classes, was squeezed. More serious for regular attendance at classes was the continuous shift system employed in the new steel works, which completely ruled out weekly attendance. The new technologies in coal and steel increased the status of craftsmen and diminished that of process workers. Pay comparisons between different grades of workers in the same workplace or between factories in the same industry were at the root of an increasing number of disputes.

In the new factories the workers were a mixture of former miners and hand mill workers, railway workers (Beeching was swinging his axe), bus drivers, forestry and foundry workers, and a host of others from a variety of industries. Despite the influx of factories during the war many were unfamiliar with the technologies, working practices and bargaining machinery within the new industries. The same point applied in many instances at supervisory level. It was indeed a strange new world. At the Abbey works of the Steel Company of Wales (SCW) 14,000 process and craft workers were represented by twelve different unions, often at loggerheads with each other; at one south Wales car plant alone there were over 10,000 piece-work prices, a situation with which no full-time trade union official could cope and which threw negotiations upon shop-stewards and foremen; at Llanelli former steel workers accustomed to a system of 'job and finish' felt trapped on continuous production lines where Fisher and Ludlow were pioneering a measured daywork system of remuneration.

It was against this developing background that the WEA embarked upon education for trade unionists. In South Wales the full-time staff consisted of the District secretary D.T.Guy and the west Wales organizer Mansel Grenfell. There were no full-time tutors, let alone specialists in trade union studies. Suitable teaching materials were scarce. The WEA provision targeted at trade unionists was in the hands of the Workers' Educational Trade Union Committee (WETUC), a joint committee of the WEA and affiliated unions. In the inter-war years the chief activity organized by its divisional committees in South Wales had been two weekend schools each year, one in Swansea and one near Cardiff. The unions paid the cost of these by providing 'scholarships' to enable members to attend. Post war the tempo increased. In 1947-48 three schools were held and in 1948-49 four. In September 1950 the divide between east and west South Wales was swept away and a Trade Union Advisory Committee (TUAC) replaced the two divisional committees. The new committee was much more active and by increasing courses called forth a latent demand. In 1951 nine weekend schools attracted 315 students

## THE WORKERS' EDUCATIONAL ASSOCIATION

# SPECIAL CONFERENCE

of

## Representatives of Affiliated Trade Unions

to discuss

## Education to Meet the Modern Needs of Trade Unions

BONNINGTON HOTEL, SOUTHAMPTON ROW, LONDON, W.C. 1.
WEDNESDAY, 11th MAY, 1949.

Sessions : 11.0 a.m. to 1.0 p.m.
2.30 p.m. to 4.30 p.m.

The Conference will be opened at 11.0 a.m. by
**MR. HAROLD CLAY,**
*President, Workers' Educational Association.*

An Introductory address will be given by
**PROFESSOR R. H. TAWNEY,**
*Vice-President, Workers' Educational Association.*

**The Conference will adjourn for lunch at 1.0 p.m. and resume at 2.30 p.m.**

but applicants far exceeded the number of scholarships available. Most of the schools were still dealing with topics such as 'The Problem of Germany' or 'The Present International Situation' but significantly two weekend schools for members of the Transport and General Workers' Union (TGWU) were on 'The Shop Steward as a Trade Union Official'. In addition, ten day schools were organised including two for members of the Amalgamated Union of Foundry Workers. In that first year the Committee discussed the appointment of a full-time Organizer 'whose main function would be to organize educational facilities for trade unionists. A full-time Organizer is essential in an area like South Wales'. But the South Wales district could not afford to make an appointment.

Meanwhile, over the weekend of 26-28 October 1951, as the newly elected Churchill formed his Cabinet, the WEA in annual conference decided to establish a committee to examine how its work with the unions could be increased. The chairman would be Arthur Creech Jones, Colonial Secretary in the Attlee government and one-time National Officer of the TGWU, with a life-long interest in workers' education.

While the Creech Jones committee deliberated, WEA involvement with trade union education in South Wales grew steadily. In 1952 eight weekend schools were organized and nine day schools. Again demand outran the number of scholarships available for weekend schools, the greatest number coming from the Iron and Steel Trades Confederation and the Inland Revenue Staff Federation. Gradually the topics at these schools began to include more on economic and political issues while day schools at Pontypridd and Cardiff dealt with 'Functions and responsibilities of trade unions in a democratic community'. The next year eight weekend schools — including one for members of the NUM, the first time that miners had attended a school organized by the WEA in South Wales — and eleven day-schools were held.

### The Pilot Scheme
In 1953 the Creech Jones committee reported. Its central conclusion was that 'the basic aims and purposes of the WEA require that it should give a clear priority to the educational needs of the trade union movement . . . this has been done in good measure over the years, but the WEA should now apply its resources to a more specific and concentrated effort in this field'. Among its recommendations was: 'three intensive development schemes should be established in carefully selected areas'. The South Wales TUAC seized upon this, proposing that 'the area between Neath and Bridgend appeared to be an eminently suitable one for these experiments'. South Wales put in an application along with seven other districts

and the three pilot areas chosen were Cleveland (in the Yorkshire North district), Tyneside (in the Northern district) and the Neath to Bridgend area centred on Port Talbot.

The Port Talbot pilot scheme was the smallest of the three. The largest single employer was the Steel Company of Wales, which drew its labour force of 15,000 from miles around. Within the area there were four WEA branches, fifteen classes and study groups, and twenty unions with over 150 branches of unions affiliated to the WETUC. But no classes were organized with the specific aim of attracting trade unionists, there were no classes in trade union studies, and the District in its application had said: 'At the moment there is next to nothing being done in this area by way of trade union education'. Not one of the 1953 weekend schools had been held within the prospective pilot area. Hugh Clegg and Rex Adams, who were commissioned by the WEA to assess the pilot projects, noted in their 1959 report that the NCLC had a history of activity in the south Wales pilot area and this had 'left a tradition of hostility to the WEA amongst some of its former students, and overcoming this tradition has taken time'. In an all-out effort to promote trade union education, funds came from the WEA head office and from the Ministry of Education to appoint an organizer and a tutor-organizer and to meet other costs in the calendar years 1955-57. In anticipation the District appointed an organizer in the autumn of 1954.

He was Dick Lewis, a colliery blacksmith at Cwmdu, Maesteg, who had won an NUM scholarship to Harlech and then after his year's course, had returned under the terms of the scholarship, to the colliery. Not until June 1955 was the tutor-organizer appointed. He was Eddie Jenkins then working as a tutor-organizer in the Cumberland and Westmoreland District but originally from Deri in the Rhymney valley. He had taken a well-trodden path for people of his generation: left school at fourteen, eleven years underground, WEA and NCLC evening classes, Coleg Harlech in 1948, a state scholarship to Aberystwyth in 1950, and a good degree in economics and political science. Supported by his wife Gwen whom he had met at Harlech, and who had also won a state scholarship to Aberystwyth (they were the first Harlech students to do so) he was the driving force in the development of work with trade unionists over the next twenty years. Hard working, with a challenging intelligence, he never lost an opportunity to open up new avenues for the work or to encourage and advise a potential student or colleague. Many had their lives changed through meeting Eddie.

There is a well-nourished myth that nothing happened in the 1950s. That intellectual, political and cultural life in Britain stood still between the fall of the Attlee government in 1951 and the appearance of the Beatles in 1962. True, the early years of the decade were staid although Orwell's *1984* first published in 1949 reverberated as it went through constant reprints and Wain's *Hurry on Down* (1953) and Amis' *Lucky Jim* (1954) struck welcome notes of irreverence. But 1955 brought events of great significance. Commercial television began transmissions and the government announced plans to build twelve nuclear power stations and to manufacture hydrogen bombs. Then came the seismic year of 1956 with Suez, Hungary, Kruschev's speech on Stalin, Becket's *Waiting For Godot*, Osborne's *Look Back in Anger*, Colin Wilson's *The Outsider*, Frank Cousins' accession to the leadership of the TGWU, and Crossland's *The Future of Socialism*. In 1957 came Hoggart's *The Uses of Literacy*, and Bevan's H-Bomb speech at Brighton. Then in 1958 appeared *Chicken Soup with Barley*, the first of Arnold Wesker's trilogy, followed by *Roots*, 1959, and *I'm Talking about Jerusalem*, 1960; the text of each play eagerly discussed as they were rapidly published by Penguin. That year 1958 also saw the foundation of CND and the publication of Raymond Williams' *Culture and Society*, Sillitoe's *Saturday Night and Sunday Morning*, and Galbraith's *Affluent Society*. Into this tumult of ideas and events reflecting and questioning the post war world the pilot scheme was launched.

The bare statistics of what was achieved from a standing start are given in Table One. For the first period from October 1954 to June 1955 Dick Lewis was the only full-time worker on the project, from June 1955 until September 1957 he and Eddie Jenkins worked together, and then from September 1957 Eddie worked alone as Dick left the project to be an NCB Area Manpower Officer and was not replaced. In effect, the Scheme was only fully manned for two years. It formally came to an end in December 1957 although some courses carried through to 1958. Both Eddie and Dick were relatively inexperienced to run a scheme upon which much depended; they operated from their homes without benefit of computers and emails, often meeting in houses and pubs to plan the programme; they had to make contact with union branches and create mailing lists from scratch; and without cars they covered the area on slow trains and buses.

**Table One**

| Type of Course | 1954-5 | 1955-6 | 1956-7 | 1957-8 |
|---|---|---|---|---|
| One Year | - | 1 | 4 | 2 |
| Terminal | - | 2 | 8 | 3 |
| Short Terminal | 4 | 13 | 13 | 9 |
| Weekend School | 4 | 16 | 19 | 7 |
| Day School | 8 | 6 | - | - |

(Source: *TUAC annual reports*)

The emphasis upon weekend schools came from a desire to make contact with a large number of students in the shortest possible time and thereby build support for the work. It also enabled a range of tutors and methods to be used. Weekend schools had traditionally been held in hostels run by educational and voluntary organizations at Glan-y-Mor, Barry, Coleg-y-Fro, Rhoose, and Dunraven Castle, Southerndown. Dick Lewis broke new ground by using the Esplanade Hotel at Porthcawl, a major innovation that took learning into unusually pleasant surroundings that included a Saturday evening dance. There was dark talk among WEA elders about young people 'enjoying themselves'.

Youth was certainly a characteristic of the students. In 1954-5 HM Inspectors in a report on the district had stated that the movement had practically no appeal to young people and very little to people under forty years of age. But analysis of Pilot Scheme weekend school students consistently revealed that three-quarters of them were under forty and nearly half under thirty. A weekend school for young trade unionists held at Port Talbot in June 1958 drew over eighty applicants between sixteen and twenty years of age for forty scholarship places, and the school was so successful that some of the students offered to pay the full costs if another could be arranged. Youth was not an attribute confined to those attending weekends. The age of students in classes ranged from sixteen to sixty with a large majority under forty. In the 1956-7 session the eldest student in one class was twenty-nine and the youngest sixteen. In another, visited by one of HM Inspectors, only one of the eleven present was over forty. Moreover, the WEA was finding a new constituency. Most students at weekend schools and classes had had no previous contact with adult education before the Pilot Scheme started, although a substantial minority was active in their union, chairing the branch, acting as secretary, or holding positions as shop steward or committee member.

The subjects taught at weekend schools and classes were predominantly those associated with trade union education at that time – trade union history and organization, industrial law, collective bargaining and arbitration. A heavy burden of teaching fell upon Eddie Jenkins although the District was able to call upon tutors employed at the University Colleges at Swansea and Cardiff. Bill Campbell Balfour from the Industrial Relations Department at Cardiff took a number of classes. Victor Hampson Jones, from Cardiff Extra-mural Department, was a popular and effective lecturer on industrial law, Brinley Thomas, an economist of international repute and District Treasurer for many years took day schools. There was also the incomparable Bill Gregory who had graduated from the barbershop in Briton Ferry via Cambridge to an extra-mural lectureship at Cardiff and whose wide experience, range of reading, wit and irrepressible zest attracted audiences wherever he went. Probably more important for the District was the involvement of Ron Mathias the Regional Secretary of the TGWU. A forceful personality, he had a ringside seat at industrial developments in South Wales, a penchant for analysing them and an original approach to wages issues that later made him a full-time member of the Prices and Incomes Board. Mathias threw himself wholeheartedly into the work, frequently lecturing, substantially increasing the number of TGWU scholarships for weekend schools and affiliating all TGWU branches in South Wales to the District. From 1964 to 1968, when he died from a heart attack, he was District Chairman.

Although the bias of the project was trade union education, in the sense described above, there was also a considerable amount of liberal education for trade unionists. The Clegg/Adams Report noted with regard to Port Talbot: 'almost any topic can attract trade unionists'. But the topics were serious, the tutors first class. In November 1956 Kingsley Amis, Andrew Vicari and W. John Morgan tutored a weekend school on 'Culture and the Worker'. At a time of concern about the uses of atomic energy and a growing interest in South African apartheid and race relations, the WEA found two highly qualified academics in Glyn O. Phillips and Ivor Isaac who spoke with clarity and vigour about these respective topics. Under the guise of courses labeled 'Clear Thinking and Expression' Tom Thomas, the charismatic Swansea Extra-mural tutor, inspired many to become serious students of literature. (During his career he was responsible for at least thirty students going to Coleg Harlech.) As the classes and weekend schools expanded so new tutors were drawn in, excited by the opportunity to reach young and enthusiastic adult learners. There was an unmistakable buzz in the district. In 1945-46 the number of trade union branches affiliated to the district had been forty-seven along with two trades councils. In 1958-59 the comparable figures were 122 and four. By 1961 one third of the WEA South Wales executive consisted of full-time trade union officers.

Two main lessons came out of the pilot scheme. First, the recruitment of trade unionists into WEA courses on a wide range of topics was perfectly possible given extra resources and clarity of purpose. As Clegg/Adams reported: 'The first impression of the Port Talbot scheme is that it has been a very successful exercise in recruitment. In 1956-57, for instance, there were 1,380 student attendances at weekend schools alone.' A major area of work had been opened up. In so doing the WEA was also contributing on a larger scale than previously to the adult education of working class women in south Wales. No statistics on the gender balance of students at those weekend schools exist, but the heavy involvement of the Union of Shop Distributive and Allied Workers, the Civil Service Clerical Association, and the Inland Revenue Staff Federation ensured that women were well represented. The second lesson lay in the specific field of trade union education and was pointed out by Clegg/Adams: 'Some of the most rewarding and apparently useful types of course for trade unionists (judging from Cleveland and Port Talbot) are short and introductory courses for workers drawn either from a single union or a single industry and dealing with subjects close to their immediate interests'. This was a pointer to the way the work subsequently developed. The scheme also uncovered the major difficulty referred to earlier. The continuous shift system in the steelworks, chemical plants and oil refineries made it virtually impossible for an individual or any group of workers to attend a regular evening class. Linked weekend schools organized at lunar month intervals went some way to dealing with the problem but difficulties with guaranteeing accommodation and scholarships made their organization hazardous. The answer lay in a different direction.

Finally, how effective was the Port Talbot scheme in educational terms? Clegg/Adams had their reservations: '. . . most of the weekend school work has, however, been at a fairly low level, and the scheme has not clearly established the best means of moving on to more advanced work, either from the weekend schools or from its successful elementary courses in evening classes'. The District in its review of the Clegg/Adams report naturally demurred from this verdict and given the quality of the tutors involved and the adult educational inexperience of most of the students it does seem too harsh. Moreover, no balanced assessment of the project could be made without seeing its impact unfold. The concentration upon working with trade unionists was, in that now familiar phrase, 'not an event but a process'. Many continued in WEA and extra-mural classes, growing in knowledge and capacity. The number of trade unionists who became WEA branch and class members steadily increased, as did the numbers taking correspondence courses and going to summer schools. In the 1950s the tradition of suggesting to working class students with unfulfilled talents that they should enter Ruskin College or Coleg Harlech was still strong. A number were encouraged to attend Harlech summer schools and then to become full-time students there. From memory Eddie Jenkins reckoned that seventeen went to Coleg Harlech from the pilot scheme, most of them going on to take university degrees. But there were certainly more. Jimmy Poole, an electrical coil winder at SCW who later became a highly successful law lecturer, remembers being one of five from the Pyle/Port Talbot area who together went to the College in 1963 after attending weekend schools and classes. Clegg/Adams, however, with an eye to the needs of the unions made the point that 'the pilot schemes should be judged rather by the subsequent careers of their students in the trade union movement, and by the number of new trade union students who come to the WEA for similar help in future years.' Here too the scheme was successful, creating a momentum that pointed the whole District in the direction of trade union work that developed leaders at local and national levels.

For example, the work of TUAC in providing courses for trade unionists continued outside the pilot scheme area but drew on the experience gained in that experiment. In 1955 in addition to the pilot scheme schools, there were five week-end schools, twelve day-schools, and six classes for trade unionists mainly in Newport and Cardiff. In 1956 developments outside the pilot area included four weekend-schools, thirty day-schools, and nine special courses. The district now felt confident enough to press for another full-time post and in April 1957 Harry Jones was appointed tutor-organizer to develop trade union education in the industrial area of Monmouthshire. Like Eddie, Harry was an ex-miner and a former Coleg Harlech student who had graduated at Aberystwyth in economics. He also had a valuable knowledge of employment law and soon began to teach and organize new courses. With the end of the pilot scheme, and the loss of Dick Lewis as organizer, fewer courses were held in the pilot area (now known as Mid-Glamorgan) but work with trade unionists was now embedded in the District as Table Two illustrates

**Table Two**

| | Week-end Schools | Day-schools |
|---|---|---|
| 1958 | 25 | 18 |
| 1959 | 20 | 18 |
| 1960 | 18 | 32 |
| 1961 | 15 | 28 |
| 1962 | 14 | 32 |
| 1963 | 10 | 31 |
| 1964 | 14 | 23 |

Source: TUAC annual reports

The decline in the number of week-end schools is accounted for by the increase in the number of such events run by individual unions, particularly the NUM, as they developed their own educational schemes. The consequence in South Wales was a squeeze upon the accommodation and number of scholarships available. In 1958 a total of 1,107 trade unionists attended District weekend schools. In 1959 attendance was down to 633 but the total number of applications for scholarships was over 1,000. In 1960 512 students attended on scholarships, another twenty-five paid, and an extra 300 students could have been taken if scholarships had been available. These were local illustrations of a national problem. To the traditional rivalry between the NCLC and the WEA for the attention of trade unionists had been added the expanding educational work of individual unions and the TUC.

Meanwhile the one area that did not have a tutor-organizer was Swansea and Carmarthenshire although Mansel Grenfell facilitated the local branches and their programmes. It was an area where important social changes were taking place with the accelerated closure in 1958 of the old tinplate works at Llanelli, Pontardulais, Gorseinon, Pontardawe and Morriston, together with the clear prospect of pit closures. In 1959 the Ministry of Education provided the funds to appoint a tutor-organizer. I took up this post based in Llanelli on 1 August that year. I had a degree in economic history and had been working as a journalist in south Wales. The district now had three full-time tutor-organizers working mainly with trade union students whereas five years before there had not been one. Around that time Eddie moved house from Port Talbot to Swansea and we began a companionable partnership in developing the work over the next eight years. It was a shock on 12 June 1961 when Mansel Grenfell collapsed and died before our eyes at a tutors' meeting in Berwick House, Swansea. Mansel had served the WEA with great devotion for thirty years.

## Day Release

The pilot scheme had revealed how difficult it was to provide regular classes for shift workers. A similar problem had also emerged for those active trade unionists who attended their trade union branch, the trades council, and Labour Party meetings. The answer lay in persuading employers to release employees from work, with pay, to attend courses. It was, after all, what many did for management trainees. And models of such 'day-release' courses existed in the courses for miners provided by the universities of Nottingham, Leeds, and Sheffield. The break-through came, however, as a result of what was perceived as the escalating number of strikes in the motor industry, many of them unofficial. Estimates put the loss of output in the industry at six million pounds per year, a substantial sum in those days. In the early part of 1961 joint talks were held between representatives of the relevant unions, the motor industry employers and John Hare, the Minister of Labour. In April there came an agreed joint statement a key part of which was:

> The employers will review their arrangements for the selection and training of supervisors, including potential supervisors. Similarly the unions will in accordance with their constitutions review their arrangements for the qualifications and training of shop stewards and will give individual consideration to specific proposals which the employers have offered to make for co-operation by management for such training to be given under independent auspices.

The employers further offered to release shop stewards from work with appropriate pay to participate in approved courses.

The first day-release course in Wales began in March 1962 for twenty-four shop stewards from the Morris Motors plant, Llanelli. The topic was 'Industrial Relations in the Engineering Industry' and the course ran for sixteen weeks, one half day each week. The stewards, who were all members of the TGWU, received payment from the company for time lost and the union paid the course fees. Ron Mathias had played a key part in setting it up, as had Glyn Morris of the Engineering Employers' Federation. There were two groups, one on Mondays and the other on Thursdays. Eddie and I each tutored a class. On 1 January that year Eddie had joined the extra-mural department of Swansea University College so that his class was under the auspices of the university while mine was under the WEA. It was an arrangement we carried through to other courses including the next to be organized which was at Prestcold, Swansea, where we set up separate classes for shop stewards and junior foremen. The pattern was rapidly followed elsewhere and that year there were courses for shop stewards at AB Metal Products, Abercynon, and KLG Sparking Plugs, Treforest, and courses for junior foremen at Radio and Allied Industries, Hirwaun, and the Celtic watch factory at Ystradgynlais. The tutors on these courses were Bill Gregory and Ken Jones of the Cardiff Industrial Relations Department. The next year, 1963, the number of day-release courses had expanded to thirteen and these courses together with day and week-end schools were dominating the work of the tutor-organizers, particularly Harry Jones and myself, whilst we continued to work closely with Eddie.

A number of implications followed. The development of shop stewards courses meant that the WEA was now concentrating, as recommended by the Clegg/Adams report, on providing education to active trade unionists drawn from a single industry. Further, the intensive process of negotiation with unions and managements could only be done by the tutor-organizers familiar with local managements and trade union officials, and not by voluntary WEA branch officials. Consequently the link between day-release courses and local WEA branches was tenuous. Similarly the day-time nature of these courses meant that generally they could only be taught by full-time tutors. It also meant that tutors were on a fast learning curve turning themselves into industrial relations specialists. Tutors learned as much, probably more, from the shop stewards as the stewards learned from them. There was no better way of research. Clegg/Adams had made the point that industrial relations, methods of collective bargaining, trade union government, work study and similar subjects were relatively underdeveloped and only half recognized as academic subjects. They therefore claimed that:

> it requires a tutor of unusual intelligence and training to make out of them an interesting, instructive and serious topic for a class of adult students. Because so little material is available it also calls for a considerable ability in research to collect together the material for a class.

The problem of finding relevant material for the courses in the motor and general engineering industry was substantially helped by making use of documents written by Arthur Marsh of the Oxford Extra-mural Delegacy. But developing our knowledge and expertise also entailed wide-ranging reading, detailed discussion and debate with shop stewards and managers, and the variety of experience gained from tutoring at trade union summer schools. Among schools I recall were those for members of the Society of Lithographic Artists and Designers, the Post Office Engineering Union, the National Union of Vehicle Builders, the national WEA and TUC summer schools and, above all, the TGWU schools at Cirencester where the range of students and tutors made it an intensive and happy learning experience for all. And quite suddenly the response of governments to 'the trade union question' – pay pauses, national planning machinery, incomes policies, a Royal Commission, pro and anti-union legislation – provided plenty of teaching material and industrial relations became an expanding academic field. WEA and extra-mural tutors right across the UK who were significantly involved in both research and teaching shared their ideas at academic conferences, and in 1968 founded the Society of Industrial Tutors with its own journal.

Day-release courses multiplied in south Wales factories and workplaces and a number established at that time continued for many years. But the most important event of this phase was the day-release scheme at the Steel Company of Wales, Port Talbot, which started in 1964. In some respects it was a delayed result of the pilot project. The classes and weekend schools had raised educational expectations among local activists and since 1962 they had been aware of day-release courses growing in the area. Steelworkers who had been in Eddie's classes, including John Foley (later a full-time official of the Iron and Steel Trades Confederation) put pressure on the Company for such a scheme. But, as with the car industry, it was economic pressures that opened the door. By comparison with the rebuilt steel industries of Europe and Japan the Margam works was already technologically outdated and over-manned. By 1964 the Company was engaged in productivity bargaining with a union joint craft negotiating committee in order to achieve major reductions in the workforce. When we met with the management to press for a day-release scheme at the works they were amenable, hoping it would help the Company to adapt to its changing environment.

The course that began in September 1964 was the first full day release scheme for trade unionists in South Wales. Fifteen people attended three classes held every Tuesday for twenty-four weeks. The day's work was divided into three teaching periods: 9am-10.30am, *Communications in Industry*; 10.45am- 12.30pm, *Industrial Relations*; 2.0pm-4.15pm, *Industrial Development in South Wales*. Eddie taught the Industrial Relations course, I taught Industrial Development, and we shared the Communications course. The Company released the men (they were all men) from work without loss of pay on working days, but they also attended voluntarily when their free day fell on a Tuesday. Attendance was high throughout the year. The students were manual workers representing five unions – the Iron and Steel Trades Confederation, Amalgamated Engineering Union, Transport and General Workers' Union, National Union of Blastfurnacemen, and the Amalgamated Union of Building Trade Workers. The unions nominated the students and paid their class fees and the students were all branch officers – secretaries, chairmen – or works representatives and shop stewards. Some were regional or national executive members of their unions. In addition to paying wages the Company provided a meeting place, refreshments, and books nominated by the tutors for reference and regular use. After initial suspicions that the scheme was merely a management gimmick the students took to the work with no-holds-barred enthusiasm. An HMI came and was very impressed and I remember those classes as being among the most stimulating ever. The first year was such a success that the next year another group began the course while the first intake went on to a second year. Then a third group began, the first group entered a third and final year, and so a three-year cycle was established.

Other unions that joined in included the Electrical Trades Union, the Plumbing Trades Union, the National Society of Painters, the General and Municipal Workers, the Amalgamated Society of Woodworkers and the British Roll Turners Trade Society. Hundreds of active trade unionists went through this scheme including at least three future general secretaries of their union, and others who became full-time trade union officers or executive members of their union, including future chairmen and presidents. Some, after time at Coleg Harlech, went on to become university graduates. The majority remained shop stewards and branch officials but continued their education through correspondence courses, classes and summer schools. In time the viability of the course was affected as the pool of potential students shrank dramatically. Negotiated redundancies continued throughout the 1970s and then, after the 1980 national steel strike, a further 6,883 jobs disappeared at Port Talbot. The labour force, which at its height had been 17,000, settled at 5,000. The day-release scheme was also affected by changes in working methods at Margam that made it harder for men to be released for a day from a working team. After many changes in tutors but with the teaching still shared by the WEA and Swansea University tutors it finally came to an end in the 1990s.

The national expansion of day-release courses had been absorbing and successful but they were the subject of some controversy. By the early 1960s the term 'shop steward training' had come into common use and there was concern as to whether this was liberal education as traditionally understood by the WEA. The older generation of tutors had a view expressed by Bill Gregory:

> I didn't belong to the generation that spent any time on training a workman to become a better branch secretary. That wasn't my type of adult education. I would say this: if you give me a student to study Plato's *Republic* in a tutorial class, he would write a much better letter as a branch secretary than if you sent him to a clerks' college to do a business administration course.

We, the tutors closely engaged with the details of the procedures of the engineering and steel industries, agreed. But in the context of day-release our teaching material had to be closer to the day-to-day concerns of active trade unionists. And that which might appear at first sight to be narrow and arid could lead to fundamental issues. For example, to sit down with a group of stewards and use their union rule book as a text in order to discuss and understand the constitution of their union instantly threw up all the issues of representative democracy, accountability, voting systems, executive versus administrative power, and processes of appeal and jurisdiction. Comparisons *between* unions could be even more illuminating. In this respect the South Wales tutors of 'trade union studies' as it became known had little time for ideological disputation over the merits of the Oxford school of 'role education' using documents focused on the role of the shop steward *versus* the broader Industrial Studies approach incorporating history and economics. We freely combined both in our work depending upon the needs of the students, as the syllabuses of those courses would show.

There was an allied issue. In those days before the Employment Protection Act 1975 required an employer to permit shop stewards to take reasonable time off for industrial relations training, day release could not happen without the employer's co-operation. There followed an understandable suspicion that really the courses were for the benefit of the employer. And certainly employers had their own agenda. So did the unions, and a left-wing criticism of the courses was that they were intended to bolster the authority of union bureaucrats against the shop stewards. Only experience of the tutors and the teaching could overcome these suspicions. As tutors we too had an agenda: to develop the students' critical faculties, to increase their understanding of the structure and functions of trade unions, and their awareness of the political and economic context within which they operated. In fact, the day-release classes were among the highest level classes the WEA was running in south Wales in terms of quality of students, student attendance and participation, and library and accommodation facilities.

However, the work was disrupted to some extent by a rapid turnover of staff. Eddie Jenkins' successor as tutor-organizer in Mid-Glamorgan in 1962 was Keith Jackson (later to be Principal of Fircroft College) but Keith left after one year and was succeeded by Rhodri Morgan, described in the annual report as 'a young Welshman'. Rhodri only stayed for about eighteen months but he was responsible for organizing a series of lectures on *Merthyr Politics: the Making of a Working Class Tradition* in the winter of 1964-5. The lectures, and the subsequent book edited by Glanmor Williams, have some claim to be the catalyst for the upsurge of interest in Welsh labour history that followed soon after. In July 1964 Harry Jones followed Eddie Jenkins onto the staff of Swansea Extra-mural department and David Mills, one of Bill Gregory's former students, replaced him. After going to Coleg Harlech he had graduated in economics from St. John's College, Cambridge. Within a year, however, he too had moved on. Stability came with the appointment in 1965 of Alan Rodgers, a geologist, to be tutor-organizer in Monmouthshire and Cled Phillips to the post in Mid-Glamorgan. Cled came from Port Talbot and was a former lorry driver who after attending classes with Eddie had gone to Harlech on a TUC scholarship and then graduated from Swansea with a degree in political theory and government. Both Alan and Cled were to become in turn secretaries of the South Wales District. The next year with the number of students still increasing the District was able to appoint an additional tutor-organizer for industrial and trade union studies and Neil Gordon Kinnock joined in August 1966. He rapidly established himself as an exciting and impressively successful tutor. In December 1967 I left the WEA for a post in Hong Kong.

## DISTRICT SECRETARIES

| John Thomas | John Davies | D.T. Guy | Alan Rogers | Cled Philips | Barry Moore |
|---|---|---|---|---|---|
| Wales 1911-1916 | Wales 1919-1925 | 1939-1970 | 1970-1979 | 1979-1984 | 1984-1988 |
| | Southern District | | | | |
| | 1925-1937 | | | | |

## Enter the TUC

While these staff moves were happening a fundamental change in trade union education was taking place. The NCLC had sponsored a motion at the TUC 1957 Congress calling for a co-ordinated education policy to make better use of the money available. Since then the TUC had been deliberating how to bring this about. By 1961 sufficient consultations and maneuvering had taken place for a policy to be agreed that would involve the TUC taking over the work of the NCLC and WETUC and the correspondence courses organized by Ruskin College. By the time the scheme came into full operation in 1964 the reality was much starker. The education of trade unionists was 'now within the TUC' as George Woodcock, the general secretary, made clear. It was to be centrally planned and organized by the TUC Education Department. Regional bodies existed — the first meeting of the new TUC Regional Education Advisory Committee for South Wales, on which I represented the WEA, was held on 5 January 1965 – but they were explicitly advisory.

The scheme came at a time of gathering concern about the impact of shop floor bargaining upon inflation and economic growth and coincided with the election of a Labour government. The TUC's priority therefore was the training of shop stewards in their constitutional functions, chiefly through day-release courses of ten weeks duration. As it developed it became a centralized scheme, standardized and prescriptive in its approach to topics and course material. The south Wales tutors (as elsewhere) became heavily involved in teaching these courses. But there was a narrowing of the approach that had been traditionally adopted by tutors brought up in the WEA/extra-mural liberal studies tradition and, successful as the scheme was in TUC terms, something important was being lost despite the individuality of tutors.

There was another change that gradually impinged directly upon the District. The number of WEA/TUC week-end schools declined over the next ten years so that whereas there had been eighteen in 1965-66 there were only two in 1974-75 and none in 1975-6. Week-end schools did not cease altogether, but the number each year remained in low single figures. From a TUC point of view the rationale for cutting back was straightforward: the cost of week-end schools per student hour was calculated to be eight times more expensive than a day release class. But they had been an important medium through which tutors could contact a wide range of trade unionists, build support for the WEA and 'spot' potential class members.

There is a final point. The expansion of the TUC scheme in order to keep pace with the growth of shop floor representatives far outran the number of WEA tutors available. Consequently, the TUC turned increasingly for tutors to the technical colleges, soon to be renamed colleges of further education. These colleges began to recruit tutors for these courses, a number of them former WEA and Coleg Harlech students. The colleges also had an advantage over the WEA in that they had purpose built teaching premises. Although South Wales District tutors continued to teach substantial numbers of TUC courses they formed a smaller and smaller proportion of the total number of tutors involved in TUC day-release classes.

## Conclusion

The work with trade unionists from 1954-75 was seminal for the post-war South Wales District. It enabled full-time tutor-organizers once again to be employed, attracted young new students, widened the range of classes and generated fresh income. It is not, I hope, mere nostalgia to see it as valuable work. Out of that work too came a tranche of students who took the route from industrial work to WEA classes to Coleg Harlech to university and then on to full-time teaching with the District that Eddie Jenkins and Harry Jones had taken before them in a tradition that stretched back to D.T. Guy in the 1930s. They included Cled Phillips, David Mills, Gareth Morris, John Morris, Terry Burns, Barry Moore, Llew Smith, and Paddy Kitson, not to mention those who became tutors for other WEA districts and for universities and colleges. It also introduced a change in teaching methods albeit as part of a nation-wide trend. The dazzling formal lecture – a direct descendant of the passionate chapel sermon – whilst still having its inspirational merits gave way more often to the close analysis of texts and documents, a method carried over into other areas of teaching.

By the late 1970s the zenith of the unions and of shop steward education had been reached. The election of Mrs. Thatcher in 1979 with her determination to deal with 'the enemy within' had an almost instant impact. In 1979-80 trade union and industrial studies teaching accounted for twenty-four per cent of the District's provision. There followed a continuous decline reflecting the arrival of mass unemployment (over three million in the UK), growing management hostility towards day-release, and a haemorrhage of trade union members. By 1989-90 work with trade unions was fractionally above three percent of the District's work.

Yet working with the unions and with trade unionists in a targeted way is now embedded in the District's work, not only through TUC courses but also in work with individual unions. The unions have had to make many adjustments since 1979 and the decline — in some cases the demise — of collective bargaining in the private sector has made unions much more conscious of the role they can play in providing learning opportunities for all their members. This is now a major trade union function and the development of workplace learning representatives has opened the door to a range of possibilities in which the WEA can collaborate. The wheel is turning and, as in the days before the TUC took over trade union education, there are opportunities for the WEA to work with individual unions and acquire funding for programmes separate from the TUC.

A final thought. The Pilot Scheme demonstrated that targeting a specific group, working with their representatives, and committing resources to that strategy can be highly successful. In the hands of clear-minded and dedicated professionals achievements do not depend upon an elaborate superstructure.

## Bibliography

This chapter is based on WEA South Wales District annual reports 1945-6 to 1990; South Wales TUAC annual reports 1951 to 1964; *Trade Union Education: A Report from a Working Party set up by the Workers' Educational Association* [The Creech Jones Report] (London 1953); H. A. Clegg and Rex Adams, *Trade Union Education: With Special Reference to the Pilot Areas* (London, 1959); a tape recording of a talk by Eddie Jenkins in the possession of the Miners' Library, Swansea; a transcript of an interview with Bill Gregory, also in the Miners' Library; discussions with Terry Burns, Garfield Davies, Tom Fellows, John Foley, Lyndon James, Gareth Morris, Alan Penny, and Jimmy Poole; and personal knowledge. A special thanks to Terry Burns for lending me his collection of annual reports without which writing the chapter would have been much more difficult.

For details of the TUC and trade union education see John Holford, *Union Education in Britain: A TUC Activity* (Nottingham, 1994). For a survey of the growth of industrial relations as a subject for research and teaching see D. Lyddon, 'History and Industrial Relations' in P. Ackers and A. Wilkinson (eds), *Understanding Work and Employment: Industrial Relations in Transition* (Oxford, 2003) pp. 89-118. For developments in the Welsh economy and trade unions in Wales since the 1960s see Joe England, *The Wales TUC 1974-2004: Devolution and Industrial Politics* (Cardiff, 2004).

# CONTINUITY AND CHANGE: THE WEA IN GWENT 1985 to 2004

## JEREMY GASS

When, in January 1985, I became tutor-organiser for Gwent I was joining a small staff group by today's standards. There were six tutor-organisers – one for each of the counties in south Wales – all of whom worked from home with minimal resources. An answering machine was an innovation in 1985 and computers would not follow until the end of the 1980s. The South Wales District Office, housed in a former brewery wages office in west Cardiff, was the base for Barry Moore, the District Secretary, and three administrative staff.

At the time the south Wales and north Wales WEA Districts were part of the UK National Association. The Welsh Districts were funded directly by a Welsh Office as yet relatively untouched by Thatcherism's obsession with accountability, although not immune at that time to cuts in public expenditure. Grants to the Districts were allocated on the basis of an understanding as to the number of courses that would be provided within a District each year and were not conditional on targets being reached, the curriculum offered or any notion of learner achievement. Accreditation of courses was not on the agenda then and, compared with today, the inspection regime could be characterised as having a 'light touch'. An HMI was assigned to the District who usually had a clear understanding of the WEA's history and purpose, and was sympathetic to the particular contribution made by the Association within the field of adult education. At that time it was hard to imagine either the managerialism and audit culture that would emanate from Thatcherism or the way in which adult education would become, from 1992, part of a further education system dominated by a vocational and qualifications ethos where funding depended wholly upon the numbers of students taking part, the nature of the course on which they were enrolled and their post code.

Relationships with most of the six county councils in south Wales were strong – local education authority grants amounted to fifteen per cent of the District's income and the Association also benefited in most counties from free use of education buildings for classes.

In the mid-1980s there were still close links between the WEA and the labour movement. The District Secretary and all but one of the tutor-organisers were active Labour Party members. At least three of this staff group had been adult students themselves, progressing from WEA classes and trade union activism to Coleg Harlech before studying at Welsh universities. Working for the WEA in south Wales was seen by many as a stepping stone to a political career. The post in Gwent became vacant when Llew Smith, who had replaced Neil Kinnock, was elected to the European Parliament, to be joined there by one of my colleagues, Wayne David, a few years later. Links with the labour movement in the form of the Trades Union Congress Education Service and unions such as the National Union of Public Employees were particularly strong. At District level there was a thriving democracy with vigorously contested annual elections for Council and for its officers.

Over the past twenty years or so there have been significant changes in the context within which the WEA operates in terms of public policy and funding for adult education, political culture, and a decline in traditional industries as well as the communities and social institutions associated with them. In this chapter I want to reflect on these changes and how the WEA has responded to the challenges posed by them. I will draw on my experience of working for the Association until 1999 and on knowledge gained in my role as a member of Council from 2000 to date. Naturally, I focus on the changes in Gwent, the area I know best.

Re-visiting annual reports of the WEA South Wales District in the mid-1980s it is interesting to note that, as the WEA today comes to terms with a new common funding system for post-16 learning providers in Wales, twenty years ago the Association was also preoccupied with the future method of its funding. I wrote, somewhat plaintively in the annual report for 1984/5:

> As Welsh Office pressure on us to raise more of our income from class fees [grows], as Gwent County Council's Urban Grant covering those fees for unemployed students expires, as the principle of free education gets left further behind, I look forward with unease to the new year and the role of 'policing' numbers and class fees. As incomes fall, as unemployment rises, as opportunities shrink, how many of those classes I'm planning now will attract sufficient numbers for the Government's magical and mysterious 'Effective Student Hours' formula?

Despite the significant changes revealed by a review of annual reports, including a very substantial increase in expenditure from £226,000 in 1984-5 to £2,787,440 by 2004-5 and a corresponding growth in staff, certain themes remain constant. These are financial insecurity and the capacity to meet demands for learning alongside an expressed commitment to addressing educational disadvantage within a democratic structure.

In 1984-5 the District provided 683 courses of varying lengths, which together consisted of 7,668 class meetings. In terms of subjects Visual Arts accounted for 141 of the courses, with trade union studies being the second biggest subject, although the emphasis was on day schools rather than courses. More than ten per cent of courses were described as Study Skills including Basic Education, and there were fifty-six courses in Welsh Language, Literature and Culture. Women's Studies courses, which were listed separately for the first time, totalled thirty-one. Subjects such as Economics, Environmental Studies, Law, Media Studies, Modern Political History, Peace Studies, Politics, Social Economic and Labour History, and Sociology made up more than ten per cent of the total. In those days International Studies (twelve) outweighed Computer Studies (ten). There were just over 8,000 students and of these forty-four per cent were men and fifty-six per cent women. The annual report also records that there were thirty-two branches across the District.

### The Mid-Eighties Programme

One third of the courses and about half of the class meetings took place in Gwent, an administrative county created in 1974 which, until the reorganisation of 1996 comprised Blaenau Gwent, the former Islwyn now part of Caerphilly, Monmouth, Newport and Torfaen. This high proportion of courses was due in part to the historic relationship with the County Council whereby the WEA provided a significant number of the evening classes in many of the LEA Community Education Centres and also received a generous level of funding compared with that provided by other authorities. For example, in 1984-5 Gwent contributed £17,392 to the south Wales District out of a total income from local education authorities of £35,781. Moreover, the County Council was able to subsidise the fees of unemployed students from an Urban Aid grant, although that ran out the following year. In addition there was a substantial programme of Art, Drama, Life Skills and Current Affairs classes within psychiatric hospitals and day centres throughout the county, made possible by the payment of fees by the Gwent Health Authority. This was mirrored to a lesser extent in neighbouring Powys. There was also a thriving trade union studies day release programme run in partnership with the TUC. One of a small number of TUC Centres for the Unemployed in Wales had been established by the WEA in Pontypool, managed by a Project Organiser, Brian Maurice, with financial support from the Manpower Services Commission and Torfaen Borough Council. WEA classes were also a feature of the Newport Unemployed People's Centre. In Tredegar a local history workshop was supported as part of a County Council initiative for unemployed adults. Whilst the hospital programme can be seen as an example of the WEA's purpose to prioritise work with those who are educationally disadvantaged and the work with trade unionists and unemployed people demonstrates a commitment to the founding principle of working class education, the relevance of much of the provision in LEA centres is less clear. Certainly some courses were offered within areas of social and economic disadvantage such as the valley communities of Crumlin, Ebbw Vale and Nantyglo but there were no resources available at that time to ensure that these were targeted at disadvantaged people.

Although on paper there were eight Branches in Gwent at the time, branch stimulated initiatives made up a small proportion of the overall programme; thus there was little democratic control over the programme's content or delivery arrangements. This would support the view that there had been a decline in the WEA's voluntarism and dedication to a democratic structure during the post-war decades. Only a minority of the courses in Gwent in 1985 could be seen as 'equipping adults with the tools and knowledge for a fairer society' which had been the goal of R.H. Tawney, a key figure in the WEA's development.

The annual reports for the remainder of the 1980s highlight the centrality of national and international politics and labour history within branch programmes and demonstrate the impact of Thatcherism on the WEA directly, in terms of funding and public policy, and indirectly, in terms of the consequences of economic policies on employment and trade union membership. Simultaneously new trends were emerging in this period as opportunities were created for innovative approaches to be tried out and as new links were made with the voluntary sector.

International topics addressed by branches in this period included Apartheid, Cuba and Central America and Glasnost and Perestroika. A day school in Abergavenny made the links between famine in the third world, European food mountains, and the future of the British countryside. During 1986, the International Year of Peace, several classes were held on the theme of Peace and Conflict in the Modern World. Domestic political issues included proposed legislation such as the 'Poll Tax' and social security reforms, and The Future of Nuclear Power on Severnside. Events in labour history in south Wales that featured in the programme included the Blaina Riots of the inter-war depression and the Chartist Rising in Newport, particularly during 1989, the year of its 150th anniversary.

The influence on the programme of the peace movement has already been noted. The impact of other social movements, such as the green and women's movements, can be seen in references to various courses on environmental issues and to increases in women's education. The latter included a course in women's studies negotiated by women shop stewards attending a TUC day release course and courses at Well Women Centres in Monmouth and Newport, both of which had affiliated to the District. Several women-only branches were to develop during the 1990s, in line with a trend in other Districts.

Numerous references to uncertainty about future funding reflected the government's determination to reduce public expenditure, at the same time as unemployment rose due to the 'slim down' of the steel industry and pit closures following the 1984-5 miners' strike. By 1987-8 it was proving harder to recruit shop stewards for the TUC day release classes. The total number of trade union studies classes in the District fell to forty-six that year, with a further drop the following year to only thirteen. During this period pressure was also mounting on adult education providers to collaborate in order to make better use of resources and to save duplication. Not only was this time consuming in view of the additional meetings that had to be attended, but also it posed the challenge of how one could simultaneously co-operate with others whilst retaining the distinctive identity and profile of the WEA – a challenge that has intensified as collaborative working has assumed even greater significance in contemporary public policy, as, for example, in the case of Estyn's approach to area inspections.

## Help for the Valleys

During 1988-89, Peter Walker, the then Secretary of State for Wales and a noted 'wet' in Thatcher's cabinet, established the 'Valleys Initiative'. As a part of this initiative the Welsh Office invited applications for additional short-term funding to support new project work in the valleys. A successful bid was made for an outreach project at Garnlydan, an isolated and windswept housing estate cut off from Ebbw Vale by the A465 Heads of the Valleys road. This involved working in partnership with the LEA Community Education Centre in Ebbw Vale and the local further education college. A part-time outreach worker was employed to talk with people on the estate and run appropriate, informal taster sessions supported with a crèche. This provided opportunities for women in particular to determine for themselves the kind of learning they wanted. During the same year a women's group began at Oxford House in Risca which was to develop several years later into a flourishing women's branch which is still active today. In January 1990 the Welsh Office funded a further five development projects in Valleys' communities proposed by the District, two of which were in Gwent. One of these aimed to provide educational guidance and informal learning for ex-miners following the closure of the last Gwent collieries at Cwm and Oakdale. Although the project had a steering group of eight former miners, various events planned to bring ex-miners together met with a poor response. The project worker noted at the time 'it is apparent that the social networks which existed prior to closure have broken down to a far greater extent than was perhaps realised by the men themselves'.

The second project, which was more successful, built on the previous year's experience at Garnlydan. The funding enabled an outreach worker and a play worker to be employed on another isolated estate, this time at Cefn Golau above Tredegar. An average of twenty women with as many children were attracted to twice-weekly informal meetings held at the Ironsides Rugby Club, the only sizeable building on the estate. The rugby club made no charge for the use of the premises and LEA staff from Tredegar Leisure Centre were closely involved in the project. This kind of work was developed elsewhere in the county that year on other large housing estates reaching isolated women and introducing them to adult education in informal ways. This involved working collaboratively with the LEA on the Bulwark estate at Chepstow and Ty Sign, Risca, as well as the Diocesan Community Work team at Pantside, Newbridge. Simultaneously new short courses in women's studies were developed such as Women and the Law and Women's History. Thus, project funding from the Welsh Office was instrumental in enabling the WEA to develop a new way of working in communities in Gwent which provided a foundation on which to build as greater opportunities arose in the 1990s when European funding became available.

During this period strong links were formed with several voluntary sector organisations which were to last well into the 1990s. The first of these was the mental health charity MIND which had branches in Newport, Pontypool and later Abergavenny. The first courses to be run with its members were held in Newport in 1986 with Pontypool and Abergavenny following in subsequent years. Subjects included drama, art, photography and current affairs. Collaboration with Mudiad

Ysgolion Meithrin (MYM), the Welsh-medium playgroups movement, began with the organisation during 1989-90 of the first Welsh language courses for parents in Gwent. These classes were part of a wider programme of Welsh language classes held across the county in LEA centres, and at the time the WEA was the largest provider of Welsh for adults in Gwent. The relationship with MYM was to develop in years to come with the delivery of courses that would qualify WEA learners to work in crèches or pre-school playgroups. Initially these courses were provided with support from the county council's European funding. The WEA also began to play a part in the training programme for members of voluntary groups organised by the Gwent Association for Voluntary Organisations. Day schools were run on topics such as Speaking in Public with Confidence, Understanding Local Government, Meetings Skills, Charity law and Lobbying. In addition Welfare Rights courses were held regularly in conjunction with Newport Advice Workers, an umbrella group of local advice workers employed mainly in the voluntary sector.

The 1990s heralded several major changes that have had far reaching implications for the WEA, notable amongst them were the Further and Higher Education Act 1992 and the re-organisation of local government in 1996. The splitting of the six county councils covering south Wales into sixteen unitary authorities, and education reforms such as the Local Management of Schools, dramatically altered the WEA's relationships with LEAs and signified a significant loss in grant income and the end of free use of rooms for classes in many areas.

The Further and Higher Education Act ended the funding arrangement between the Welsh Office and the WEA in Wales with the establishment of the Further Education Funding Council for Wales (FEFCW). From 1993, after years of being funded with a block grant the WEA, was to be treated as a further education institution subject to the new Recurrent Funding Mechanism (RFM) which would allocate funding according to the number of students enrolled, the subject area, the hours of study undertaken and the qualifications attained. Additional income would be gained according to the level of social disadvantage of the area in which the student lived. Whilst the WEA (and the YMCA) were accorded special status in the Act as organisations that could be funded for non-accredited work the emphasis was upon funding courses included in Schedule Two of the Act. The list of permitted courses reflected Government priorities for sixteen to nineteen year olds – the emphasis was on recognised vocational and academic qualifications such as NVQs, GCSEs and A levels. Other categories included the Access to Higher

Education Certificate, Basic Skills, English for Speakers of Other Languages (ESOL), Welsh Language, and Independent Living/Communication Skills. One other category that became particularly significant for adult education providers allowed for courses aimed at progressing learners onto the courses offering vocational and academic qualifications. It soon became clear that whilst the WEA could still offer non-accredited provision the number of such classes would be capped and the funding received for them would be lower than that for accredited provision. In the early years there was no cap on accredited provision and all providers were encouraged to expand.

### The Accreditation Debate

There had already been considerable debate within the WEA nationally about the appropriateness of accreditation within a movement which was committed to the notion of learning for learning's sake. On one side there were those who argued that accreditation was not appropriate on the grounds that learning with the WEA was not about taking examinations. They would be a distraction from the main purpose or would be a barrier to people's participation because, either they already had all the qualifications they wanted, or they would fear failure. Those in favour of accreditation made the case that it was a way of ensuring that learners could gain recognition for their achievement and that this was particularly relevant for those who had not fulfilled their potential in the past and who wanted to progress into higher levels of learning or gain more interesting jobs. The argument persists today as WEA members make the case for non-accredited learning both as something valuable in its own right and as a stepping stone for those who would be put off from starting if they were expected to seek accreditation. As Sue Wiltshire, a member of the Risca Women's Branch, said at a seminar in London in 1996 to launch *Recognising Good Practice in Women's Education and Training,* a book in which the Branch was featured :

> We need to persuade the funders that accredited courses aren't
> everything. Can't liberal courses be seen as an important stepping
> stone on the path to further education? With care and consideration
> I'm certain that women will enjoy the benefits of accreditation if
> they do not have to participate initially.

Nevertheless, by 1993 the WEA had already started to provide courses with accreditation through the Open College Networks (OCN) in Wales. Whilst some of the 'traditional' branches chose not to embrace accreditation, newer branches with younger members developed programmes with a mix of non-accredited sessions, usually on a 'drop-in' basis to encourage new members at any stage in the term, and accredited courses. The opportunity to gain credits was clearly welcomed as is evident from an article in *Hysbysu*, the WEA South Wales newsletter, written in 1994 by another member of the Risca Branch, on her experience of an OCN accredited course. She anticipated accepting her first credits 'with much pride and satisfaction' whilst explaining that the assessment was ongoing and 'the absence of a formal examination also eliminates any pressure'.

Accredited provision expanded and with it came additional funding and the need for more staff in the Cardiff office to handle the bureaucracy entailed in providing the Funding Council with the data required. The WEA was not alone in growing its provision. In Gwent the LEA was to expand its community education programme with FEFCW money channelled through Coleg Gwent. Over the next few years WEA provision in LEA centres, especially Welsh classes, reduced as centres chose to fund courses from this source. At about the same time cuts in the occupational therapy budget and the shift towards community care resulted in the Health Authority withdrawing funding for the hospital programme across the county. Whilst MIND groups expanded the new funding regime threatened provision for some of the most vulnerable learners whose attendance was often erratic due to their health. With funding being determined by numbers in classes and the time spent in learning, minimum numbers became more pressing and classes with low numbers and erratic attendance had to be closed. The pattern of WEA provision in Gwent which had begun to change in the latter part of the 1980s was about to change again.

Whilst local government reorganisation and the 1992 Act brought substantial challenges there were also new opportunities at the time, not least the availability of European funding. There were significant changes within the WEA also when, in 1993, the two Districts in Wales, together with Northern Ireland became independent organisations distinct from what had been known as the national WEA.

### Informal Learning
The availability of European funding, initially through the Gwent Tertiary College's 'New Opportunities for Women' scheme and later as a result of the WEA's own applications, enabled the development of a distinctive programme building on the experiences of the Welsh Office funding for projects in the Valleys. Outreach

146

projects were developed in Risca, Bettws (a large estate on the periphery of Newport), Maesglas (also in Newport), Markham and Cwm (both former mining villages) and Trevethin (another large estate above Pontypool). European funding ensured that all courses were free as was the crèche provision alongside them. Crucially, it also covered the wages of skilled outreach workers who networked with partner organisations, liaised with tutors, recruited and supported learners, and encouraged them to identify their learning needs and to engage in the democratic processes of the movement.

Informal learning was a key feature of the early days of these projects, and some such as Bettws began alongside existing playgroup or parent and toddler group activities. In Bettws it was the Under-Fives Development Officer who contacted the WEA outreach worker in Risca because the mothers needed 'company, support and things to do'. At first the group met once a week alongside the playgroup with the women choosing 'tasters' such as Confidence Building, DIY, Second Chance Learning (English and Maths). Whilst numbers were erratic to start with, 'lots of new people' were attracted by two excellent workshops on First Aid and Resuscitation run by the Ambulance Service. Further sessions included Drawing, DIY and Computer basics (with the Risca WEA Branch), Safety and Self-defence, Women and the Law, and Creative Writing. Less than six months after the initial sessions numbers had grown sufficiently for a programme of four courses to be offered for the summer term – Children's Development through Play, Living in a Changing Society, Women's Writing Group, and a choice between Make Your Experience Count or Assertiveness Training and Confidence Building. Equally important, six women and eleven children had attended a WEA Women's Residential School at Llwynypia and a few months later members of the group attended A Taste of the WEA event at Penarth and the Summer School at Coleg Harlech.

At the end of 1993- 4 – the first full year of the project – Suzi Pari, the outreach worker, was able to report that more than sixty women had taken part in Child Development courses, over fifty-five in First Aid for Workers with the Under-Fives, thirty or more in Social Sciences, more than forty in Personal Development and Return to Learn and a similar number in Arts, Crafts and DIY. Sixteen had taken an Introduction to Computer Literacy and Information Technology course. She added that the numbers included women who had completed several, if not all the courses available. More than sixty women gained vocational qualifications in work with the under-fives and more than half of them found paid employment in crèches and playgroups all over Newport, including the project's own crèche. Some participants moved on to further studies including vocational training or accredited WEA provision. Other outcomes recorded were increased self-esteem and enhanced parenting skills, and voluntary work in schools and the community. Within a couple of years of the project starting the women at Bettws decided to form a WEA Branch. Later, in 2000, the Branch would become a partner with the wider WEA in South Wales and University of Wales College Newport in a successful funding application under the Assembly's Sustainable Health Action Research Programme which would result in branch members becoming researchers in their own right examining health and social issues in their community.

The Risca Women's Branch, which was formed in late 1992 around an outreach initiative of the local community education service and WEA, was able to expand its programme with the arrival of ESF funding so that by 1996 over thirty hours of learning activities were offered each week, from seven community buildings in and around the town all with creche and during term time. One of the members recalled; 'we became eager participants in an educational programme that we, the students, had helped to devise'. The branch's curriculum was a mix of women's studies, social studies, art and crafts, personal development, child development and play training as at Bettws. In addition the branch had internationalist leanings with courses such as Women and Europe and a Taste of European Languages, One World Week events including a talk on Ethiopia, and links with groups in Denmark, Sweden and Nicaragua as a result of welcoming visitors to Risca.

Like Bettws, WEA activities developed in Cwm around an existing parent and toddler group set up in the village in 1990 and meeting in the Tirzah Chapel. During 1995 the group's leader contacted the Valleys Women's Roadshow – a European funded initiative to raise the profile of women's education and training – about holding an event in the village. The event, which took place over three days, attracted a lot of interest and resulted in the women asking for more. The local organizer for the Valleys Women's Roadshow advised the group leader to contact the WEA just in time for her to attend a training event for outreach workers. Once again the availability of European funding was crucial in order to respond swiftly to the women's interest and, after some initial meetings, to plan the first courses. First Aid and Women and Health began that September. By January 1998 a branch had been formed and ten classes per term were being offered. A few years later funding from the Coalfields Regeneration Trust allowed for an expansion of WEA activity in the village and a presence within the Cwm Community Café. It was a pleasure to return to Cwm in 2005 for a very well attended party to celebrate ten years of WEA activities there.

Although by the late 1990s the WEA had made good and strong links with a variety of women's groups in Gwent valley communities, there were few contacts with women from other cultural groups. An opportunity presented itself when some of the workers involved with the then Newport County Borough Council ESOL programme began to look for ways that women they were working with could continue to have opportunities to learn together. Many of the women were beginning to outgrow the ESOL programme and needed to extend their use of English and widen their educational experience. Out of a series of meetings with two of the ESOL workers, June Gumsley and Angela West, and some of the women involved, an organisation called Ta'Aleem Alnyssa was born. Ta'Aleem Alnyssa means 'education for women' in Arabic. The group began to work with the WEA in the way any branch would work. They discussed programme ideas, and negotiated with the then tutor-organiser, Enid Hankin, to enable courses and sessions to take place in a centre local to their homes.

Yemeni, Somali, and Pakistani women had been working successfully together for some time under the umbrella of Ta'Aleem Alnyssa and the WEA when they agreed to write a book together. The idea of the book, *Faith, Family and Friendship,* was to write stories with their new skills in English to help other women attending ESOL classes to have stories to read that would be from their own community and experience. The book was launched on 11 September 2001 at Newport's Millennium Centre in the company of Rosemary Butler AM. The significance of the pictures to be seen on TV in the centre's coffee bar that lunchtime was not to be fully understood until much later. In 2002 Ta'Aleem Alnyssa was the NIACE Dysgu Cymru Adult Learner Group of the year, going to both Llandudno and London for award ceremonies. The group continues to work together. As well as widening the courses they ran in conjunction with WEA to include Arabic, Driving Theory, Desk Top Publishing and Word Processing, they have also become successful fundraisers in their own right and have responded to Welsh Assembly Government consultation documents such as the Refugee Inclusion Strategy.

By the mid-1990s the profile of WEA activity in the county had changed considerably with resources concentrated more in areas of social and economic disadvantage and an emphasis on involving people in learning who had few qualifications. Accreditation had been embraced with enthusiasm by many of those engaged in European funded courses so that plans were developed for the first community-based Access to Higher Education Certificate. Learners enrolling for the Certificate met together for core units such as Interdisciplinary Study whilst the credits they gained from a wide range of courses from the branch programmes counted towards the total required for the qualification. By the end of 1998 twelve students had completed their Interdisciplinary Study on topics including attitudes to euthanasia; poverty and single parents; what support exists for the families of drug abusers? images of women and the novels of Thomas Hardy; and cholera in Merthyr and India. This highly innovative Access to Higher Education programme involved women from several branches meeting together and its success depended upon the support of a dedicated Access tutor. After a period where resources were no longer available to continue this level of support the Access Certificate has been re-launched as part of the ESF supported Progression through Partnership project within which two part-time Access tutors are employed.

As in many voluntary organisations, branches start and others come to an end. After ten years of activity the Chepstow Branch wound up in 1995 and Abergavenny followed a year or so later. By this time the Abertillery Branch had ceased to operate also. However the European funded projects had spawned new branches in Maesglas and Markham as well as Bettws, Cwm and Risca. All these branches were bringing a younger age group into the movement. Crucial to the development of these new branches was a combination of outreach workers, who themselves were committed to the democratic empowering ideals of the WEA, and activities that provided opportunities for potential branch activists to meet with people from existing branches, thus gaining a sense of the WEA being greater than their own local activities. These included women's weekend schools, branches' weekends and taster events (several of which were held at Oxford House in Risca, followed in the evening by a Twmpath).

## New Learning Opportunities

It would be misleading to give the impression that the only work during this period was with women's groups. Other new developments included the partnership with UNISON to deliver the Return 2 Learn programme. The Welsh programme, though smaller than before, assumed a more distinctive character as new courses with MYM were developed. A Cylch Trafod – Welsh medium discussion group was held for advanced learners and Welsh speakers in Chepstow — and a beginners' class took place at the offices of the Gwent Association of Voluntary Organisations for staff and members of voluntary organisations. In Cwm, a community affected by both coal and steel job losses, a project aimed at involving unemployed men attracted a small, but very dedicated group that decided to paint a mural depicting the village's history which was subsequently hung in the local library. With the opening of a WEA centre in Cwmbran and a designated tutor-organiser for trade union studies, there was a revival of TUC course activity and as a result close links were developed with local unions which led to workplace learning at Trico at Pontypool and Burtons Biscuits in Cwmbran. Information Technology courses were a major attraction at both factories and the classes held at Burtons required a particular commitment from students and tutor alike as they ran from 9-00 till 11-00 pm, with the employer releasing workers for an hour of their shift.

In the mid 1980s, the WEA provision in Gwent was a combination of evening classes - which could be described as being traditional, liberal adult education and indistinguishable from other classes delivered in LEA centres across the county, a sizeable daytime programme of art, drama and current affairs classes in psychiatric hospitals, TUC day release courses for shop stewards and health and safety representatives as well as daytime classes in the two TUC centres for the unemployed, and a small branch based programme concerned with a variety of contemporary and historical issues. Twenty years later, after social and economic changes, together with major shifts in public policy, this pattern is unrecognisable. The WEA has had to work within a funding and quality regime designed primarily for Further Education Colleges and their students aged sixteen to nineteen with the emphasis upon vocational and academic qualifications. Since the 1990s the policy of both Tory and Labour administrations has been to prioritise economic at the expense of social goals, emphasising skills for employment and economic competitiveness rather than learning for social purpose and democratic citizenship. The meaning of 'life' in lifelong learning policy has tended to be working life. The 1992 Act resulted in a funding mechanism that rewarded accredited provision whilst 'capping' the amount of non-accredited learning. In an increasingly audit driven culture, a new quality management regime has demanded 'continual improvement' with inspections that are both more frequent and more intrusive, often undertaken by assessors with little or no understanding of the WEA. Simultaneously, a decline in the labour movement brought about by a transformation of the economy, and ambivalence towards formal politics has resulted in little interest in the political education that the WEA offered in the past.

Within this environment the WEA has sustained a commitment to challenging educational disadvantage. European funding has been used effectively to offer learning in communities where few or no opportunities were available before, with support such as childcare to enable parents of young children to take part. Sets of lap top computers have brought the possibility of learning essential IT skills into isolated estates and villages. The curriculum has responded to rapid technological change by offering an increasingly wide range of IT courses which now represent a large proportion of the programme. Other subjects on offer include communication skills, complementary medicine, counselling, crafts, history, social studies, trade union studies and women studies.

In an era when the decline of social institutions such as chapels, political party branches and trade unions means that there are fewer opportunities to learn the skills for and to practice democracy, WEA members and staff work to foster the democratic spirit of the Association. Across south Wales, long standing branches as well as those that grew in the 1990s survive, and new branches are being formed, amidst a commitment to the promotion of active citizenship in keeping with the vision that Raymond Williams had of the WEA standing for 'an educated democracy'.

## Bibliography

B. Elsey, 'R.H. Tawney – Patron Saint of Adult Education', in P. Jarvis, (ed) *Twentieth Century Thinkers in Adult Education* (Croom Helm, 1987)

R. Fieldhouse, 'The Workers' Educational Association', in R. Fieldhouse, and Associates (eds) *A History of Modern British Adult Education*, (Leicester, 1996)

J. Grewar, 'Students on an accredited course', *Hysbysu*, June, 1994.

Presentation by Sue Wiltshire and Suzi Pari at NIACE 's 'Recognising Good Practice in Women's Education and Training' Book Launch and Seminar, 8 March 1996, London Voluntary Resource Centre

S. Robson, 'Focus on Cwm Branch', *Hysbysu*, November,1998

WEA South Wales District Annual Report 1985

WEA South Wales Finance Statement 2006

R. Williams, 'An Open Letter to WEA Tutors', in John McIlroy and Sallie Westwood, (eds) *Border Country – Raymond Williams in Adult Education* (Leicester, 1993).

# THE WEA IN WALES 1990-2007: A NEW WORLD?

## GRAHAM PRICE and ANNIE WILLIAMS

At the beginning of the 1990s the North and South Wales Districts of the WEA, and Coleg Harlech, seemed a family of like-minded organizations whose distinctive role of 'adult education with a social purpose' was an established and accepted traditional part of education in Wales. A number of key developments in the following years gave rise to fundamental changes in the structure of these organizations that caused them to re- consider their mission and purpose. Following the Further and Higher Education Act of 1992, and the creation of the Further Education Funding Council (FEFCW), a new funding regime was introduced in 1993. This was the most obvious but only one of a series of changes in the early nineties which together brought the WEA in Wales into a largely new landscape. As in England, the Welsh Districts and Coleg Harlech became 'designated institutions' under the 1992 Further and Higher Education Act. They retained their existing constitutional arrangements but were no longer funded by central government as Responsible Bodies. Instead, they were funded on the same formula as the newly-created Further Education College Corporations, by the Further Education Funding Council Wales (FEFCW). The formula was based on units of delivery driven by FE targets and was matched by a model of provision in which the new FE corporations were to compete with each other and other providers in a business efficiency model, and generally behave like private companies.

## Before the Further and Higher Education Act 1992

A closer look at the WEA across the United Kingdom in the period before the funding changes suggests that the organization was already undergoing change. In the post Second World War period the advent of universal secondary and higher education in the 1944 Education Act had, some thought, vindicated and completed the work of WEA. The academic and radical elements in the WEA tradition tended

153

to separate into a liberal education programme mainly through branches, and education for trade union members which as time went on concentrated increasingly on role training for workplace representatives in conjunction with the TUC. By the 1970s the WEA was defining a new role for itself. In evidence to the Russell Committee on the future of adult education it argued that, in addition to liberal education and work with trade unions, it had expertise in developing greater social and political awareness and in taking education to socially and culturally deprived individuals and communities.

To give a flavour of the WEA programme prior to the creation of the Further Education Funding Council for Wales (FEFCW), in 1989/90 we can see from the annual report of the North Wales district that the largest number of courses was offered under four headings: Local History; Welsh Language Literature and Culture; Visual Arts; and Welsh as a Second Language. In that same year, of the 2,103 students whose occupations were known, only 535 were in paid employment and of these only 111 were manual workers.

Within the WEA tradition of offering liberal adult education, most courses were non-accredited. That is, they did not offer qualifications and students did not see qualifications as the end goal of learning. Students would often remain with the WEA for many years with different tutors taking classes and offering their own perspectives on the topics covered. The profile above suggests that a good proportion of students were professional and retired, having gained their qualifications in the past, but keen to maintain their engagement with education and learning.

The South Wales District had continued an older radicalism with an emphasis on courses for trade union activists, alongside a healthy branch programme in some areas. By the mid-eighties the industrial work was in decline as trade union membership plummeted. As in North Wales, most courses provided liberal adult education, with a significant programme in art and craft. There were areas of growth, particularly in classes for students with disability or with mental health issues, and the beginnings of a women's education programme followed the first appointment of a woman as an organizer in the District in 1986.

### New Work
In South Wales one of the current authors, the then newly-appointed District Secretary, took on involvement in the new Access to Higher Education movement

as a personal crusade for a traditional WEA aim of involving working class people in higher education. Three consortia of education providers led by the University of Wales colleges were set up in Wales to promote and regulate the new route into higher education through study for an Access certificate in local colleges. Within two years the Access consortia were becoming Open College Networks (OCN) offering custom-made credit for 'small bites' of learning at all levels up to HE entry, and WEA South Wales was with considerable hesitation offering OCN credits for a small number of courses. Later, OCN credit was to become a predominant feature of WEA learning, and the South Wales District developed a ground-breaking community-based Access to Higher Education programme which enabled students to accumulate credits over six years to attain a full Access certificate, alongside family or other responsibilities. In the new century more rigorous conditions cut this flexibility to three years

Traditionally some West Wales branches had offered Welsh lectures, but the District's involvement with teaching Welsh to adults had been minimal. However, the enthusiasm of the Tutor-Organizer for Gwent introduced the idea of Welsh for Adults initially through classes for workers and parents in conjunction with Mudiad Ysgolion Meithrin. The first computer literacy classes began, using laptop computers resourced jointly with Gwent County Council. Computer classes developed into a major element in the WEA's work in South Wales, leading the growth of accredited classes.

In north Wales there was also a new focus on studies generally described as 'Return 2 Learn' and developed by the Unison trade union. These were offered in a variety of curriculum areas but with a shared emphasis on providing generic skills like communication, key skills and information technology (IT) in an integrated fashion. During this period one of the tutor organizers concentrated her efforts on developing the women's education programme. There was a clear shift of emphasis driven by individual tutor organizers who were keen to nurture this new area of work. A contract with TARGED (the Training and Enterprise Council for North-West Wales) was secured to provide advice and guidance as part of the Return 2 Learn programme and European funding was used to support these initiatives. This work was largely concentrated in Anglesey and Wrexham. Welsh for Adults was also developed across the district. Some tutor organizers continued to concentrate on the liberal arts but it was becoming evident that this area was showing signs of decline. At the creation of the FEFCW in 1992, the new work was increasingly becoming a significant part of the overall provision.

## *After the 1992 Act*

The need to operate within a different funding regime began to raise tensions around the principles underpinning the WEA. The funding methodology privileged accredited learning and the traditional non-accredited liberal arts classes were funded under a lower unit value and were capped. At the beginning only formal qualifications were securely funded and OCN credits had to be part of designated progression routes to 'proper' qualifications, though this was relaxed later. The introduction of formal qualifications ran counter to WEA traditions. It could be argued however that introducing accredited provision in disadvantaged communities was a positive way of re-asserting the founding principles of the movement. This provision was aimed at people who had been failed in one way or another by the state system. The WEA's manner of working by involving students in the learning process and providing courses in sympathetic and accessible environments was entirely fitting in drawing new learners back into education. It could also be argued that the WEA had become an organization that served the needs of middle class professionals and that the new work it was now promoting was bringing it closer to its roots. An uneasy tension existed between the traditional programme and the new work in disadvantaged communities, replicating the earlier dichotomy in the wider WEA between traditional branch programmes and TUC-sponsored courses. The groups were quite distinct and it posed a challenge to the organization to bring them together and to recognize shared interests. This undercurrent has continued to trouble the WEA.

There were more positive features for the WEA. There were no restrictions on Welsh for Adults funding, TUC courses were funded by the FEFCW and so higher education institutions could no longer provide them (though oddly, this restriction did not apply to Welsh for Adults funding for which university departments were eligible). Above all, anything which met the funding criteria could be funded. In practice this included approved qualification-bearing courses, an increasing range of OCN-accredited courses, Welsh for Adults, Trade Union Studies, and some courses for adults with special learning needs. All could be developed and receive funding without restriction. General unaccredited provision was capped at the level of the previous funding of the WEAs as Responsible Bodies.

For the WEAs this represented a real opportunity to grow. WEA in the South doubled its provision partly through extra classes, partly through increasing the class period from 1.5 to 2 hours, and partly through an increasing number of accredited courses. It took on a large share of TUC courses and appointed a tutor-organizer for trade union studies. FEFCW required Welsh for Adults consortia to be set up in each of the then eight counties of Wales, and the WEA took a prominent role in South Glamorgan, employing a Welsh for Adults officer in collaboration with the local authority. In other areas of the south where there were established arrangements to deliver Welsh for Adults, courses were diverted from the WEA to local authorities. There was a general trend for local authorities to abandon arrangements with the WEA to provide general courses in their centres and instead put on classes themselves. This happened more often after 1995 when local government reorganization in Wales increased the number of local education authorities from eight to twenty-two, and WEA could no longer rely on long-established relationships. Nevertheless the WEA South Wales provision doubled in this period. Government policy changed and the freedom to grow was suddenly curtailed in 1997, but by then the additional provision was embedded in the District's work.

The WEA district in north Wales was much slower to adapt to the changes brought about by the creation of the FEFCW. The district retained its traditional programme without engaging fully in the implications of operating with a lower funding unit for non-accredited work. Had the analysis been done it would have become clear that the courses were no longer viable and that a strategy to introduce more accredited provision should have been adopted early on to retain the financial stability of the organization. Decisions were taken too late to introduce additional accredited programmes and the organization faced very serious financial problems that threatened its continued existence.

The other principal factor which made growth possible was European funds. In 1995 the WEA successfully applied for European Social Fund project funding. South Wales WEA secured projects from that year in both South-East Wales and the Valleys and West Wales Objective 1 area, and has continued to access similar funds up to the end of the second programme in 2008. The additional funds enabled WEA to employ staff to develop courses and support students in new areas, and to provide childcare alongside classes. This lay the foundations for the 2007 position where thirty-five per cent of students live in high-deprivation Communities First areas and eight per cent are from black and minority ethnic communities, compared to just over one per cent in the population.

The effect of European funding on the curriculum was to confirm the move towards personal development education, 'applied' social science, and creative arts. The extra funding also gave impetus to a community-based access to higher education course which initially provided a very flexible period of six years to gain the access certificate. The community provision of information technology training, using laptop computers, was hugely expanded through European funds and capital equipment funding from the FEFCW, which was a novelty for the WEA. So by the late 1990s the WEA South Wales curriculum featured courses to build personal skills and confidence, ICT, creative arts, Welsh for Adults, English as a Second Language, and provision for those with additional needs, alongside a strong trade union education provision and a continuing traditional branch programme. The WEA could have been left behind by the government-sponsored internet 'University for Industry' (UfI) which was to be provided through large 'hubs' managed by colleges or local authorities. In Wales this did not happen, and each FE college made its own arrangements with UfI. This gave an opportunity for the WEA, which was funded as a college, to develop as a well-regarded community UfI provider from 2000, with support from ESF-funded projects for the considerable staffing costs. In contrast to a provision dominated by a largely male student body in the 'industrial studies' period of the sixties and seventies, two-thirds to three-quarters of students in the years around the beginning of the new century were female.

Coleg Harlech was also faced with challenging decisions. Government policy to increase participation began to impact on Coleg Harlech in the 1980s. In particular, the Second Chance initiative and the growth within further education colleges of Access provision targeted at adults who had failed to benefit from education in the past, and based upon links developed with higher education institutions, offered adults a progression route that would have been much more difficult through traditional 'A' Levels. The courses, which usually lasted for one year, were local, accessible and structured around the needs of adults with caring and other responsibilities. This development, that was very successful, was bound to affect Coleg Harlech as more people opted to stay in their own locality rather than move away from home.

In 1991 the Welsh Office, influenced by the apparent success of Access courses, decided that Coleg Harlech students would receive maintenance grants for one year only. As most of them were pursuing a two-year course leading to the University of Wales Diploma in General Studies that gave entry to British universities, the effect of this decision was to reduce study for the Diploma from two years to one. In turn, this required the College from 1994 to double its recruitment to the Diploma course from around seventy students a year to 140. This, with the other pressures on recruitment, was a challenging target at a time when the cash limited Welsh Office grant to the College was not keeping pace with overall costs and when increased marketing would require further expenditure.

The creation of the FEFCW brought the College under the same regime as further education colleges in terms of funding, financial accountability and planning. Previously, Coleg Harlech by its tutorial method of teaching, the qualifications of its tutors, and its connections with the University of Wales had seen itself closely aligned with higher education. It had also seen itself as one of the small family of long-term residential colleges for adults which formed a distinctive sector of British adult education. As a residential college, and the smallest college in Wales, the cost of educating students at Harlech was nearly double the further education average. The Funding Council sought to bring the College's 'unit of resource' down to the level of the rest of the FE sector in Wales. The College argued, unsuccessfully but in its view logically, that the valid comparison should be with the long-term residential colleges in England, like Ruskin, which had similar missions and were of comparable size.

At the same time as the WEA Districts were responding to the changes brought about by the new funding regime in Wales, a major upheaval was taking place in the Association itself. The WEA had been a federation of regional Districts (of which North and South Wales were two) receiving separate funding but bound together in a National Association which guided policy largely by consent. At the beginning of the 1990s, governance and employment law issues were driving the WEA towards being a single unitary national body, while the new funding arrangements confirmed the separateness of the regional bodies in Wales, Northern Ireland and Scotland. The preferred solution of the Celtic nations, a UK federation for the WEA, was not acceptable to the national body and so, as the new funding arrangements began in 1993, the WEA became four independent bodies – England with Scotland, Northern Ireland, North and South Wales. Some contact continued, particularly between staff engaged in women's education and trade union studies, and through the International and European WEA networks. Delegates from North Wales continued for a time to attend 'national' meetings in England. Major changes in the England/Scotland association enabled a fresh start and following discussion between UK delegates at the IFWEA Conference in Portugal in 2003 an initial meeting of a WISE (Wales-Ireland-Scotland-England) group was held in Belfast the following November. The WISE group has continued to meet at regular intervals and has restored the sense of a UK-wide WEA movement.

The separation of 1993 left the Wales ex-Districts to find a form of independent organization. Much anguished discussion led South Wales to form itself into a company limited by guarantee in 1995, while North Wales opted for some revision of its existing District constitution. Discussions about a federation or merger between the Welsh bodies were inconclusive, though following a launch conference for 'WEA Wales' in 1994 at Harlech there have been continuing if intermittent attempts to hold joint events and develop joint initiatives.

In the North, such moves were overtaken by the financial crisis in the WEA. The underlying cause was a failure to engage fully with the consequences of operating under the new funding regime. The new Director, appointed late in 1997, was faced with near bankruptcy in the first months of her tenure. The FEFCW agreed to continue funding the Association on the understanding that a recovery plan was agreed and implemented. A number of changes were therefore introduced very rapidly. This included a revision of the constitution that created a smaller and more accountable management committee. A complete re-evaluation of the curriculum was undertaken in the light of the funding methodology and tight controls introduced on class sizes and the cost effectiveness of learning programmes. Finally, sources of external funding were sought to support key priority areas of work particularly Return to Learn, work with the voluntary sector, Welsh for Adults, workplace learning and the creative arts.

This combination of measures coupled with the commitment and dedication of staff and trustees led to a steady improvement in the financial position of WEA(N). In 1997 the Association had generated a deficit of £44,000; by 2000-01 this had been reversed and a surplus of £170,700 had been achieved.

During this same period discussions had been taking place between WEA(N) and Coleg Harlech regarding a merger. The Warden of Coleg Harlech was to retire in December 1998 and it was felt that both organizations would gain from amalgamation. The process took three years to complete and a number of constitutional issues became interlaced with the new powers that were conferred on the Welsh Assembly Government. This led to a hiatus in terms of planning as both organizations remained separate during this period and there was a lack of overall strategic management. FEFCW treated the organizations as one in terms of student recruitment as Coleg Harlech during this period was failing to meet its target. The WEA(N) generated additional units between 1997 and 2001 to compensate for the under-achievement in Coleg Harlech during that time.

Coleg Harlech and WEA North Wales finally merged in August 2001 and the newly merged organisation, Coleg Harlech WEA(N), was faced with a financial crisis in its first years that required urgent action. This was largely focused on the Harlech site and involved a re-evaluation of the curriculum and arrangements for student support. The College had been increasingly recruiting students from very difficult backgrounds and a shift of resources was required to meet their needs in terms of advice and guidance, basic skills support, counselling and security. The estate also required attention and as a first step the opportunity was taken to upgrade Crown Lodge, mainly for short course students. The Association generated a deficit of £363k in 2002 but as the result of implementing a recovery plan this was improved and small surpluses were achieved in 2004. The College is now recruiting very well and reaching its targets but a number of issues remain to be resolved about its future and how its mission fits with current Welsh Assembly Government priorities.

In more recent years the WEAs and Coleg Harlech have been burdened by the level of reporting for data and for systems of control, governance and audit. As small organizations they are subject to the same level of reporting and monitoring as much larger institutions. The need to operate within the ethos of further education has also caused a narrowing of the curriculum at Coleg Harlech and in the community and a stronger emphasis has been placed on qualifications as the end goal. There have also been a number of re-organizations taking place and these have all had an impact on planning.

### The Legacy

The landscape steadily changed so that with each reorganization – from Welsh Office to the Further Education Funding Council Wales, to ELWa (the National Council for Education and Training Wales), and in 2006 to the Department of Education, Lifelong Learning and Skills (DELLS), government agendas increasingly focussed on vocational skills. The WEAs and Coleg Harlech were able to respond positively to these agendas and increase the number and range of courses provided and benefit from the funding available. This enabled the Welsh WEAs to broaden their reach to groups of students who had been failed by education in the past, in a process of reinvention within the founding principles that had happened several times before in the WEA's history

This came at a cost to an important aspect of WEA's overall mission, in that it became increasingly difficult to support a broader 'education for a social purpose' which enabled WEA students to see their local concerns in a wider analytical framework. This took place at a time when the prevailing if largely unstated ideology was one of possessive individualism, contrasting with the wider citizenship philosophy which drove the WEA's educational mission. What was largely lost was university-level study which did not lead to qualifications. The best branch classes continue to provide this, but on a small scale. The link with higher education has been actively pursued through the Access to HE programme, joint work with the Community University of the Valleys and the Open University, and Coleg HarlechWEA(N).

It was inevitable that these trends would have an impact on the branch structure of the WEA. The branch had always been at the heart of the WEA's mission and management structure. In the early years, branches would inform tutor-organizers of their needs for the year and the tutor-organizer would then make the arrangements. This bottom-up approach ensured that officers were answerable to members. The branch structure was a central component in maintaining links between learners and the centre, an important element of local democracy. Branch representatives were then elected onto the central management in the District and from there the larger UK-wide organisation.

The concerns of branches, tutor-organisers and management centred on issues to do with education, and the WEA attracted voluntary members who had a keen interest in promoting the values of the WEA in society. Increasingly, the branches came to rely on the efforts of middle class professionals with confidence and experience of sitting on committees. Some branches stand out as being particularly strong and active offering a wide variety of classes and additional educational visits and lectures. While there is no doubt that these voluntary members made an enormous contribution to the WEA and were in many respects its life blood, some hard questions do need to be asked about how open branches were to new members and how diverse they were in terms of their membership.

There were two factors that led to the weakening of the branch structure. The first followed from the increase in the levels of reporting, monitoring and audit of the Association's activities. It was apparent in the north, for example, with the creation of the FEFCW that the management committee had continued to concern itself largely with the education programme and that financial viability had been given insufficient attention. The demands on trustees/governors became increasingly centred on meeting statutory regulations and the requirements of funding bodies. This began to sever the connection between the branch and its locally focused educational needs, and the management structure with more professional concerns around compliance and regulation. The constitutional changes brought about by the merger caused a further separation in the north as governors were recruited via public advert and a 'search' committee that matched the skills required on the Governing Body to the applications received. Efforts were made to encourage volunteers and branch members to apply but the automatic link was severed.

In the south the structure of a company limited by guarantee adopted in 1995 continued the democratic election of Council members from branches, individual members and affiliate bodies. Affiliates were historically important in south Wales as much of the provision had been made in conjunction with trade unions and trades councils. Some branches relied heavily on trade union and trades council support. In the mid-eighties the affiliate group was small but membership was lively and active and elections to Council were keenly contested. The same problems of divorce between the programme concerns of branches and members and the formal requirements of running a closely-regulated, publicly-funded association have also affected the south. Marrying a democratic structure of governance to an effective management structure able to meet the demands of government regulation has proved a difficult process – especially as WEA South Wales was successful in delivering programme targets and financial stability and so there were not the same imperatives as in the north. The problems in the north led to addressing systems deficiencies, although eventually the merger with Coleg Harlech added additional infrastructure to help meet monitoring demands. In the south the same process of restructuring was completed only in 2005. Meanwhile considerable efforts have been made in training Council members in their new role, and the relationship between governance and management is much better understood.

The second factor was a more general change in the nature of volunteering and the decline in the numbers attending the WEA's traditional liberal arts programmes. In the north this decline had been apparent prior to 1992 and an assessment of actual numbers attending liberal arts classes showed very small numbers of students in many cases. There were strong branches in Colwyn Bay, Penllyn, Rhyl and Wrexham and the programmes in these areas were extensive and varied but in most other areas, it was a case of maintaining what already existed. Classes offered through the medium of Welsh were a strong feature of the traditional programme in north-west Wales supported by the branch. In south Wales the number of active branches was smaller, and more classes were provided with partner organisations, but the same pattern of successful branches, such as Llanelli, Neath and Swansea, and some smaller ones obtained. The generation that had gained from universal education in the post-war period had been particularly active on branch, district and national committees. There was a sense of giving something back to society behind their volunteering and a commitment to the broader principles and values associated with liberal adult education. While branches were very stable, it became apparent over time that very few new people were joining and as branch officers retired it was difficult to find replacements in these roles. Vigorous attempts to found new branches were made in the pre-1992 period, such as at Barry and the DVLA, Swansea, and those which continued relied heavily on the hard work of a few volunteers and practical support of WEA staff. Branch programmes in some areas continue to be very successful.

It has been necessary to re-define branches to meet the needs of a more diverse range of learners. The formal structures involving branch officers and the taking of minutes have given way to a looser association: for example, bringing groups of learners together from different classes around a shared area of interest, such as creative writing or the visual arts and organising visits or speakers in these areas. Close support from WEA development staff has enabled some of these groups to develop into full branches and offer candidates for Council membership. The more established are beginning to offer support to newer groups, as happened between Risca, Bettws(Newport) and Maesglas branches, and more recently between Caerphilly and Merthyr.

Branches in the WEA express not just a method of organisation but a relationship between student and tutor based on equality of respect in deciding both what is the topic of learning and how the learning takes place. And this is real, hard-edged equality where tutors have to justify themselves and students get to decide.

The redefinitions of learning over the past twenty years seem to have pointed government policy in Wales in conflicting directions. In one direction, dominating the 'education' agenda, has been the notion of 'skills' rather than 'skill' – developing techniques and aptitudes for specific (mostly vocational) roles, rather than a framework in which to assess what is necessary and what is the best way to do it. In the other direction, policies of social justice and community development are informed by notions of empowerment, collaborative informed decisions – the citizenship agenda. Both are needed. The skills are empty without the ability to see them in a context, and to assess that context.

WEA in Wales has not only survived but profited from this series of redefinitions of the purposes of lifelong learning since 1992. Looking to the future, it seems likely that a large part of public policy will concentrate on skills that will be closely defined by the needs of the economy. The WEAs and Coleg Harlech can contribute to that, particularly in the areas of countering economic inactivity and responding to demographic change. The WEA is well placed to help adults who have experienced long-term unemployment and who lack the skills and confidence to enter the labour market. As people will be working longer, there is a clear need to work with the trades unions to provide education in the workplace that will improve life chances. In a more heterogeneous society, migrants will need language skills and how to cope in a new culture.

Whilst the WEA is able to operate well within the economic agenda, there is another. Education in its broadest sense both for personal development and effective citizenship lies at the heart of the WEA's mission and to concentrate on one to the detriment of the other would threaten its reason for existence. Although governments in Wales and Westminster promote the principles of social justice and citizenship, it has been difficult to find a framework within which the WEA can operate to promote this side of its work. 'Education' has become rather divorced from the wider concerns of culture, politics, and citizenship. There are strong indications too that education can contribute towards improved health and well-being. As different departments are responsible for health, regeneration, social justice, culture and education it is becoming increasingly difficult to find suitable sources of funding for the WEAs wider programme. In order to guard against a narrowing of the WEAs mission and purpose, government policy will need to encourage a closer fit between education for employment and career development, personal development and active citizenship. The recent move by the new government in the Welsh Assembly to bring culture, sport and education into one department may offer opportunities to bring these strands closer together.

As the WEA has worked more closely with the economic agenda for education, it could be argued that it is now competing in the same territory as other providers, particularly FE colleges. In assessing its position more than a decade after the Act of 1992, it is therefore important to pose the question, 'Does the WEA still have something special to offer, over and above what is provided by others?' In the preceding paragraphs central characteristics of the WEA have been enumerated: a real equality between learners and tutor in deciding what is to be learnt and how learning happens, a concern for the personal, social and political as well as the economic outcomes of learning. The traditional WEA mantras – 'creating an educated democracy', 'knowledge is power' still, to these authors, have force. WEA is centred on these things. Being driven by these principles gives WEA privileged access to overlooked parts of the community and can bridge the divide between them and the education mainstream.

Promoting the value of education as a measure of the individual's engagement and responsibility in a civilised society and concern for fundamental issues will become more possible if public provision firmly recognises the interdependence of these facets of policy. The ability of the WEAs and Coleg Harlech to retain their unique place as specialist providers of adult education in Wales will depend on the policy framework that is established in coming years. They have survived and adapted to a new environment since 1992 and gained in presence and stature in the process but in order to maintain their *raison d'etre* a more sympathetic policy framework is needed that encompasses the full range of their principles and purposes. To invest in the WEA and Coleg Harlech is to affirm these principles in society as a whole.

*A joint project between the charity, New Sandfields and the WEA in Port Talbot in which men are taught carpentry has been awarded two national awards by the National Institute of Adult and Continuing Education*

# REMINISCENCES

## MEMORIES OF GEORGE DAVISON

### JAMES GRIFFITHS

In 1910 two anthracite miners, D. R. Owen, Garnant, and Jack Griffiths, Cwmtwrch, returned home after two years residence at the newly established Labour College in London. The Anthracite Miners' District of the South Wales Miners' Federation arranged that classes would be organized at selected centres in the coalfield at which the returned students would teach industrial history and Marxian economics. One of these classes was established at Ammanford with D.R. Owen as our teacher. I was appointed secretary of our class. We met in the ante-room of the Ivorites Hall – the only place available at that time as our efforts to secure a room at one of our schools were rebuffed by the County Education Committee, at the advice, we were told,of H.M. Inspector of schools.

It was a dingy, stuffy room and our only light was an oil lamp set on the table at one end of a long room which ran the whole width of the hall. One evening just before the Christmas break our teacher brought a visitor to our class. When we entered the room we were all curious as we beheld this strange man dressed in a thick black and white tweed suit. He looked like a visitor from a different world to ours. D. R. Owen introduced him to us as George Davison, a friend of Dennis Hird the founder of the Labour College, a supporter of the College, and a generous friend of the students. He stayed with us throughout the two hours of the class and then spoke to us.

He said he had been impressed by our keeness and ability both in our questions to our tutor and in the ensuing discussion. He went on to say he had been distressed to find us meeting in such dingy surroundings, and that he would like to help us to find a more suitable home. Some time later our teacher informed us that the next day George Davison had asked him to take him to an estate agent at Ammanford and straight-away that morning he had completed arrangements for the acquisition of the old vicarage in the High Street at Ammanford. I was instructed to write to him to express our appreciation of his kindness. From him we had a reply that he had set his agent to the task of arranging for the old vicarage to be adapted into a suitable place to hold our class.

Eventually, we were informed that the old mansion had been reconstructed with a hall to seat about fifty people, a smaller classrooom, a library, and with living quarters for a caretaker. The whole building was to be for our use free of any rent except that we had to provide for a caretaker and for cleaning the premises. This was soon arranged for one of our members, Harry Arthur, volunteered to move into the caretaker's quarters and to look after the premises. When all was ready for opening we found ourselves the proud occupiers of an ideal meeting place. Each room had been furnished by Maples of London and the library was already partly provided with a series of books all about Anarchism.

We had all been curious about our benefactor and this is what we eventually found out. George Davison had been a civil servant whose hobby was photography. He was a member of a camera club and one day a representative of the Kodak company of the USA had met members of the club. He told them that his company proposed to establish a British subsidiary and he invited members of the club to take up shares. George Davison promptly became a shareholder in British Kodak. He was, by the time we first met him, an obviously wealthy man. He had a house in London and a cottage on the Thames near Henley. The cottage was white and was known as The White House. This was why he had the old vicarage painted white and renamed it The White House of Ammanford. He had, we gathered, in his youth come under the influence of Anarchist writers, and had known and been much influenced by (Prince) Peter Kropotkin and his circle. Another member of the then 'revolutionary circle' who influenced him was the writer Wyndham Lewis. Both of these were fully represented amongst the books in the White House library on that auspicious opening day.

In course of time we formed ourselves into an organisation to which we gave the name of 'The Workers' Forum' and I continued to be the secretary until I entered the Labour College in 1919. During the first world war we became the home for the pacifists and anti-war members of our trade unions and Labour Party. We held several classes on week nights, and on Sunday evenings we held public meetings at which speakers – all of the left – addressed our gatherings. The White House, during those war years and the immediate post-war years, became the Mecca of the left in our valley and our influence became powerful in the labour movement.

In 1914 George Davison invited our class as it then was, to send four of our members to visit Harlech and stay for two weeks at a camp he had set up in the grounds of Wern Fawr, the large house he had had built at Harlech. I was one of the four selected and together with some twenty young people from all over Britain spent two weeks at the camp. Twice in each week we were invited to attend a concert in the Great Hall. These would consist of organ recitals by Davison himself interspersed by songs and dramatic recitals by some of the guests who were staying in the mansion. I remember particularly a talk on folk music given by a friend of Davison who lived in Harlech, Alfred Percival Graves, and being introduced, with my fellow campers, to Mr. Graves' young son Robert. The end of our visit was clouded by the grim news of the outbreak of war. Each pledging our resolve to oppose the war we dispersed and returned to our homes.

The four years of war followed by the struggles of the twenties and thirties were to involve all our energies in work for our unions and the Labour Party. The dream period of the White House, Wern Fawr, and Anarchism was over, but the memory abides. I still treasure a beautiful photograph by George Davison of the Harlech sand dunes and as I gaze at it the memory of that first stay at Wern Fawr returns vividly to mind.

[This memoir was written by the Rt. Hon. James Griffiths, C.H. for Coleg Harlech in October 1970]

# AN UNUSUAL CHARACTER

## TOM JONES

In 1905 I attended a Fabian Summer School at Llanbedr, Merioneth. I shared rooms with Professor Tawney and Professor Namier. Sidney and Beatrice Webb, George Lansbury and many others were there. We were asked out to tea to a new house which was being extended at Harlech called Wernfawr. Our host was an unusual character, George Davison, who had made a fortune in Kodak Ltd and had retired to this residence in Wales. He lived largely on fruit and nuts and his political views resembled those of a Tolstoyan anarchist.

I liked him and got to know him well enough to tell him that such a house on such a wonderful site ought not to be monopolised by one man or even one family but should be put to some public use. I do not claim credit for the fact that he proceeded to adopt a number of children of ex-cabmen from the mews behind Addison Road, London, about a dozen of them and brought them to Harlech where he provided teachers for them. Later he bought a villa at Cap d'Antibes on the Riviera which had belonged to the King of the Belgians and took his big family there. Wernfawr was thus free and he offered it to me for £25,000. I am not myself, in the ordinary sense, a rich man, but twenty-five hundred pounds might have been within my range.

When I was at Pengam School I had known a Pontlottyn boy, Henry Gethin Lewis, who had prospered in business. I asked him to dine in London, I think in the Hotel Cecil, and I brought along to meet him Lord Haldane and Lord Eustace Percy, then Minister of Education. They developed the case for Adult Education and at the end of dinner Henry Lewis handed me an IOU for £7,500, which was the figure to which I had reduced George Davison's price for what was to become the house now known as Coleg Harlech, a residential college for adult education which opened its doors in 1927.

[This is an extract from *Moments in Eighty Years: A Birthday Talk* broadcast by Dr. Thomas Jones, CH

# HARLECH'S WARTIME OCCUPATION

## JOE ENGLAND

At 11.30 on the morning of Saturday, 3 September 1927, Henry Gethin Lewis formally opened Coleg Harlech the first, and only, long-term residential college for adults in Wales. Exactly twelve years later on a sunny Sunday morning came Neville Chamberlain's broadcast – '.. . and consequently we are now at war with Germany' – and Ben Bowen's telephone rang. It was a call the Warden had been expecting. Arnold McNair, the Vice-Chancellor of Liverpool University, was on the phone confirming that in accordance with instructions from the Ministry of Home Security he was sending one of his professors to take charge of the College buildings. As early as 1937 the College had considered its position should war break out and an arrangement for Liverpool University to rent the College in those circumstances had been concluded in July 1939.

The University stayed for the next three years. Initially some ninety students and seventeen staff from departments of the Faculty of Arts moved to Harlech, finding accommodation in Wern Fawr itself, in Crown Lodge, and in the St. David's Hotel. Later the entire Education Department went to Harlech. College rooms were used for teaching and the library, not yet officially opened, was the chief venue for private study. Altogether more than 150 Liverpool students passed through Harlech and, as the Vice-Chancellor wrote in 1940: ' the students learned many things which only the intimate corporate life of a residential College in such surroundings could teach them'. They developed an impressive range of activities. During the session 1940-41, for instance, country dancing was held on a Monday, first aid on Tuesday, drama on Wednesday, music society on Thursday, Friday and Saturday were left free, and the badminton group met on Sunday. Christmas parties were organized for the evacuee and other children in Harlech and an open invitation given to local people to attend discussion groups and gramophone concerts. Not everyone was happy. Some missed the larger university surroundings and contacts, others felt guilt at being safe in Harlech when they heard of heavy bombing on Merseyside, and there were those who were just plain homesick. But for many it was one of the happiest times of their lives.

Gilbert Marson, one of the education students in 1939-40, rembered how:

> . . . we worked hard; we walked and cycled widely; we enjoyed the late Saturday breakfast of hot buttered toast, honey and tea in the Plas Cafe; there were eminent visiting lecturers; we attempted Welsh and learned first aid; we had dances; we helped with evacuee children in the village; we learned and performed an oratorio; we performed plays; we had our own students' union; we men 'enjoyed' wooden-hutted quarters below the College and near the kitchen and dining-room.

Anne Doherty, a second-year Arts student in 1939-40 recalled that the oratorio was Mendelssohn's 'Hymn of Praise' with the student choir augmented by local people. She remembered too a day in mid-June 1940 when a train arrived packed with soldiers who had been rescued from Dunkirk. 'Two days later we held a dance for them in the Hall – men students to stay in the background and provide refreshments!' Jean Macleroy, an education student in 1940-41, was charmed by the College building itself which 'was a delight with its nooks and crannies' while 'the beautiful surroundings and lovely wild flowers were a constant joy' forming a sharp contrast with the bomb damage on Merseyside.

The Liverpool staff threw themselves enthusiastically into organizing activities with the students, encountering for the first time, as did many of the students, 'the joys and responsibilities of residential education'. Some of the staff joined the Home Guard

> ,,,which used to patrol the castle and College at night, a rather eerie experience sometimes but on the whole not bad; they had to do this duty about once in every nine days. In the middle of September 1940 they were called out for about thirty-six hours and the trenches were dug from which they were not expected to retreat when the Germans invaded.

In fact, the only tangible signs of the war were the sound of enemy planes going to and from

171

Merseyside, and the dropping of a bomb across the bay at Pwllheli. By the close of the 1941-42 session bombing in Liverpool had ceased to be a danger and the University voluntarily relinquished its tenancy of the College in September 1942.

But no sooner did Liverpool move out than the War Office in the shape of the Army School of Education under the aegis of the Army Bureau of Current Affairs (ABCA) moved in. When, in May 1942, Tom Jones had learned that Liverpool intended to vacate the College in the autumn he had made an agreement with his protege W.E.Williams, the Director of ABCA, that it would move in and set up a centre for training officers in lecturing and leading discussion groups, using the pamphlets issued by ABCA. The intention was 'to provide as many units as possible with officers capable of instructing, assisting and stimulating other officers in their units in the duty of discussing Current Affairs with their men'. Each course lasted five days and around fifty officers attended each week. Army Council Instructions for 13 January 1943 proclaimed 'Officers will bring service or battledress, revolver, ammunition, steel helmet and respirator . . . their own sheets, pillow cases and towels . . . Officers will not bring soldier servants. ATS batwomen are provided by the school'!

By the end of the war the Harlech centre had trained 4,600 officers. One was Gwyn Illtyd Lewis who had been a student at the College in 1936-37 (and who later became a tutor in Swansea Extra-Mural Department). He recalled in 1977 how, on the first night, the colonel had tried to explain to everyone on the course the College's original purpose.

> It was obvious that the whole matter was a complete mystery to most of them. They could understand the purpose of a university, or a teachers' training college, or a technical college, but an adult education college? The idea was beyond their comprehension . . . . .!

It was not until after Dunkirk and the announcement that all men were to be henceforth engaged in National Service that the College's own residential course came to an end. Until then eighteen students and three tutors carried on. The summer schools continued in the College buildings, with the co-operation of Liverpool University, until 1942 and were well attended. After that, accomodation was found in Beck Hall, Swansea, in 1943 and 1944 and in 1945 at the Maesglas Hostel, at Pencoed near Bridgend. Meanwhile, 'non-residential summer schools' were held in various parts of the country and became a significant joint Harlech/WEA institution that continued well after the war.

[This note is based on information in the *University of Liverpool Recorder* No. 64, January 1974; P.E.H. Hair (ed.) *Arts. Letters. Society: A Miscellany Commemorating the Centenary of the Faculty of Arts at the University of Liverpool* (Liverpool, 1996); Coleg Harlech *Official Re-opening Programme 1946*; and personal communications from Miss Anne Doherty and Miss Jean E. Macleroy.]

## BLISS WAS IT IN THAT DAWN TO BE ALIVE
### G. B. OWEN

One fine evening in May 1946 I alighted from the train at Harlech station and made my way to the College. I was taking up the position of Bursar, to which I had been newly appointed, and joining I.D.Harry, the Warden, and Edna Lloyd Williams, the Housemistress, in the task of re-opening Coleg Harlech after the war years. I had come that morning from Bristol, changing at Rhiwabon and, in those days before Beeching had started wielding his axe, travelling through the beautiful vale of Llangollen and along the Mawddach estuary to Barmouth and then following the coast to Harlech, surely one of the finest scenic rail journeys in Britain.

I fell in love with Harlech and its environs from the beginning. The castle stood on its mighty rock looking out over the Morfa to Cardigan Bay and the mountains of Snowdonia. In its shadow was Wern Fawr, the noble mansion built by George Davison in 1910 and now the home of Coleg Harlech. From the terrace we saw the great sweep of Harlech beach and, beyond, the little hills of the Llyn peninsular. I wandered in the hills and fished for trout in the rivers and lakes.

Our main object in the College was to prepare for the session beginning in September, but before that, summer schools were to be held for three weeks from 3-24 August. A distinguished panel of tutors had been engaged to teach a wide variety of subjects in English and Welsh. These included international relations, literature, philosophy, politics, history, and drama. A total of 127 students were enrolled, twenty-four of them staying for two weeks. They included miners, steelworkers, clerks, teachers, housewives, and a surgeon. In addition to lectures and seminars, informal events were arranged: concerts, a *noson lawen*, and coach trips to Snowdonia. The summer schools were a resounding success, combining study and recreation, with tutors and students mingling freely in the best tradition of Harlech.

On 31 August a distinguished company of the great and good assembled for the official opening of the library and the re-opening of the College. Sir Wynn Wheldon, chairman of the Council, presided and Dr. Thomas Jones was there to receive a painting in appreciation of his great achievement in founding Coleg Harlech and developing its work. Ben Bowen Thomas made the presentation and TJ in his reply said that 'the workers of Wales and other nations would come once more to seek knowledge and wisdom, to understand the world we live in and to recall it to peace.' An address was delivered by Sir Philip Morris, Vice-Chancellor of the University of Bristol and a good friend of adult education. The Bishop of Bangor offered prayer and former students of the College and the local Member of Parliament spoke. Appropriate Welsh hymns were sung and the students of the University of Wales Council of Music, who were at a summer school, gave a fine rendering of a majestic piece by Palestrina. It was a notable occasion and as a young administrator I felt relieved and rather proud that my first test had gone off without a hitch!

The first sessional students came into residence in September. Tutors had been appointed: M.J. Jones to teach Economics, Tecwyn Lloyd to teach Welsh Literature and Welsh History, and Mansel John to teach History and Sociology. The Warden took charge of English Literature, Music and Psychology. Ten students were enrolled; they came from north and south Wales and one from Brittany. Taking into account all grades of staff – academic, administrative and household – we outnumbered the students! However, we all settled down happily,facing the future with confidence. Two additional students joined us in the spring term and a further five in the summer term.

Despite their small number, the students led a full and varied corporate life. A literary and debating society, gramophone club, Students' Christian Movement branch, keep fit class, arts club and Welsh dramatic society were formed. Local friends were invited to many activities and thus a good relationship was established between town and gown. There was a stream of distinguished visitors from home and overseas, many of whom gave us memorable lectures on their specialities.

Sir Wynn Wheldon came to see us from time to time and with his vast experience of men and affairs, was a tower of strength. Dr. Thomas Jones, though now retired from the chairmanship, continued to take an active interest and visited us occasionally. He would ask me to accompany him on a tour of the College, starting in the library. He would pick up a volume here and there and comment upon its contents or its author, revealing the great breadth of his knowledge of books in both English and Welsh. In the Great Hall he would pause in front of the portrait of Sir Henry Jones, his old philosophy teacher at Glasgow, of whom he always spoke with admiration and affection.

Apart from work there were all kinds of activities that occupied our time: there were long walks along the seashore when we discussed philosophy, literature and religion; we played the occasional game of golf or tennis; there were excursions to Cwm Bychan lake and the Roman Steps and to eisteddfodau in little country chapels; sometimes of an evening we just sat on the terrace watching the sun setting over Llyn. We gathered around the grand piano in the Great Hall and sang, more or less in tune, under the guidance of Ceridwen Lloyd Davies, an accomplished musician. Recitals were given by professional artistes sent by the Welsh Arts Council and others. The Arts Council also sent an exhibition of paintings and drawings. A choral society was formed and, supplemented by members from the town, performed excerpts from the *Messiah* at the end of the autumn term. We had a hop at the end of each term, to which friends from the neighbourhood were invited; the standard of dancing improved with the advent of women students in September 1947. One of these, Meinir Evans, a miner's daughter from the Gwendraeth valley, taught me to dance the waltz!

In the session 1947-48 we had an influx of foreign students from Austria and Denmark together with a German who had been a prisoner-of-war in Wales. Two from Denmark arrived before the session had started and to help in keeping them happy I took them one day to the summit of Snowdon. Not being used to hills they found the going rather heavy but Ralph, our deaf and dumb houseman, who was with us, bounded ahead like a greyhound. When we got to the cafe on the top we were dismayed to find a notice, 'Customers must not consume their own food on the premises'. We bought cups of tea and surreptitiously ate our sandwiches from under the table!

Gradually, student numbers improved, from eight in residence for the full session in 1946-47 to twenty-seven in 1947-48 and fifty in 1948-49. There was also an increase in those staying for just one or two terms. Finance was a problem. Nevertheless, with growing student numbers, improved grants from the Ministry of Education and other bodies, and support from individual subscribers and donors, the situation gradually got better.

The coming-of-age of the College in 1948 was taken as an opportunity to make an appeal for public support. Friends old and new responded generously. Among the donations received I recall one from Idris Davies, the workers' poet from Rhymney, who accompanied his cheque with a poem written in his own hand on the back of the remittance slip:

## Harlech

She listens on a summer day
To martial music far away,
And as she turns unto her sleep
She dreams of Branwen on the deep;
And there, above each starlit height
Her warriors guard her through the night.

I left Harlech in 1949. Looking back over the three years spent there I have a sense of having been greatly privileged by sharing in the life of the College and, in some small measure, helping in a worthwhile task.

## HARLECH STUDENT MEMORIES

*In October 1948 twenty year-old J. Hefin Jones left his village of Y Fron, near Caernarfon, for Harlech.*

We were accommodated in wooden stable-like dormitories down near the railway line. These were freezing cold in winter. I remember an African student arriving during this cold spell with all the other students contributing either hot water bottles or a blanket to keep him warm. He spent most of his time in a bath of hot water.

There was food rationing at that time and each student had two jam jars, one held a few ounces of sugar, the other two small pieces of butter and margarine. They had to last a week. I shared a section of this dormitory with Mr. R. Wyn Jones whose mother from time to time sent him half-a-dozen eggs. There was no kitchen available for student use. We found an empty two pound tin can, 'borrowed' a piece of wire from the fence opposite, connected the wire to the tin can which was then filled with hot water, placed the eggs inside and very discreetly went to the boiler room at the far end of the dormitories and lowered the contraption into the fire inside the boiler. The result was very lovely boiled eggs, black but slightly hard boiled.

*The twenty-five year-old Eddie Jenkins from Deri was there at the same time.*

I was working at the coalface on the Friday before arriving at Harlech with £30 to last me the session. Some were worse off than I was so the general picture was one of low standards of living and low expectations among students. Only one student, an ex-policeman had a car. I remember that very well because he gave me a lift back to south Wales. I would have difficulty otherwise as I could not afford the fare and could not afford to have my shoes repaired. I remember having to go to the National Assistance for the week of my return home, to tide me over until I had my first pay on returning to work in the pit.

But at the College, although we still had food rationing, I was amazed that life could be so good. I was treated with respect that I had not known previously. There was no respect like that in the pit. The teaching was superb – exciting and rigorous, especially the marking of essays, in which spelling and grammar were corrected exactly without undermining motivation. Encouragement was found in all comments.

... Visits by men to female hostels was not permitted, and such was the 'spirit of the age' that this was accepted. This did not stop men, at the end of term, waking women early by throwing bits of gravel at bedroom windows to catch the 6.40 am train. It was also possible for ladies in Crown Lodge to open the front door to the few love-sick men, who could make an early morning cup of tea, while the subjects of their affections dressed and finished packing.

A major feature of College life was the morning assembly at which all staff and students were expected to be present. Each student was expected to read to the gathering a piece of text important to him/her and explain why it was chosen. This was intended to develop confidence in people in whom it was lacking and provide an opportunity for all to participate in a common activity and build respect for the opinions of others. The reading was followed by an open discussion chaired by the Warden which I found very helpful in learning about the ideas of others.

*In September 1962 twenty-six year-old Anne Thomas left Neath for Harlech.*

For the first time in my life I became aware that despite not succeeding in conventional terms in the selective education system **I was not a failure**. The feelings of inferiority and lack of achievement engendered by my school experience were reinforced by the class and status structure within the factory system where I spent the next eleven years after leaving elementary school at the age of fifteen. What the ethos at Coleg Harlech offered was equal treatment and respect for one's ideas and opinions from staff and fellow students which boosted my self-esteem. I had previously only encountered this philosophy when attending the extra-mural classes taught by Tom Thomas in Briton Ferry and in trade union education.

The two years I spent at Harlech changed my life from one of limited expectations to one where I was encouraged to believe I was capable of achieving anything I aspired to. Since leaving Harlech I have worked within the adult education field where I have sought to be a facilitator for other people in the way that Harlech was for me. Coleg Harlech offered to me not 'a second chance' but the first opportunity I ever had to achieve my intellectual and personal potential.

*In 1968 twenty-four year old Michael Shaw went to Harlech from Liverpool*

My year was the first of the new two-year Diploma and the Hall of Residence was built and completed for our second year. The change of atmosphere and the development of student independence from the College authorities was very clear. It was like attending two different colleges in two years.

On the walls of the 'refectory' were paintings of former students done in that dull brown realistic style of the nineteen thirties. They seemed to be symbols of the traditional 'feel' of

Coleg Harlech, men (and they were all men) who were having a well-earned academic holiday from their back-breaking, sooty existence, in the coalfaces and factories of Britain, before being shipped off overseas to save the world from fascism. If you contemplated this too deeply they seemed to be challenging your post-war, free orange-juice, full-employment molly-coddled existence.

Being the sixties, music obviously featured highly in our lives, and not just The Beatles. Bob Brett, from Bethnal Green (later Director of Housing at Tower Hamlets) brought his portable record player and a copy of Vivaldi's Four Seasons out on to the lawn between the old College and the yet to be built accommodation block (the site was our much loved football pitch). In the early summer sunshine of 1969 the music seemed to have been written especially for the scenery we were now surveying. I don't remember such a shared state of bliss, except when Everton won the cup in 1966.

Moving into the new hall of residence in 1969 released the students from the last vestiges of College supervision. Men and women now lived in close proximity – women occupied the top two floors – and were separated physically and emotionally from the College authorities. Strangely enough, though, those who wanted to smoke illicit substances and explore the sexual freedoms of the late sixties, and those who wished to lead quiet conventional lives were seldom in conflict. In those heady free-thinking days, tolerance was very much a buzz word. This feeling developed and grew to its apex in the first few years of the seventies. It was a lovely time.

*In 1983 twenty-six year-old Catherine Marvel entered the two-year Diploma course.*

It was a unique and memorable time allowing great personal as well as academic development. One of my many memories is of the peace and solitude of sitting in the library after dinner watching the sunset whilst reading and absorbing new knowledge, the air seemed golden with pleasure and contentment.

*On the same course was twenty-three year-old Julie Sarker.*

Coleg Harlech provided me with the courage to say to myself 'I can do that'. This remains at the root of my own teaching career. I hear myself saying – you can do that – and that magical discovery on a child's face makes all the hard work more than worth it.
It was hard work at Harlech. Seminars were not my best friend during the first few months. They were akin to the first reading of a Shakespeare text, unfathomable and incomprehensible, yet rattling at a sense of conscience and tapping at a mind which had for so long wanted to take on a greater depth of understanding. Without the tutors Graham Allen, Richard Poole, and David Wiltshire who persevered with my learning that potential may never have seen the light of day. A poem by Gerard Manley Hopkins sums up my time at Harlech.

> ... do but stand
> Where you can lift your hand
> Skywards: rich, rich it laps

Round your finger gaps.
. . . the glass blue days are those
When every colour glows,
Each shape and shadow shows.
Bloom breather, that one breath more
Earth is the fairer for.

I doubt for me there was any other way to learn. They were my glass blue days.

## WEA MEMORIES

### DEREK G THOMAS

As a young journalist I learned of the existence of the WEA through the National Union of Journalists and the extra-mural class in current affairs that I helped to establish in Cowbridge in 1947. I also learned about various summer schools and attended one at Coleraine in Northern Ireland. There I met the then secretary of the Northern Ireland District, W.G.McCullough, who took me under his wing and introduced me to the strange politics of the province. Fortunately, in 1947 it was going through a lull. One day he took me to Londonderry for a conducted tour. Twenty-three years later I returned in much more troubled times when I was the Army press spokesperson for the 1970 Apprentice Boys rally – a considerable contrast with the 1940s.

In 1951 I was granted a union scholarship to attend the Anglo-German summer school at Frankfurt am Main. It was the first since the Nazis had come to power in 1933. My hosts were a German family – one of the sons worked for the *Frankfurter Neu Presse*, a prominent Frankfurt newspaper. I was anxious to find out what had happened to the Nazis, apart from those who had been executed for war crimes. I met a woman who had been director of education for Frankfurt in Hitler's time and was rapped over the knuckles by the course leaders for talking to her – it was considered quite improper. My overall impression was one of dynamism and effort by the Germans to recover from the war years. It was easy to understand why they led Europe in the years that followed.

After I married in 1953 I lost touch with the WEA until I was asked in 1980-81 to become chairman-elect of the Brecon branch. I discovered that the branch was a little out of contact with the tutor-organiser, Robin Cain, through no fault of his. I quickly remedied the situation and also discovered that Brecon was rarely represented at meetings of the South Wales District Council. Here too I was able to effect a change and with Elsie Pritchard, the founder of the branch, attended Council meetings. Subsequently, several District secretaries came to address the branch including the late Barry Moore and his predecessor Cled Phillips.

The South Wales WEA has experienced a number of crises over the years. The sudden death of the District secretary Barry Moore and the breakaway from England were both in their different ways traumatic. However, we have survived and I deem it a privilege to have helped with a new constitution and new charity status, having been vice-chairman and chairman during this difficult phase.

## CHRIS O'CONNELL

My experience of working for the WEA as a tutor was during a period of teaching the trade union studies courses at the Channel View Leisure Centre, Grangetown, Cardiff. I taught in the bar which had been used on the previous night for functions; ash-trays still full, floor and tables still sticky with an array of substances. Despite being moved from room to room on a weekly basis, with a kitchen which would have made a chip pan look clean, myself and a committed group of shop stewards managed to have a wonderful course. They put up with ten weeks of me, wearing patches on my arm to stop me from smoking and a peg on my nose to stop me smelling the over-flowing ashtrays. It never ceases to amaze me, how when you want to learn, you will, no matter how difficult the environment.

## JOHN MORRIS

I was an assistant storekeeper active in the local trade union movement, works committee, union branch and trades council etc. At a branch meeting one piece of correspondence referred to a WEA/TUC linked weekend school to be held at Porthcawl. I applied, and surprise mingled with some alarm was my response to the letter of acceptance I received shortly afterwards.

I duly arrived on a Saturday afternoon. My first impression was that most of the other students knew each other, knew their way around and were obviously old hands at the game. The actual content of the school is, of course, lost in the mists of time but my impressions will always remain with me. The feature of the course that astonished me, and I use the word in the dictionary sense, was the way in which many of my fellow students reacted. Generally they listened to the lectures in a polite, but what turned out to be an ominous, silence. Once the speaker invited comments or questions they were at him (and here I record my impression) like a pack of wolves. If they agreed with him, he had not gone far enough. If they did not he'd been influenced by the media not scholarship.

I freely admit that up to that time I had never seen anything like this during any educational activity I had been involved with. Although the format was commonplace at trade union meetings and the like, I had never imagined that education could be so dynamic. My astonishment was compounded by the fact that each lecturer actually seemed to relish the experience: sometimes claiming that criticism was irrational, sometimes confused, and sometimes wholly warranted. (Egads! Can this mean that teachers are sometimes wrong?)
By the time we reached the end of the course we all knew each other fairly well and I discovered that one of the students, now a long lost friend, had applied for a place at Coleg Harlech that year. The two main lecturers on the course were Cled Phillips and Dave Gidwell, both WEA tutor-organizers at the time, and they had both been mature students. Late on the final Saturday night/Sunday morning of the course, I turned to Dave Gidwell and said: 'I wouldn't mind a job like yours; how do you get into this Coleg Harlech then?' Well you never know.

# NORTH WALES 1945-1996

## RUFUS ADAMS

At the end of June, 1954, I had just completed my 'A' levels and in the Welfare Hall, Tumble, I saw a poster:

Cross Hands School  WEA
Non-residential Summer School
Monday- Friday 7.00 – 9.00 pm

## Lecturers

Dr Glyn O. Phillips, Cardiff University: Nuclear Energy
Mr Huw Bevan, Swansea University: 'Beirdd yr Ugeinfed Ganrif'
Mr Brynmor Thomas, Aberystwyth University: What is Civilization?

I enrolled and joined Brynmor Thomas's group. Non-residential summer schools were a splendid idea started with the non-availability of Coleg Harlech during the war years. It's worth noting that all three tutors came from University of Wales' colleges, an example of the close working relationship that existed throughout the twentieth century. I had discovered, without realizing it, what Professor Sir Richard Livingstone, Vice-Chancellor of Oxford University had described as: 'One of the most important educational movements of the twentieth century.'

Thirteen years later, in 1967, when history tutor at Coleg Harlech I was invited by the Aberystwyth extra-mural group at Barmouth to lecture on the anniversary of the 1917 Russian Revolution. Afterwards, I tutored there for 20 weeks and in the following autumn/winter took WEA classes at Corris and Trawsfynydd. I enjoyed these immensely and, in 1970, I successfully applied for the post of WEA tutor-organizer with the challenging brief: 'to develop liberal adult education in Flintshire.' Then, from 1980 to 1996 I was the District Secretary.

The years immediately following 1945 saw many changes in North Wales. Mrs Silyn Roberts, secretary of the District since 1930 – and the first woman secretary in Britain – retired. She was succeeded by C. E. Thomas, 1945-1966 and then Ray Rochell took over until 1980. Both had

## North Wales District Secretaries

| R. Silyn Roberts | Mary Silyn Roberts | C.E. Thomas | Raymond Rochell | Rufus Adams |
|---|---|---|---|---|
| 1925-1930 | 1930-1945 | 1946-1966 | 1966-1980 | 1980-1996 |

been students at Coleg Harlech, and both referred to Mrs Silyn as the strongest influence on their convictions and ideals. The Association was fortunate, too, in its dedicated office staff, and two of the senior clerks must be named: Jennie Allford 1950-1974 and Doris Williams 1953-1994. For many years Doris typed *Lleufer*, often at weekends, ready for the printers. Neither clock nor calendar meant anything if there were still work to be done and for over forty years they were the WEA's friendly telephone voice.

From the beginning over fifty per cent of courses and lectures organised by the District have been in the Welsh language, whatever the topic. And over the last thirty years the District has responded to a new demand by adults to learn Welsh, providing courses which consolidated learning already acquired. Banks, councils, the Inland Revenue and the National Library of Wales have all invited the WEA to help their staff gain greater confidence in speaking and writing the language.

As tutor-organizer, Flintshire, I was conscious that the English speaking students did not have a magazine where they could publish their work, unlike the Welsh speakers who had an outlet in *Lleufer*. My aim to start an English magazine received the full support of the committee and Raymond Rochell and a competition was held for a suitable title. Perhaps, not surprisingly, *Silyn* was chosen. Many issues had a short story by Tom Pratt, Deeside, and we were all delighted when one of the stories was read on Radio Four.

It was always a pleasure when Tutor Organizer and District Secretary to be invited by art classes to their end of year exhibitions. I still recall the sense of pride and admiration I experienced when looking at the work. They made me acutely aware of the talent in our communities, talent that the WEA was encouraging and refining. Housewives, young mothers, the retired, all had artistic skills which WEA tutors nurtured and developed. Important public recognition of the quality of the work was the granting of a month-long Exhibition at Theatr Clwyd, Mold. It was also a pleasure to inform visitors to the WEA Office that the paintings displayed were the work of students.

Why do people go to the Opera or, rather, not go? The question, of course, would not be asked in Italy where it is as normal as going to a football match. My brief as tutor-organizer, 'to develop liberal adult education' was an opportunity to approach Welsh National Opera with the suggestion to stage 'Workshops'. Would their producers and soloists take us behind the scenes, as it were, before the Llandudno season? The Company's Musical Director, James Lockhart, took up the idea with enthusiasm and the North Wales Arts Association agreed to help financially if we attracted over one hundred. On Sunday, 6 June, 1971, at the Rhyl Town Hall the first Opera Workshop was held and 107 attended. The lecturers were James Lockhart, who was helped by the internationally renowned soprano from Monmouthshire, Margaret Price, singing various arias; John Moody of 'Nabucco' fame, and Michael Geliot. Immediately after his lecture on *The Magic Flute* Michael Geliot flew from Manchester to San Francisco to produce the opera there. For the next ten years workshops were held in Rhyl, Connah's Quay, Mold, Llandudno, Conwy, Bangor, Beaumaris, Dolgellau and Harlech. In the 1980s, with the Arts Council, the Opera Company and WEA facing financial difficulties, reluctantly the workshops had to be abandoned. But, not entirely: today, at every venue in England and Wales, pre-performance talks are given by WNO personnel to help people better understand and enjoy the opera. An offshoot was the illustrated talks given before orchestral concerts at the North Wales International Music Festival at St Asaph Cathedral which in turn led to the Festival lecture, all of which have been published.

A significant social development in the last quarter of the twentieth century was the increase in the number of people for whom retirement meant at least twenty years of active life. From 1976 the District organised Preparation for Retirement courses to help individuals and, whenever possible, couples to adjust to their new life. It was particularly gratifying that so many firms and companies accepted the premise that retirement was as important a change for the partner as it was for the person retiring and paid for both to attend. Participating companies included Wales Gas, The Inland Revenue, Pilkington's, Egatube, Marks & Spencer's, Rhuddlan and Flint Borough Councils and the Forestry Commission. The courses were very popular and over a thousand attended.

The WEA has never been financially strong; 1983-84, and the following years, were therefore particularly difficult since the Welsh Office informed both Welsh Districts, a week before Christmas, that the grant was being reduced by 7.5 per cent over two years. This was a loss of £9,000, a great deal of money for North Wales. Other Districts within the UK were facing the same reductions. Although there was a determined campaign against the cut there was no change in government policy and the effects were soon evident. For the first time in the history of the WEA a District went out of existence: North Staffs amalgamated with the West Midlands District to form West Mercia. In the early 1990s Southern District, ceased to exist. As well as the reduced grant from central government it became far more difficult to obtain grants from local authorities since they also were facing considerable financial pressures. The three Scottish Districts were particularly vulnerable and the solution was to have but one Association with its office in Edinburgh. In the mid 1980s there were twenty-one Districts, by the early 1990s there were only seventeen

What did the WEA achieve in the twentieth century? Members and students would have their own answers but its significance should not be underestimated in an age which tends to count everything in millions. It served a minority, but it was a significant minority of men and women who contributed greatly to the social, educational and political life of their communities. The WEA in north Wales achieved much with relatively few resources because of the commitment and loyalty of the volunteers. It always faced a double challenge — attracting enough students for classes to continue, and encouraging students to become active members for the Association to continue. Much of its history is one of tensions, crises and warnings from treasurers that the future was bleak without increased funding. Yet in spite of all the disappointments and challenges, members remained steadfast since they strongly believed in its aims and in the ideal of a participating democracy.

# MY ROAD TO DAMASCUS

## TERRY BURNS

This is an outline of my educational development from leaving school at fifteen to entering Coleg Harlech at twenty-three. My starting point is my first contact with the WEA. That life-changing encounter took place, as far as I can recall, on a wet Monday night at my union branch meeting in the upstairs room of the Tredegar Junction Hotel, Pontllanfraith. This was about four years after I left school. Prior to that I was an active, some would say an over-active, teenager in the labour and trade union movement. I had no clear idea of where I wanted to go, in life, education, work or public activity. The WEA and its local tutor-organizer encouraged me to seek a direction, a new road to travel.

The road to the Tredegar Junction wasn't new. I passed that way twice a day, Monday to Saturday, on my way to and from work. I lived in the small mining village of Markham, five miles north of this pub and worked in South Wales Switchgear's main factory in Pontllanfraith, half a mile to the south.

Our branch of the AEU (Amalgamated Engineering Union), like so many others, consisted of a small group of union activists, who met once a fortnight — every other Monday in our case — to take members' dues, handle the correspondence from the union head office, and discuss local union and political issues. Sometimes, a guest speaker would be invited, and on this particular evening we had taken up an offer to speak from the local WEA tutor-organizer, Neil Kinnock. He proved to be the most effective speaker we ever had. Three of the branch officers joined the WEA and for two it was to be a life altering experience. It could be described as the moment I saw the light on my personal road to my equivalent of Damascus. Not that I realised this at the time. Nor was it a single flash. It was a gradual process of gaining knowledge, understanding, experience, confidence, and being presented with alternatives.

Up until that time the branch had participated in educational activities restricted to AEU/TUC weekend schools and a few of the officers taking correspondence courses. Some years before this our AEU regional organiser Bill John encouraged me to become involved in the union's youth activities. As a result I started to go to TUC and AEU general weekend schools, some youth schools, and I attended the union's National Youth Conference, postal courses through the NCLC (National Council of Labour Colleges) and two national Labour Party Youth Summer Schools at Ruskin College, as a union sponsored student. I was also an active member of the Bedwellty Labour Party, being assistant secretary and youth officer of the Bedwellty constituency party and a delegate to Blackwood trades and labour council.

I began to recognise that my level of education was really of poor quality and did not provide me with the tools I needed. Increasingly, I found myself lacking knowledge or information when debating with my much older comrades. My formal education consisted of attending my local village school. This was the largest building in the village, a long grey stone building and a couple of demountables. At the age of four or five you entered the school via the Infants Entrance. As you grew older new entrances became available until at the age of fifteen you finally left for a life of work via the Senior Girls' or Boys' entrance. All in the same building you moved through Markham Infants School, Markham Junior School and completed with Markham Senior Mixed. Most of the boys entered the village coalmine.

I did not pass the eleven-plus and completed my school education at the age of fifteen, obtaining 10 subject passes in the recently created Monmouthshire Certificate of Education. My year was the third year of students to gain this qualification. My older brother Tony was amongst the first, along with Barry Moore who was to become a future District Secretary of the WEA in south Wales. All three of us found our way to South Wales Switchgear as apprentices.

It is impossible to ignore the influence of this past: my school, the mining community I lived in, my time as an apprentice and then engineering worker. Also there was the enormous influence of my family and their experiences. There were the stories of my mother as a domestic servant for the high and mighty, her time on the line at the Weetabix factory or at the munitions factory. My father's life as a miner, an experience he neither would nor could forget. It made him the man he was. Although he retired through ill health in his mid-fifties, he talked of that life until he died. Equally I cannot forget this was the same work that caused his premature break from work, with the guilt he felt about not earning a wage and finally leading to an early death. I recall the talk about my grandfathers and the General Strike. I was receiving an education. An important education but it lacked structure and direction. A major signpost was erected on that eventful night at the AEU branch meeting in Pontllanfraith.

### The Kinnock Influence

Neil addressed the meeting on the theme of trade union and adult education and the possibility of forming a local WEA branch. The union branch chairman, treasurer and I agreed to assist and with Neil gathered around us twenty or so local Labour Party members and union activists. Within a short time the WEA branch was attracting quite large audiences for a series of lectures on diverse topics. One of the most memorable from a local headmaster who delivered a talk on the local Chartist Movement. I can remember to this day how he held the class mesmerized as he brought to life the local Chartist leaders such as Williams, Frost and Jones and their drive to create a democratic system of government. The following week the WEA class might replace this highly charged celebration of the Monmouthshire Chartists with an equally important but more reflective class on why the Labour County Council still favoured grammar schools.

Following the meetings a large part of the WEA Branch would move down to the local pub, the Greyhound, where we would discuss the important topics of the day, most of which consisted of the errors of the Wilson government. Neil of course would be a leading participant in these discussions. He did not hide his ambition to become the next MP for Bedwellty, replacing the ageing MP Harold Finch. Nor was the group restricted to supporters of his goals. The result was quite often a lively discussion sometimes reflecting the issues already discussed at the Branch meeting.

Neil was also trying to develop his skills, not as a leader but as someone who could carry drinks from the bar to a table without spilling them or how to get involved in a discussion without knocking a drink over. He was still at the practice stage when I left for Harlech.

It would be fair to say that without the influence of Neil and Glenys and the WEA I would not have considered entry into Harlech. Together they provided an enormous amount of stimulation, educational development and the vital confidence to apply. Through them I was introduced to new discussions and my reading, which included some of the Marxist classics and the novels of authors such as Orwell, was widened. Neil loaned me his copy of Jack London's *The Iron Heel* that even today I return to as an inspirational piece of literature. Neil claims I can return to it because I never returned his copy. My memory unfortunately lapses at this point. Glenys provided history textbooks and a copy of *The Essential Trotsky* — which I did return because she was trying to get Neil to read it!

During this period I became the AEU shop steward for my workshop – Fab B. A colleague of mine, George, was the AEU branch treasurer and also present on the night Neil spoke to the branch. George also became heavily involved in the local WEA branch and was also convinced by discussions about the potential and opportunity offered by Harlech. Like me, he saw a opportunity to undertake a life altering experience with a chance of improving his economic and work prospects.

All this was not happening in isolation. The trade unions were under attack from the then Labour Government, accusing the leaders of being unable to stop wildcat strikes, the membership of being out of control, and shop stewards of having too much power. The Royal Commission on Trade Unions and Employers' Associations was about to report, soon to be followed by Barbara Castle's White Paper *In Place of Strife*. Added to this were international events that shocked almost everybody and the 'left' in particular: Paris 68; the movement against the Vietnam War; the Civil Rights marches and demonstrations in Northern Ireland that became bigger and bigger. The troops went in just after I started my first year at Harlech. These events provided a background against which my decision to apply to Harlech was being made.

I decided to apply. My decision was based on the premise that two years at Harlech would make me more effective in my ever-increasing political activism. There was also a tinge of careerism, the possibility of a job in the future with a union. A more cowardly reason for applying was that the decision to go or stay would be made by someone else. I might not be accepted as suitable material for entry into the College. So along with George I put my application in. Both of us were subsequently called for interviews.

### The Interviews
Entry into Harlech required us to successfully complete two interviews. Harlech's own interview to be accepted as a full-time student and the County Council's interview for a grant. The Harlech interview was held in the WEA office in Charles Street, Cardiff. I remember the interview room was very small and I faced two tutors from Coleg Harlech. I am quite clear that one of the tutors was Alan Parfitt, who was not only to be one of my tutors but also a friend during my days at Harlech. Of the other I am not absolutely sure but I think it was Graham Allen the literature tutor and acting Vice Warden. I was exceedingly nervous; this being my first interview of this nature ever. I was not sure that I came up to the standard required and being only twenty-two I was at the bottom end of the age group Harlech wished to attract.

George's interview was even tougher. Being a married man with two sons he had to demonstrate he was clear about the important step he was about to take. He needed to demonstrate that he was sure he understood the gravity of his decision. He was about to give up a fairly well paid job on the gamble of a better future presented by Harlech. Within days we both knew that we had been accepted.

Our next hurdle was the County Council Education Committee. And I mean the Education Committee, all thirty-two of them. I had a short interview that asked me about my plans for the future. George on the other hand had a grilling, centring on his family status and his decision to give up a good job at Switchgear. I was fairly confident of being awarded a grant. This was based on the long established policy of the county council to support Harlech students and I knew at least twenty of the thirty-two councillors involved. Some would be supportive of my goal to improve myself and a few would welcome the opportunity of seeing the back of me for a few years. We were a bit more concerned about George. We retired to the local Chinese restaurant, a big treat in those days, to run through what had happened and to cheer ourselves up. I tried to convince George that everything would be OK.

We left Newport and decided to call for a pint in one of the local pubs. As we entered we could hear a fairly heated discussion in the lounge bar. It was obviously political so we thought we'd have a look. On entering we found Councillor Bevan, Nye's brother, who had just been chairing the Committee deciding our grants, berating the Wilson government for some proposed cuts in educational spending and their determination to force the County Council to scrap its Grammar Schools. I asked one of the Councillors whether the grants had been approved. He replied, 'That's confidential so I can't tell you but I hope you enjoy yourself at Harlech'. I asked him the same question about George to get the same reply about confidentiality, but he also wished George well in his new venture. All we had to do was wait for September. The management of South Wales Switchgear foreshortened the wait by declaring a fairly large redundancy! On a personal level this redundancy was a bonus, as it would give me an extra few weeks pay. As a shop steward I was committed to fighting any redundancy and in particular compulsory redundancies. I am pleased to say that in my workshop all the proposed redundancies were defeated. I then negotiated two of us onto the list for voluntary redundancy, retaining the posts, which were filled by two workers from the compulsory redundancy list in other parts of the factory.

The decision to go to Harlech was without doubt the biggest I had ever made. Give up my job – even if I had started to dislike the work, it was reasonably paid. Leave my comrades in an increasingly volatile labour and trade union movement; I ate, drank and slept politics. So here I was moving to north Wales where I suspected I would not find an active role in political life. Leaving my family, my Valleys Mam — I would need to learn how to wash and iron my own clothes. Worse was to face me when I went on to university, I had to learn how to cook.

One group of people who were a further spur to going were those who thought I was mad. They thought I was wasting my time. Almost all held similar views to society in general and education in particular. You were either born with brains or not. The education system was perfectly geared to identifying those who had the brains. These were your actual working class Tories or 'I know my place' people. But undaunted, I signed on the dole for the first time in my life as I waited for summer to end and the arrival of September 1968.

The previous three or four years had been a watershed in my life. The three most important organisations to me — the WEA, the Labour Party and the Trade Unions — had begun to merge into one large social and learning experience. All three demanded I raise my educational level and all at the same time assisted in stimulating the educational process. If I was going to continue to develop within these spheres of activity I would need to develop the formal side of my education. The activities themselves had provided an enormous opportunity for informal and non-formal improvement and the means for achieving that development and for the creation of new ideas.

All these activities, the new and old friends, colleagues, comrades and opponents had developed a growing desire to learn. My reading had expanded from SF novels to *The Iron Heel* and other socialist novels. In my daily journey to and from work I read the standard socialist works of Marx, Engels, Lenin and Trotsky. I was ready for my new journey into Coleg Harlech. George and I arrived in mid evening, in fading light and we were not able to get a complete view of the College. George was sent to Crown Lodge, whatever that was, and I was directed to the dorms.

## *My First Night*
All the formal activities, information giving and so on have long been dislodged from my memory. What remains are the impressions and events that were to have the most effect on me because of the element of surprise, almost disbelief. The first surprise was the dorms. They consisted of two pre-war huts joined together by a toilet, washing facility area. I was allocated a shared room, in dorm One. What faced me on entering was a long corridor with four or five rooms to either side. This accommodation did not seem to fit in with the pre-conceived ideas that I had drawn from photographs of the College. These were of a well-built stone building with a tower at one end providing the library, and a tower at the other end providing the Great Hall (unfortunately destroyed by fire the previous year). What I did not expect was something that looked like a large garden shed or national service barracks. But I was here and I would have to make the best of it. In fact I became a strong defender of the dorms requesting that we be allowed to remain there for our second year rather than move into the then under construction tower block to be opened early in September 1969.

Meeting my room-mate, John, was another shock for me but I feel a disaster for him. John was an ex-merchant navy seaman. It was as though the authorities in Harlech had deliberately selected the tidiest, most clean living person who had years of experience of living in cramped quarters and then subjected him to share with the universe's most untidy individual. Our room was approximately ten feet by twelve feet and had two single beds, separated by three feet of floor space with a small dressing table with three shelves above it. At the bottom of the bed, the door end, were two 'fitted wardrobes' on each side of the door with a sliding loose cloth blind acting as wardrobe doors. John who was first had proceeded to allocate each of us space. A shelf and a half each, half of the top of the chest of drawers, one large and one small draw each. His half of the shelf was immaculately set out on a perfectly folded brilliant white towel and everything was in its place. My stuff was thrown on the bed. This was the odd couple writ large. John found alternative accommodation within a few weeks.

The next adventure was the welcome reception provided by the second year students held in the Saint David's Hotel. I was a bit surprised to find this event taking place in what was the local boozer for the bourgeoisie. But I have another confession. Like my early judgement on the dorms, my rejection of the St David's Hotel was premature; I became a more than frequent visitor to its bar. It was at this reception that I entered into a relationship with a small number of fellow students, both first and second years that was to help shape my future as a political activist. Individually they were a very eclectic group of Marxists of the Trotskyite and Stalinist varieties, a Plaid Marxist, an Anarchist or two and a couple of stray Labour Leftists and one who thought he could be a Maoist today, a Fannonist tomorrow and a follower of Che on weekends. Although this sounds like a mad collection it made me finally plant my feet in one of the political camps I was flirting with. The choice was either Tribune or Militant; I chose the latter.

Also in that group was Nigel, the Plaid Marxist, poet, and guitar playing, ex-shepherd from Ebbw Vale who became my closest friend. Nigel and I spent many an hour in one pub or another trying to read Lipsey's standard work on economics. We were both convinced he was a dipsomaniac who wrote the book while drunk. We thought we should be in a similar state to understand it. After many attempts we agreed we could never get that drunk.

### My arrival at Damascus

The three or four years that I have outlined here had an enormous influence on my personal and educational development. The events and people I experienced in those four years and the two to follow at Harlech, and my first year at university — which after Harlech was one of the greatest disappointments of my life — were to set the shape of the rest of my life. The influences on my life must include my family, community, work, activity in the Labour Party and the trade unions. But I have to give enormous weight to my meeting Neil Kinnock and, just as importantly, Glenys, and finding the WEA.

Entering Coleg Harlech in September 1968 was the next chapter in a mind-expanding and life-changing process that includes a further thirty years with the WEA as a member, and on and off periods as a student, a tutor, a member of Council and District Committee and tutor-organizer.

# WEA TUTOR ORGANIZER 1966-1970

## NEIL KINNOCK

From August 1966 until May 1970 I was Tutor Organizer in Industrial Studies for the South Wales District of the WEA. The work was demanding, the hours were long. There could be disappointments when an under-subscribed course had to close or when a class failed to magnetise enough students to even start. But no pressure or frustration was ever great enough to outweigh the *main* experience of being part of the WEA – unalloyed delight, spiced with inspration.

The South Wales District Secretary at the time, and long before it, was David Thomas (DT) Guy. DT, a former industrial worker, adult student, university graduate by his early thirties, acquaintance of Mansbridge, friend of Tawney. DT was a cultured, thoroughly Welsh, benign giant of a man. He led his district committee, students, tutors and organizers by appearing not to *insist* on anything whilst at the same time making it mildly but absolutely clear that he expected – and tolerated – nothing but the best. The reason for that was strong and simple: to him the purpose of the WEA was to conduct an unstinting mission of enlightenment. Of course, he never articulated his purpose in such a grandiose way – but the result of his mixture of zeal and benevolence, passion and kindness was compelling. It meant that everyone on DT's staff would do anything to avoid letting him down. No management was ever less theoretical or didactic. No management ever provided a sharper spur to effort.

Naturally, the students had much the same effect on me. People who have done a day's work and can show insatiable curiosity, can consume everything on a reading list, can sustain their attention for a two-hour lecture and discussion session are testing students. When they approach a class series on 'The Economics behind Today's News' with piercing questions about the welfare of the yen or the shortcomings of incomes policy, they are impressive. But they become terrifying to the tutor when they can listen to thirty minutes on 'Mao, the Cultural Revolution and the Contradictions of Communism' – and then demonstrate that visits to China as merchant seamen, or to Hong Kong as soldiers, or a life long interest in the People's Republic have given them encyclopaedic knowledge. Imagine being a twenty-five year old, damp-behind-the-ears tutor turning up at the Aberdare Trades and Labour Council to speak on 'The Rise of Fascism' and being confronted by a group of twenty-seven, eight of whom had been International Brigaders in the Spanish civil war . . . Such experiences were *very* character forming.

Bill Gregory, autodidact, barber by trade, student of Marxism when travelling the USA, Cambridge graduate and post war extra-mural and WEA lecturer was one of the finest teachers that any graduate could hope for. Brilliantly laconic, funny, an instructor-by-aphorism, he was my role model. I was starting in adult education as he was in semi-retirement in his early seventies so I naturally asked him for professional tips. 'Oh, I don't give advice. It's much better for you to find your own way' he said. But, pressed insistently, he eventually said reluctantly, 'Well, I suppose there is one little bit of guidance I *can* give. In adult education – and in politics too if you are the right kind of stuff – always aim a little above their heads. If you do that, people will reach up. But if you aim at their bellies, like some teachers do, then they'll think with their balls'. It wasn't elegant I suppose. But to me, it was the innermost secret of the trade. So I tried, without Bill's charisma arsenal, to follow his guidance.

Kindness, tolerance, the willingness of experienced students to teach fresh faced tutors made survival possible. That, in turn, strengthened performance, particularly in the then novel shop stewards' day release courses. As Eddie Jenkins, Harry Jones and Joe England of the South Wales WEA broke new trails at BMC, Hoover, ICI, and other large and small employers in the sixties, I followed their inspiring lead and learned very quickly that the key to successful and fulfilling workers' education was the development of students' self confidence. Assertive, capable shop floor representatives had only negative memories of their last encounter with education and training in school or National Service. For much of the time they'd been taunted by teachers and instructors with what they *didn't* know and what they *couldn't* do. So, despite being tigers across a negotiating table, they naturally began the courses with inhibitions and self doubt.

The WEA classes where encouragement was a teaching method, where emphasis on what students *did* know was essential, and where hectoring or humiliating teaching techniques were completely absent, disoriented some at first. But as familiarity and security grew, self assurance quickly flourished and the classes became places of vitality and enjoyment. Many of the men and women who came to our courses blossomed manifestly. Most stayed in their jobs but, among the ones that didn't, several went on to become full-time union officials and eighteen men and one woman who came to the classes run by my fellow WEA tutors and me between 1966 and 1970 were university graduates by the mid 1970s. There cannot really be much that is more fulfilling for any teacher to see students taking the risks – and making the sacrifices – involved in changing the whole course of their lives through using the opportunities of adult education provided by the WEA.

The innovative industrial classes were quickly and easily established in some places, and several companies gradually extended day release courses on industrial relations, labour economics, communications, organizational and representation skills from union representatives to middle management. Other encounters were not as easy. A departmental boss in a south Wales steel works expressed his disgust at the provision of workers' education in company time by complaining, 'You are just going to turn these bastards into bright bastards'. I couldn't help responding with 'Well, we'll take care not to waste time on a hopeless case like you then'. It was not diplomatic or well advised; and it could have been disastrous. But fortunately the managing director thought it was very funny and the course got under way.

As word of the industrial day release courses got around, demand increased. By the autumn of 1968 it was obvious that our limited resources for daytime teaching were very stretched. In the belief that it would ease the pressure from the firms asking us to set up courses, I encouraged my colleagues to make a market response. We increased the charges from the absurd maximum of five shillings a day to £5 a day. The twenty-fold price increase didn't work. The inverse demand phenomenon set in as companies equated higher fees with higher quality. Applications for our services increased. It certainly helped District finances but it also meant an extra heavy work programme. Happily, after 1970, more tutor-organizers were recruited and supply moved towards demand.

The evening class programme, the most traditional of WEA activities, had particular attractiveness for me. The students really were choosing between learning and less demanding leisure. Classroom conditions varied from the perfect in a local scondary school, to the challenging in a pub back room, to the dire in a run-down damp, stained, under-used Miners' Institute. Friendships flourished, often lubricated by post class pints. I had wonderful experiences of the loyalties that developed – none more impressive than in the 'Economic background to current affairs' class that I ran in Oakdale from 1967 to 1970. In the second year of the course – properly and democratically organized in the best WEA style by an elected class secretary, Albert Williams – we received an unannounced visit by Her Majesty's Inspector. He sat at the back of the room and, when the class broke for coffee at eight o'clock, he was approached by Albert Williams.

'Welcome!' said Albert, 'would you like to sign up to our class?' 'I would' replied the stranger, 'but I can't come back again because I'm only here to inspect Mr. Kinnock's work'. 'In adult education, are you?' asked Albert. 'No. As it happens, before I became an Inspector, I was a lecturer in university'. 'In economics, was it?' inquired Albert. 'No, in history', came the reply. 'Well, I'm damned' declared Albert to the class, 'Here we are with an Inspector who hasn't taught adults or economics looking over Neil's shoulder'. And turning to the perfectly pleasant HMI, he said, 'If you go on like that butty, they'll make you a boss in South Wales Switchgear. You've got the perfect qualifications – no bloody experience and you know bugger all about the work!' Thankfully, the HMI joined in the laughter and came to the Cross Oaks with us afterwards, giving Albert an opportuity to learn about the skills of education inspection and the Inspector the chance to buy a round. 'Well', said Albert, 'it was the least he could do after coming to the class without paying his fee!'

The day classes and the more conventional evening classes were followed by Saturday schools and week-end courses, mainly for the TUC. Those events presented a logistical challenge for any tutor with a love of sport, and the most important documents at our District course planning meetings were rugby, soccer and cricket fixture lists. It wasn't just my obligations to the local cricket club that made it a necessity – any *Workers'* Educational Association that fixed a Saturday school which clashed with a rugby international would deserve no mercy. On the one occasion that a Saturday school at the Bluebell Inn, Caerphilly, did collide with an international – Wales v Ireland in 1969 – we conceded to culture and watched the game on TV in the pub. The title of that particular class was then extended from the originally intended 'Why Enoch Powell is wrong' to 'Why Enoch Powell is completely wrong' and held six weeks later so that the lecture didn't go to waste . . .

My enjoyment didn't just come from being a tutor. Organizing others for classes had its appeal too. Jeff Cocks, later Principal of Pontypridd College, used to pack Rhondda classes with his spellbinding twentieth century history courses – mainly because, he said, 'I did ten minutes of ignition and then the students blazed away about their own ideas and experiences for two hours. I learned a lot more than I taught'. Merthyr-born Gareth Griffiths, later of the University of Western Australia and brilliant author of 'The Empire Writes Back' and many other works, did a week-end school in Caerleon College on Joseph Conrad and the students from other courses deserted their classes to learn what *Heart of Darkness* was **really** about. Glenys, my wife, taught a Co-operative Women's Guild evening class in the Rhymney valley for three pre-pregnancy years. It was a sort of educational love-in as far as I could see: and it had pedagogic benefits too. Glenys would start to speak when the big hot water urn at the back of the class was switched on and she would end exactly eighteen minutes later when the gushing steam signified that brew-up time had arrived. The result was the nicest file of less-than-twenty-minutes lectures on 'The Pankhursts', 'Development depends on Women', 'Equal Pay for Equal Work' and many similar consciousness raisers that anyone could wish for.

Although, over a gap of nearly forty years, there is always a danger that 'distance lends enchantment to the view' I must say that the memories of my time with the WEA are marvellous and all my mind pictures are sunlit. Or nearly all . . . I began my job on 22 August 1966 and one of the first courses that I managed to arrange was a weekly series of Thursday night current affairs classes in the Social Democratic Club in a Merthyr valley village whose name was then, even in the rest of south Wales, almost unknown. With the enthusiastic support of two local councillors, Dai Tudor and Maldwyn Brace, the class quickly took root.

The sessions were lively and argumentative, and they usually extended to closing time. By 20 October there were over fifty students on the register. I was proud, exhilarated, eager. This was what I *really* wanted to do.

On the morning of Friday 21 October 1966, the gigantic Pant Glas tip towering above the primary school in that village slid down in a massive avalanche of slurry. It killed 116 children and twenty-eight adults. The name of Aberfan became instantly known across the world as a definition of preventible tragedy. I heard the news on the car radio. With Glenys – on half term holiday from teaching in Abersychan Grammar School – I was in Aberfan within half an hour. We had formed no real idea of the appalling scale of the disaster. I even took a shovel to help with the digging. One look at the total devastation told us how puny that hope was. We left the village to make way for the miners with their equipment. No-one knew then that even their skills would not be enough.

*D.T. Guy 'a Benign Giant'*

Two weeks later, I started the Thursday evening class again – not with any serious educational purpose, but because going into the village as someone who was not an insider but not quite an outsider just seemed the right thing to do. Amazingly, the class re-formed, although, naturally, with smaller numbers. Gradually, as the months passed, it moved from being an opportunity for conversation to divert minds to becoming a mixture of current affairs discussion and rehearsal of arguments to put to the Official Public Inquiry. When I went to the village years later, former class members said to me that it was useful. In the words of one, 'It helped us to *organize* our anger'.

The Aberfan class continued until my time with the WEA ended when the 1970 General Election campaign began. The people who came to the Thursday night sessions, like their families and neighbours in the village, dealt with misery in superhuman ways. Their grief was indelible. But so was their spirit. Like countless others that I met only because I worked for the WEA, those people gave me much more than I could have ever given them. My gratitude has never faded.